"This is a creative introduction to h(ancient text for today. To engage this that we need appropriate attitudes an(works carefully through multiple texts ~~~oss the Old Testament canon to demonstrate the payoff of his exhortations. Not overly technical, this helpful tool by an important Latino Old Testament scholar should serve a wide audience."

—M. Daniel Carroll R., Wheaton College and Graduate School

"In this creative and helpful book, Hernández encourages us to approach the Old Testament as an honored conversation partner, listening carefully to what it has to say. Hernández explains that engaging the Old Testament well means reading humbly, not arrogantly assuming we already know its message or meaning. It means reading successively, not believing a single section of the Old Testament contains all the information about God and God's plans. It means reading entirely, not skipping the disturbing or confusing sections. And it means reading deliberately, not hastily or distractedly. With chapters covering much of the content of the Old Testament and analogies drawn from literature, this book demonstrates what riches we can gain through genuine engagement of the Old Testament."

—Sara M. Koenig, Seattle Pacific University

"What a delightful book! Hernández invites readers into a virtuous and careful reading of the Scriptures. Well-written, honest, and approachable, the volume both forms and informs its readers, so that they may engage Old Testament texts in all of their literary artistry and theological depth. Hernández meets beginning students where they are and provides all the tools necessary to begin reading—really reading—the Old Testament."

—Michelle Knight, Trinity Evangelical Divinity School

"This book is exemplary not only because it consists of a number of examples of how to read the Old Testament but also because those readings demonstrate the humble, successive, entire, and deliberate engagement with Israel's Scripture that Hernández rightly claims is required if we are to hear it speak. Hernández combines clear and careful exegesis with an infectious enthusiasm for reading the Old Testament, conveyed in fresh and lively prose peppered with literary and cultural references."

—Will Kynes, Samford University

"Reading and interpreting the Old Testament is a daunting task since the writings are over two thousand years old and since they come from a culture dramatically different from ours. Hernández provides expert guidance in understanding narrative, poetry, and prophecy. Hernández wisely admonishes us to read the biblical text slowly, and the book is stocked with examples where the author has clearly followed his own dictum. This is not an ordinary textbook because it not only provides wise guidance for beginners but also offers bold interpretations that will provoke the most experienced reader to reflect anew on the biblical text. This is an ideal textbook both for new students and for those who want something fresh and challenging."

—**Thomas R. Schreiner**, The Southern Baptist Theological Seminary

"The first word in the title of Hernández's book, *Engaging the Old Testament*, says it all. This book is truly an engaging introduction to the Old Testament as inspired Scripture. Hernández's use of classic and modern literature outside the Bible to illustrate his points is a creative and effective way to stimulate one's appetite to read the Bible more and to appreciate its message better in our modern context. This book will become a standard for introductions of the Bible for years to come."

—**Seth D. Postell**, Israel College of the Bible

"A tremendous resource for interpreting the Old Testament that is as accessible as it is wide-ranging! Contrary to the modern proclivity for rapid results, Hernández invites readers to slow down and listen carefully to the biblical text, all for the purpose of fellowship with God. Hernández patiently walks readers through every major genre of the Old Testament with sage counsel and practical examples of how to listen to an ancient text that is living and active. This book should be read by all interpreters who wish to take the Old Testament seriously."

—**Andrew M. King**, Midwestern Baptist Theological
Seminary and Spurgeon College

ENGAGING

THE

OLD TESTAMENT

HOW TO READ
BIBLICAL NARRATIVE,
POETRY, AND
PROPHECY WELL

DOMINICK S. HERNÁNDEZ

Baker Academic
a division of Baker Publishing Group
Grand Rapids, Michigan

© 2023 by Dominick S. Hernández

Published by Baker Academic
a division of Baker Publishing Group
Grand Rapids, Michigan
www.bakeracademic.com

Printed in the United States of America

Library of Congress Cataloging-in-Publication Data
Names: Hernández, Dominick S., 1980– author.
Title: Engaging the Old Testament : how to read biblical narrative, poetry, and prophecy well / Dominick S. Hernández.
Description: Grand Rapids, Michigan : Baker Academic, a division of Baker Publishing Group, 2023. | Includes bibliographical references and index.
Identifiers: LCCN 2022033380 | ISBN 9781540962836 (paperback) | ISBN 9781540965585 (casebound) | ISBN 9781493436583 (ebook) | ISBN 9781493436590 (pdf)
Subjects: LCSH: Bible. Old Testament—Hermeneutics—Textbooks. | Bible. Old Testament—Criticism, interpretation, etc.—Textbooks.
Classification: LCC BS476 .H4668 2023 | DDC 220.601—dc23/eng/20220906
LC record available at https://lccn.loc.gov/2022033380

Baker Publishing Group publications use paper produced from sustainable forestry practices and post-consumer waste whenever possible.

23   24   25   26   27   28   29   7   6   5   4   3   2   1

Contents

    of Metaphors   192

16. Metaphors and Retributive Justice in the Poetry of Job   208

17. How Prophets Prophesy   226

18. How to Engage Poetic Prophecy   242

19. Who Is Isaiah's Suffering Servant?   257

    Postscript   277

    Bibliography   281

    Scripture Index   285

    Subject Index   295

En memoria de mi querido padre,
SAMUEL PÉREZ HERNÁNDEZ
(10 de diciembre 1945 al 27 de junio 1985),
cuya memoria perdura a través de sus hijos

In memory of my dear father,
SAMUEL PÉREZ HERNÁNDEZ
(December 10, 1945–June 27, 1985),
whose memory lives on through his children

Acknowledgments

This book developed as a result of my former and current students serving as delightful conversation partners, asking good questions, and challenging my readings of the Old Testament. This book began in the first Bible Introduction course I taught at Moody Bible Institute–Spokane in 2016. In this course, I strove to encourage Christian undergraduate students to engage well with the *entirety* of the biblical text on account of their reverence for the Scriptures. My advocacy for engaging the Scriptures well zeroed in on the Old Testament upon my transition to the Southern Baptist Theological Seminary. In Old Testament Introduction classes at this seminary, I encountered an array of students who were training for different vocations yet commonly aspired to establish their professional activity on principles derived from the Scriptures. These graduate-level students were already acquainted with information *about* the Old Testament, so together we were compelled to examine how to engage these texts in ways that advanced their relevance in the life of the Christian community. My current students at Talbot School of Theology have uniquely challenged me to develop a posture of reading the biblical text faithfully, despite the legitimate difficulties encountered by serious students of the Bible in courses such as Critical Issues in Old Testament Studies. I express my sincerest appreciation to my students who have sojourned with me while I worked some of these ideas out and to those who continue the journey alongside me.

The vision, patience, and encouragement of Jim Kinney, Executive Vice President of Baker Academic, are what practically brought this book to fruition. I am superbly grateful to Mr. Kinney for the opportunity to write for Baker Academic and for his careful attention to the initial stages of the manuscript. Other eyes and hands also made this book much better in a variety of ways. Melisa Blok provided invaluable line-level feedback, which made for a smoother reading experience and an improved presentation of the content.

Gratitude is due to the team of designers and typesetters at Baker Academic for creating such an aesthetically pleasing book.

I am much obliged to friends who have incessantly listened to my ideas about the topics broached in this book, have pored over my work, and have provided invaluable feedback that has sharpened the expression of my thoughts in writing. A special word of gratitude is due to Katie Merrifield, who read the entire manuscript and whose keen eyes saved me from many mistakes. I would also like to thank Jose Luis Quintana for quotidianly functioning as an informal consultant, harsh but affable critic, and encourager of my writings over the past decade.

Le quiero agradecer a mi esposa Gaby, a nuestra hija Yael, y a nuestro hijo Yair, por dedicarse conjuntamente conmigo a la misión de crear espacio en nuestras vidas para que pudiera escribir este libro. Reconozco y aprecio el hecho de su disposición de mudarse a diferentes partes del mundo y a aprender nuevos idiomas para facilitar mi oportunidad de perseguir el sueño de ser profesor y autor.

My greatest aspiration is that this book would serve as an asset to students of the Scriptures so that the God of the text would be honored and glorified in the lives of the readers of the text.

Preface

"Look at the Bible. What is it saying?"

These words were normally followed by Professor Ed Greenstein tilting his ear toward the Bible he was gripping in his hand, and a repetition of the question. After a few rounds of progressively intensified rhetorical questioning, a smirk emerged on the faces of some of the students who were present.

During my PhD studies at Bar-Ilan University, I took every class taught by my academic adviser, Professor Ed Greenstein. Thus I saw him stand at the front of his class with his Hebrew Bible open on multiple occasions, staring at it, and with humor asking the class, "What is it saying? Tell me what the Bible is saying!"

The point of Professor Greenstein's dramatic illustration was immediately clear to all who were present on every occasion: inanimate objects do not speak. Paper and ink literally *cannot* speak. Rather, texts *speak* when a person engages with them. The better a reader engages with texts, the clearer and louder they speak.

Doctoral students frequently adopt the practices of their PhD advisers, and in my case this was no different, though the context in which I teach is distinct from the Israeli university where I completed my PhD. The Christian communities to which my students and I belong have a robust view of the inspiration of the Scriptures and claim that the Bible is God's Word. Since the Bible is God's Word, we believe that it is invariably relevant to all of humanity. Nevertheless, I have found myself on numerous occasions standing before a class with my Bible open, my ear tilted toward the text, and asking my students, "What is the Bible saying? Can you hear it? Tell me!"

This illustration is exceedingly applicable in contemporary Christian communities that champion the entire Bible as being the Word of God while simultaneously spending little time considering the genius of the inspired writers. Modern Christians may declare the Bible to be the living Word of God, but the paper and ink of our Old Testaments will remain effectively inanimate in our lives unless we learn to read and listen to those texts well. Being a good reader involves bridging the gaps between the information derived from ancient texts and the application of the principles therein to contemporary communities.

Hopefully this book is a resource that promotes hearing the Scriptures loudly by encouraging engagement with the Old Testament in a manner that establishes meaningful connections between these hoary texts and the modern Christian community. Relishing the grandeur of Old Testament narrative, poetry, and prophecy facilitates an appreciation of the genius of the biblical authors and provides contemporary readers with insight into both what the authors might have been striving to teach and how that would have impacted the ancient readership. As we pay close attention to how the inspired writers tipped off their readers to what they were trying to communicate, we are shown how the teachings of those ancient texts remain applicable today.

Since this book is meant for all who desire to improve their reading of the Old Testament, it seemed oxymoronic for it to participate in the common scholarly practice of pointing readers to a catalog of secondary readings of other scholars. Thus I have not undertaken this task for the most part throughout the text, and in its place, I strove to direct readers to observe the phenomena of other writings within the Old Testament. Additionally, I present readings of Old Testament passages in which I refrain from engaging with the minutiae of historical, textual, philological, and other critical issues. I trust that readers will charitably excuse me for intentionally, for the sake of simplicity and clarity, forgoing the standard convention of citing many resources within the book.

My desire to relate to readers was a driving factor in the multiple references to classic literary works in this book. I trust that many readers will easily see how the rhetoric and examples from classic literature illustrate some of the Old Testament writing techniques and scenes examined in this work. Hopefully many of the classic works are already familiar to the reader, but if not, please consider this your spoiler alert.

As you are about to turn the page to the first chapter of this book, I encourage you to administer the following exercise as a tangible reminder of everyone's need to continuously improve as a reader of, and listener to, the Old Testament: grab the Bible that is closest to you, hold it by its spine, flip it open to any page of the Old Testament, lower your ear to the ink and paper, and listen closely.

What is the Bible saying? Can you hear it?

If you do not hear anything, set the Bible back down and turn the page of this book. Then be prepared to hear from the biblical text the next time you engage with it.

Dominick S. Hernández
La Mirada, CA
March 15, 2022

ONE

What's the Old Testament "God" to Do with Me?

What's your man got to do with me? . . .
I'm not trying to hear that, see.

—Positive K, "I Got a Man"

The emerging hip-hop culture of the 1980s and 1990s was a predetermined component of my personal life. Every household in my neighborhood (Lacey Park, Pennsylvania) had a boom box through which we blasted our favorite rappers' music until the neighbors banged on the shared residential walls to demand a bit of relief from the vibration of the bass track. Break dancing on flattened cardboard boxes in the middle of the street on hot, humid summer nights was almost a daily activity during the school-less summer months. This was my youth, and I loved it.

During the early stages of the hip-hop movement, many of the popular songs featured slick and humorous rhetoric with which the artists cleverly amused and entertained the listeners by playing on words. I had an uncanny knack for memorizing large portions of rap songs. I credit this to my then-developing aspirations to become a rapper and beatboxer, combined with the fact that rap music is particularly repetitive.

This repetitiveness might be the reason why rapper Positive K's song "I Got a Man" is still fixed in my memory decades after it hit the Billboard chart. This song portrays a conversation between a would-be Casanova who repeatedly makes advances and a young lady who has a boyfriend. Even though the female protagonist communicates time and again that she is spoken for, the rapper voices that he does not care about her boyfriend by repeatedly and obnoxiously asking, "What's your man got to do with me?" When the young lady reiterates that she is in a relationship, the young-man-turned-combatant predictably speaks up and declares, "I'm not trying to hear that, see." Positive K is ironically "positive" that the young lady will be happier with him than she is with her current boyfriend. Positive K's overconfidence leads to one rejection after another; hence the repetitive nature of the song.

> "What's your man got to do with me?"
> (Rejection)
> "I'm not trying to hear that, see."
> (Rejection ad nauseam, ad infinitum)

The repetitive nature of this song contains another glaring irony. Upon hearing Positive K spurning perpetual rejection from the young lady, one might admire his apparent persistence and internal fortitude in the face of disappointment. However, what the song actually reveals is that the rapper walks away with his pride and his ego but no new girlfriend, because he is a fool. He refuses to acknowledge fundamental information that is critical to understanding why he is at a roadblock: the woman he is flirting with has a boyfriend!

The rapper is told this information over and over again and dismisses it, acting as if it were not important to him. In actuality, the information should be profoundly disturbing to this supposedly valiant stud. He cannot acknowledge it, or it will weaken his personal assurance. Positive K intentionally overlooks a fundamental truth so many times that he seemingly grows to believe that it is not important.

Many of us will likely not be able to relate personally to Positive K's unrequited attraction toward a spoken-for love interest. But have you ever continuously encountered a roadblock that is so difficult to deal with that you tried to work your way around it by constantly ignoring it? Have you ever repeatedly dismissed information that is crucial to dealing with a problem, to the point that you began to doubt its importance to your situation?

How about in your Bible reading?

Readers of the Bible repeatedly encounter obstacles—textual, theological, historical, and others. When these problems are encountered head-on, information sometimes emerges that discloses how to best deal with the quandary. This information does not—in fact in many cases cannot—materialize if the reader intentionally evades the difficulty. For readers of the Bible, it is convenient to ignore unpleasant or obscure sections of the text by simply questioning, "What's that got to do with me?" It is painful to grapple with Bible difficulties—especially theological ones—and attempt to reconcile them with our experience. Perpetually evading Bible difficulties by ignoring them is the same pattern of behavior exhibited by Positive K: information that readers consider difficult is treated as unimportant and, therefore, becomes inconsequential to the reader, even though it is actually quite significant to the situation at hand.

A Christian Conundrum

For many Christian readers of the Bible, it can be particularly tempting to treat the Scriptures of ancient Israel—which Christians call the "Old Testament"[1]—as being less significant than the documents of the New Testament. One reason this disposition is enticing is because of the difficulty of reconciling common perceptions of the character of God in the Old Testament with the portrayal of God (especially through Jesus) in the New Testament. Cursory readings of the Old and New Testaments in juxtaposition seemingly relate perplexing descriptions of who God is and how God behaves in and toward creation. It is intellectually and emotionally convenient to effectively disregard one of these witnesses in order to develop essential beliefs about the God of the Bible. For Christians, the section abandoned is frequently the Old Testament, for the sake of understanding fundamental truths about Christianity that are primarily established from the pages of the New Testament.

There are, indeed, numerous doctrines fundamental to Christianity that are explicitly taught throughout the New Testament. On the pages of the New Testament Jesus is revealed as the Son of God and displayed to be fully God and fully human (John 1:1, 14; Col. 2:9; Heb. 1:3). Jesus is portrayed as God's chosen Messiah, who serves as the culmination of God's redemptive plan. By way of God the Son, humankind is restored to and reconciled with God the Father (John 3:16–17; 14:6; Rom. 3:23–26; 5:10–12). Jesus lived a sinless life (2 Cor. 5:21; Heb. 4:15; 1 Pet. 2:22; 1 John 3:5), died a wrongful death (John 19:4), and conquered the grave by resurrecting from the dead (Matt. 28:1–10; Mark 16:1–8; Luke 24:1–7; John 20:1–9). Jesus's resurrection is essential in bearing witness to his divinity (Rom. 1:4). Jesus is divine and reigns over the

1. We will further discuss what Christians mean by the phrase "Old Testament" and the implications of using this title for the Scriptures of ancient Israel in chapter 4 of this book.

dominion of death that affects all mortals. Therefore, believers in Jesus also maintain a hope in the future resurrection of their bodies because, through the power of Jesus, believers in him will also conquer the misfortune of death (1 Cor. 15:12–28).

This is by no means a comprehensive list of doctrines that are fundamental to the Christian faith. These are, however, a few examples of Christian dogmas that are clearly illuminated in the New Testament. Without these doctrines, Christianity would be a fundamentally different religion.

Equally true to these fundamental Christian doctrines is the fact that Jesus's advent occurs toward the end of the time period in which the Scriptures were written. The entire Old Testament, approximately 75 percent of the Bible, was written prior to Jesus's incarnation. This imbalance testifies to the indispensable backstory that relates the historical, sociopolitical, religious, and literary records leading to the ultimate disclosure of God in the person of and through the work of Jesus the Messiah. The Old Testament Scriptures, which cultivate the emergence of the New Testament, are thereby absolutely crucial to wholly interpreting God's culminating act through Jesus (2 Tim. 3:16–17; see also chap. 2 below). We cannot dismiss or evade any part of these texts for any reason and are compelled to engage with them as we would with the New Testament.

This charge is especially pertinent as it relates to sections of the Old Testament that we might find confusing, problematic, or even disturbing. The New Testament is where many Christians start reading the Bible, and, consequently, it is also the part of the Bible where many Christians exclusively (or at least mostly) develop their understanding of God. As Christians browse the Old Testament, they inevitably encounter portions of the Scriptures of ancient Israel that can be disconcerting or bewildering in light of the clear teachings of the New Testament. Thus reading "backward" from the New Testament into the Old Testament, readers frequently hit roadblocks in balancing the depiction of God in Old Testament texts with how God is revealed, especially through Jesus, in the New Testament.

The Unrelatable Testament

Because of some of the potential theological difficulties that Christians might encounter when reading the Old Testament, some of us might be hesitant to engage with it as Scripture on its own terms. We understand that there are those who might ask, "What's the Old Testament 'God' to do with me?" In other words, "What does this bizarre and arbitrary God, as portrayed in the

Old Testament, have to do with me, a Christian, in light of God's subsequent revelation in and through Jesus?"

Additionally, if the God of the Old Testament can be eradicated or redefined either by avoiding the Old Testament or by selectively reading the Old Testament and replacing the unpleasant sections with ideas from the New Testament, then Christians might be justified in asking, "What's the Old Testament 'got' to do with me?" Or, "What does this ancient compilation of books filled with antiquated laws, difficult poetry, and visions of apparent monsters (e.g., Dan. 7) really have to say to modern Christians, who can just read about the culmination of this weird stuff in the New Testament?" Whether by premeditation or not, when we avoid a holistic reading of Scripture, we appropriate the words of Positive K:

> "What's the Old Testament got [God] to do with me?"
> (Christian reader skips sections of the Old Testament and states . . .)
> "I'm not trying to hear that, see."

The more Christians rehearse this response, whether consciously or simply by bypassing difficult texts and issues in the Old Testament, the more we marginalize approximately 75 percent of the Bible. Despite the difficulties that studying the Old Testament presents, the answer to our Positive-K-type questions is strikingly obvious: the Old Testament has everything to do with contemporary Christianity!

If Christians pass over this fundamental truth and ignore or renounce attributes of the revealed character of God (in either the Old or the New Testament), then we necessarily disregard parts of the plan of redemption and, thereby, embrace a fragmented Christian faith.

So how do we go about working through some of these issues?

We turn to this question in the next chapter.

TWO

The Commitment
to *Really* Reading

> But this is one of the rewards of reading the Old Testament regularly. You
> keep on discovering more and more what a tissue of quotations from it
> the New Testament is.
>
> —C. S. Lewis, *Reflections on the Psalms*

In the last chapter, we discussed how we have the tendency to read the Old
Testament sparsely while favoring the New Testament. I proposed that one of
the major reasons we read the Old Testament less than the New relates to the
difficult theological issues that arise when we compare how God is depicted in
the two testaments. In order to even make this type of comparison, Christians
have to be at least somewhat familiar with sections of the Old Testament. If
this is the case, do we experience difficulty understanding and applying the
Old Testament because we engage with these Scriptures less, or do we engage
with the Old Testament less because we perceive it as difficult and, thereby,
less applicable to our lives? Which scenario causes the other?

This question might be as unanswerable as the conventional chicken-versus-
egg scenario. In fact, just as we currently have chickens and eggs in the world
despite the ongoing debate concerning the exact sequence of their material-
izations, so we are left with the reality that many Christians study the Old
Testament less and struggle with its contemporary application because of its
difficulty. Let's discuss the reasons why this situation is ironic and consider
the best way forward.

Let's Iron(y) This Out

Questioning the relevance of the Old Testament to modern Christianity is strikingly ironic for at least two reasons.

First, the New Testament authors based their Christian teachings on the Old Testament writings. They derived a holistic and integrated conception of God by both considering what was revealed through Jesus and reading the texts given to their ancestors. From the Old Testament, early Christians derived and developed the beliefs that are fundamental to Christianity to this day, as the fledgling Christian community began to receive the emerging New Testament documents as authoritative. Early believers in Jesus were instructed about God's plan of redemption, understood prophecies of Jesus's birth (Matt. 1:22–23; see Isa. 7:14), received him as the chosen Messiah (Mark 8:29; Acts 18:28; see Dan. 9:26), grasped the symbolism relating to his sacrificial death (John 1:29; 1 Cor. 5:7; Heb. 10:1–10; see Exod. 12; Lev. 16; Isa. 52:13–53:12), and recognized other fundamentals of nascent Christianity through an astute study of the Old Testament. The authors of the New Testament received and elaborated on doctrines that have deeply influenced the church up to today. This alone necessarily indicates the responsibility we have as contemporary readers to pore over the primary source documents of the early Christian writers.

Second Timothy 3:16–17 is one of the most well-known examples of the early church being instructed to depend on the Old Testament in order to explain the emerging Christian movement: "All Scripture is God-breathed and is useful for teaching, rebuking, correcting and training in righteousness, so that the servant of God may be thoroughly equipped for every good work." These verses are particularly important and deserving of close examination. Paul is encouraging his mentee, Timothy, to engage with the written, God-breathed Scriptures for the sake of producing effective Christian teaching, reproof, correction, and training in righteousness. Paul's reference to actual written texts to teach and guide in the practices of the early Christian movement raises the question, To which written texts was Paul referring?[1]

Paul seems to be referring, for all intents and purposes, to the Old Testament. Given that 2 Timothy is traditionally considered to be Paul's final letter, it is *possible* that Paul is referencing other portions of the New Testament that may have already been written by the time he wrote to Timothy for the second

---

1. Paul had access to other sayings of Jesus that were not written down, which he also held in a high regard. For example, see Paul's quotation of Jesus's words recorded in Acts 20:35: "It is more blessed to give than to receive." Yet in the context of 2 Tim. 3:16–17, Paul is specifically referring to God-breathed writings. This is evident through mentioning the γραφή (*graphē*), a word that refers to written texts, in this passage.

time. Supporting this idea is the fact that both Peter and Paul seemingly refer to other sections of the New Testament as "Scriptures" (2 Pet. 3:16; 1 Tim. 5:18). Thus Paul may have been alluding to additional texts, but, given the prevalence of the Old Testament in Paul's other writings, it does not appear as if Paul is implying anything less than the Hebrew Scriptures.

Along these lines, it is principally the Old Testament that Paul asserts is "God-breathed." Notice that Paul argues that "all" of the Scripture (i.e., a written text) is "useful for teaching, rebuking, correcting and training in righteousness." Paul communicates with Timothy that the written text of the Old Testament is completely inspired by God and should therefore be used for teaching and application within the life of the community of faith.

To some contemporary readers, this might be hard to believe. Some might ask questions like these: "Did Paul really believe that even the genealogies were inspired?" (Well, he did say "all" of the Scriptures were inspired.) "Is Ecclesiastes really applicable to the church?" (According to Paul, evidently so. He told Timothy that "all" Scripture is useful.) "Are the words of Leviticus *really* as important as the red letters of Jesus in modern Bibles?" (Since "all" of these words are recorded as God-breathed Scripture, the answer—according to Paul—is yes.)

This 2 Timothy 3:16–17 passage is perhaps most famous for communicating the reliability of all Scriptures, since they are depicted as being God's very breath (i.e., inspired) and applicable to multiple areas of life and ministry. What is often overlooked is that this passage also demonstrates that the early Christian community was instructed by Paul himself to delve into the Old Testament as the primary method for learning what to believe and how to act as Christians! According to Paul, the Old Testament texts were inspired regardless of how applicable the early Christian community perceived them to be to their circumstances or situations. Paul commanded Timothy to teach from the pages of the Old Testament because these texts were inspired by God, and, consequently, they unquestionably applied to the lives of early Christians. This model of understanding the Old Testament as fundamental to the life and practice of the Christian community is what Paul left behind to be lived out by all Christians who would adhere to his pastoral guidance to Timothy. Thus there is an element of irony in questioning the relevance of the Old Testament to our lives in this day and age, because the New Testament writers and early Christians that we love to read now drew extensively from the texts with which we struggle to engage.

The second point of irony relates to the self-propagating theological quandaries that emerge from seriously engaging with only a portion of the Scriptures. I alluded to this issue above, but it is important to clearly state that principally focusing on the New Testament for guidance on Christian life and practice, while minimally consulting the Old Testament, might actually be one of the main reasons readers perceive apparent discrepancies among the portrayals of God between the two testaments. Favoring the New Testament in Bible reading facilitates a misperception of the nature of God by embracing only a portion of how he has revealed himself. This habit creates expectations in readers concerning the character of God and how he "should" behave that are, quite frankly, not met by Christian readings of the Old Testament.

Though the New Testament writers present Jesus as the apex of God's progressive revelation of the divine character to humankind (Heb. 1:1–2), there is no evidence that the authors of these texts perceived their writings to be of greater significance than those of the Old Testament. On the contrary, it appears as though the New Testament writers recognized that the validity and authority of their writings were based on an awareness that they were continuing in the tradition of the Old Testament writings. The writers of the New Testament do not demonstrate any issue with regard to how God is portrayed in the Scriptures of ancient Israel compared to how Jesus reflects God in their New Testament writings. Evidently, this did not present theological embarrassment for the New Testament writers; this suggests that the quandaries relating to how God is described in the Old and New Testaments are generated by how we engage with the biblical texts, not by the text itself.

Interestingly, the New Testament actually helps contemporary Christians recognize that the major issues do not mainly lie within the pages of the Old Testament but, rather, predominantly with how readers engage these sacred texts through the following paradox: We might expect focusing on the New Testament to improve our understanding of the character and plan of God. However, this expectation is foiled when we realize that mostly devoting ourselves to sections of a composition only increases difficulty with the portions of the Scriptures that we do not engage with or understand.

Toward a Solution: Engaging the Old Testament Well

Christians are compelled to engage with the text of the Old Testament in a posture that upholds legitimate questions, on the one hand, and prevents unsettled issues from festering in their hearts like rotten food hidden in the back of a refrigerator, on the other hand. If left alone long enough, putrid food can turn the refrigerator into a septic monster, growing and ruining other good items around it. Something similar happens when readers of the Bible encounter difficulties in the Old Testament without a plan for how to work through them. A legitimate question can grow into a malicious theological toxin with the ability to spread and influence other areas of theology (e.g., one's views of God and the revealed word). Some questions concerning the Old Testament that grow sickening are facilitated by an incomplete and inadequate reading of the Scriptures and could be abated by a more complete and holistic reading.

Four Core Reading Commitments

Reading literature well is a question of stewardship. The Bible is literature par excellence, meaning that we are unequivocally called to be good readers of its texts—especially those sections that might be considered difficult. If we can learn to engage in a responsible reading of the Old Testament texts, we will come to understand that they are supremely applicable to our daily lives.

In the remainder of this chapter, I expound on four core commitments that put Christian readers on the right trajectory for reading and applying the Old Testament to their lives—despite some of the difficulties that we might encounter as we read. These four core commitments are reading humbly, reading successively, reading entirely, and reading deliberately.

Reading Humbly

A humble disposition engenders teachability, which constantly refines, nuances, and, ultimately, improves our understandings of the biblical text. The "Act of Apollos" narrated in Acts 18 portrays a person with an exemplary disposition to receiving new instruction and conducting his ministry in a more excellent manner because of it. Apollos was a first-century Jewish Christian who makes a cameo in Acts 18. During this brief scene, Apollos is depicted as a gifted teacher. Yet Apollos's knowledge of the message he is teaching is incomplete. Upon hearing Apollos teach, Priscilla and Aquila—a Jewish couple who have also come to faith in Jesus—confront him and provide him with further information about how to explain the way of God more completely. The text relates this account, which came to pass in Ephesus, in the following manner: "Meanwhile a Jew named Apollos, a native of Alexandria, came to Ephesus. He was a learned man, with a thorough knowledge of the Scriptures. He had been instructed in the way of the Lord, and he spoke with great fervor and taught about Jesus accurately, though he knew only the baptism of John. He began to speak boldly in the synagogue. When Priscilla and Aquila heard him, they invited him to their home and explained to him the way of God more adequately" (Acts 18:24–26).

This passage exhibits several correspondences to the modern Christian's study of the Old Testament. Apollos is a bold and dedicated believer in Jesus—an evangelist even. Apollos is a gifted teacher who waxes eloquent in the synagogue concerning the things of the Lord. It seems Apollos has a "successful ministry." However, Apollos's ministry is not as edifying as it could be, because his teaching is incomplete. Apollos faithfully teaches all that he knows in an accurate manner, but he is not teaching the entire message that needs to be communicated to his listeners. Thus Priscilla and Aquilla "[invite] him to their home and [explain] to him the way of God more adequately" (Acts 18:26).

After the conversation with Priscilla and Aquila, Apollos has a choice to make. He has the option of being receptive to Priscilla and Aquila's advice, though he barely knows them. After all, this is the only time he is portrayed as interacting with this couple in the New Testament. Apollos also has the choice to spurn humility, ignore instruction, and feign that more comprehensive information is not important to his already successful ministry.

Apollos chooses to humbly listen when he is presented with more thorough information regarding the message that he has already, in a way, been successfully teaching. The book of Acts does not record the conversation between these three early disciples of Jesus, so the reader does not know how the content of Apollos's message changed. Rather, the narrator shows the reader how Apollos's teaching ministry continues to be effective with more extensive knowledge of the way of God. "When Apollos wanted to go to Achaia, the brothers and sisters encouraged him and wrote to the disciples there to welcome him. When he arrived, he was a great help to those who by grace had believed. For he vigorously refuted his Jewish opponents in public debate, proving from the Scriptures that Jesus was the Messiah" (Acts 18:27–28).

The "Act of Apollos" is the humble response to new information concerning an incomplete message that might, in a way, have some success if taught on its own. Apollos's reaction to the teaching of Priscilla and Aquila provides a supreme example of humility that leads to teachability and thereby serves as the model disposition for engaging with the Old Testament. Christian appreciation of the Old Testament grows in proportion to how much Christians act like Apollos—embracing humility, accepting instruction, and deepening their comprehension of these ancient texts in order to better understand the character of God and the divine plan.

Reading Successively

The second core commitment that will help improve our reading of the Old Testament is the pledge to read the text successively. Successive reading does not necessarily mean starting at the beginning of the Bible or even at the beginning of any given book. Rather, it means that we consider where we are reading in terms of a succession of revealed information. We cannot obtain all the information we need or want in one moment; sometimes, we must wait things out (see the next section, "Reading Entirely"). Readers committed to successively reading the Old Testament acknowledge that further information is revealed about God's character and God's plan(s) when we simply continue to read.

Throughout the extensive period of time covered by the pages of the Old Testament—from the creation of the universe to the Persian period—the authors of the Old Testament progressively reveal particular aspects of the character of God and provide select reasons for divine actions. When we consider this progressive discovery of new information to be part of the Old Testament reading experience, we will thrive in our reading. By recognizing that we are discovering information about God and his plans little by little, we are able to best interpret what exactly is being portrayed about these important topics at distinct points throughout the Old Testament. This will ultimately lead us to form integrated perspectives on various matters that may initially seem confusing.

Reading successively contrasts with outcome-based readings—that is, spending an abundance of time in the latter portions of the biblical text (i.e., the New Testament) and consequently attempting to make sense out of the rich, but sometimes perplexing, compositions that came beforehand.[2] As previously mentioned, this type of "reading in reverse" could ironically be a wellspring of various theological problems for Christians, since it might facilitate an understanding of a preferable "New Testament God" who seems incongruous with the God depicted in the Old Testament. Since the authors of Scripture revealed information about God and his plan in a progressive (i.e., forward-looking) manner, Christians must strive to understand that revelation is disclosed in certain ways, at certain times, and for distinct reasons that primarily relate to a moment along the progression. Reading successively is one of the best ways to grasp this. Readers are then able to incorporate this information into what the Bible reveals about the overall character and plan of God.

---

2. Authors sometimes use certain aesthetic devices to intentionally push the reader to continue reading and then to encourage the reader to reinterpret that which has already been read (e.g., foreshadowing). I am not referring to literary devices per se, but I am pointing out the difficulty of following the storyline of any document (or compilation of documents) that is intended to be read as a whole, when we are primarily engaging the material that appears toward the end of the composition.

As readers of the Bible successively work their way through the Old Testament and into the New Testament, the character of God does not change, but the reader becomes privy to more details related to who God is and what God does. From the creation account, we observe that the God of the universe possesses certain attributes that never change. For example, God is omniscient (all-knowing), omnipresent (existing everywhere), and omnipotent (all-powerful). Yet the characterization of God develops and is rounded out as the Scriptures progress from one scene to the next, from one literary style to the next, and from one aesthetic device to the next. Our perception of God's overall character is transformed as the reading process continues, even though we know that God possesses certain attributes that are essential to the divine character and do not change.

As we read the Bible humbly and successively, some of the reasons God does things we might consider peculiar become intelligible. Additionally, some of the dissimilarities we perceive in the character of God between the two testaments are diminished. Let's be clear: every potential difficulty is not easily worked out or decipherable. However, the difficulties should be approached in a manner that reduces unnecessary interpretive problems and facilitates an understanding of some of the possible issues. Reading in a forward-looking manner, recognizing that more information is coming, provides Old Testament readers with hope that at least some issues will work out if we simply persevere in our reading.

Reading Entirely

In his renowned book *Mere Christianity*, C. S. Lewis brilliantly points out the resourcefulness of skipping certain sections of compositions while reading. He states, "It is a very silly idea that in reading a book you must never 'skip.' All sensible people skip freely when they come to a chapter which they find is going to be no use to them."[3] Glancing at passages, judging their relevance to our goals, and moving on is a way in which we can steward our time well while simultaneously reading efficaciously. Lewis's advice is eminently useful—unless, of course, all the sections of a particular composition are equally valuable to the overall argument and storyline of the work and unless, of course, all the sections of a work are crucially important to the overall characterization of the work's protagonist. In this case, the astute advice offered by the ingenious writer C. S. Lewis would not apply.

One of the primary ways of working through the legitimate difficulties related to the Old Testament is by actually reading the entire Bible—both the

3. Lewis, *Mere Christianity*, 91.

Old and New Testaments. Intentionally skipping "boring," repetitive, confusing, or disturbing sections results in deliberately un-integrating parts of an entity that is intended to be understood as an integrated whole. Of course, it is possible to develop a partial understanding of the whole by just reading parts. Nevertheless, intentionally overlooking and discounting sections of the Old Testament is analogous to ignoring the background information of a story, the character development of a drama, and the subtle, yet vital, motifs that accompany a metanarrative. Frankly, we can get the gist of what is going on throughout the Bible by reading parts of it, but it will be a partially informed gist that might occasionally lead to disconcerting theological quandaries.

There is a good deal of correlation between how one reads and understands the Bible and how one reads and understands the writings of someone else's diary. Diary entries are normally somewhat autonomous in the sense that individual accounts can *basically* be understood without knowing what was written in previous or following entries. Thus if the reader wants to know exactly what happened in the author's life at a particular moment in history, it is completely appropriate to read one diary entry. From this, it could be possible to figure out what was going on in the state, country, or world at the time the author wrote. It might even be possible to discover certain character attributes and a bit about the author's personality. If written well, one diary entry can communicate a good deal about the author and the world surrounding the diary.

However, it would be bizarre to think that any one entry of a sizable diary written over a long period of time could provide a comprehensive account of the writer's character or life circumstances. Take, for example, perhaps the most famous diary of all time, *The Diary of a Young Girl* by Anne Frank. This classic diary-turned-book consists of a collection of entries by Anne Frank as she and her Jewish family are lamentably forced to hide from the Nazis in a secret annex of a business building in the Netherlands during the Second World War. Anne addressed her entries to her personified diary, which she called by the name "Kitty," and almost all of the "letters" that Anne writes to Kitty are understandable if they are read on their own terms.

Anne Frank wrote very honestly about the violent circumstances that led her family to hide, about her sometimes unpleasant sentiments toward others, and about her burgeoning curiosity about her adolescence. Given these mature themes, it is not surprising that there is an abridged version of this important work that is intended to be read by children. If spliced well, abridged versions can be of great assistance in providing a portion of a whole text for a particular audience. Admittedly, however, the smaller portion of entries that appear in any abridged version necessarily prohibits readers from grasping the fullness of the person behind the work. What a reader learns from and about the author of a diary is contingent upon the quantity of entries that are read.

By reading only a portion of entries in a given diary—especially if analyzing exclusively the latter portion of journal accounts—readers are not privy to many of the foundational pieces that develop in other periods of the writer's lifetime. For example, if the entries containing Anne's harsh words were removed from her diary, the reader would not be able to follow the emotional turbulence connected to Anne's growing frustration with her mother and, conversely, her adoration of her father. If entries concerning the Van Daan family were removed, it would be difficult to appreciate the relationship that Anne has with Peter that progresses from friendship to a nuanced relationship to a seemingly one-sided crush. If the editor were to remove all the entries that might be perceived as sensual in nature, the reader would not be able to observe how Anne perceives her own adolescence, which she communicates by relating curiosity about her development between the tender and formative ages of thirteen and fifteen.

The Diary of a Young Girl details the experiences of one person who presents herself from a variety of angles. Thus the reader's perspective on who she is develops in proportion to how many of her individual entries we read. These entries might be coherent on their own, but when they are read successively and entirely, they work synergistically to present an integrated picture of Anne Frank's life and circumstances. As the individual entries are considered in light of the whole, the reader can put together a holistic representation of the characters mentioned in the diary and the state of affairs behind its writing.

It is possible for Christians to understand much about the Bible by focusing only on parts of the biblical text—especially if those parts are toward the end (i.e., the New Testament). However, if we read only partially, we will lose and miss out on much. If we read only snapshots of certain sections of a larger work, it is difficult to see how the biblical characters develop; it is challenging to track the main motifs and images that the biblical writers use and reuse to accomplish their theological purposes; it is hard to understand why God relates in certain ways to certain people groups throughout the long period of time represented in the Old Testament texts; and, perhaps most importantly, it is difficult to discover nuanced connections across biblical texts relating to the character and work of God in order to observe how God develops as a persona and how he carries out the divine plans.

Dedication to humbly, successively, and entirely reading the Old Testament facilitates a deepened understanding of the overall structure and plot of the whole Bible. Reading in this manner also expands our awareness of the development of primary characters. This is particularly evident in the case of observing how the main protagonist, God, is depicted throughout the text.

Reading Deliberately

Reading deliberately consists of intentionally slowing down the process of reading in order to pay special attention to "how," "what," and "why" biblical writers communicate in order to provoke a response from their readership. Reading deliberately is placed at the end of this list of core commitments to Bible reading because it is an ambitious goal that must be constantly pursued by even the most dedicated readers of the Old Testament. In other words, readers who are totally committed to engaging with the text of the Old Testament humbly, successively, and entirely still must *consciously* strive to fully consider exactly what the authors are doing with their words.

This final reading commitment emphasizes the word "consciously." We must read slowly in order to carefully focus on how an author uses rhetoric to communicate with their audience and call them to respond. This is a practice that does not come naturally to many Old Testament readers today. Perhaps this is because we believe that there is a contemporary, living message in the words of Scripture, and we are anxious to search it out; perhaps it is because we promptly desire further information that can assist the process of interpretation; perhaps it is because of the daunting size of the Old Testament and our yearning to conquer it as a reading project. Whatever the reason might be, even committed readers tend to read the Old Testament too quickly.

While reading through the Bible hastily has benefits—like acquiring information about the Bible quickly and feeling encouraged by having read such a large text—one major downside is the potential of missing out on observing the genius of the author. By slowing down and observing the creativity and ingenuity of the biblical authors, we are able to ask the questions that these authors were trying to answer. Reading deliberately permits us to read the Old Testament on the writers' terms.

Old Testament authors wrote to be read. We as contemporary readers owe it to them to read their writings well. Reading well entails permitting them to communicate exactly what they desired to convey. This can hardly be accomplished by hurrying through the careful rhetoric and aesthetic devices that they use to communicate their messages.

The four core commitments of reading humbly, reading successively, reading entirely, and reading deliberately encourage Christians to holistically engage with the Old Testament as Scripture. Reading deliberately, however, is a pledge that transcends the typical Christian obstacles of not sufficiently interacting with the Old Testament and struggling to understand some of its most difficult parts. This is a disposition toward reading that all Christians can adopt to improve their interpretations of the Old Testament. This core commitment speaks less to the quantity that readers *should* read and more to the quality of reading that readers can *receive* from the written text.

As contemporary Christian readers, we are motivated to engage with the Old Testament because it is written, verbal communication from God. God has entrusted his community with his Word, and reading deliberately is our responsibility. In the next chapter, we will further discuss the Old Testament text as the Word of God and thus the injunction to read it deliberately.

THREE

From Talking to Tablets to Tabernacle to Today

Speech is the most specifically human form of action.

—Assnat Bartor, *Reading Law as Narrative*

From Narnia to Louisville

"Dear Mr. Roberts . . ." begins the handwritten correspondence.

I stared intently at this letter, which is currently housed in the library of Louisville Presbyterian Theological Seminary, and tried to make out the considerable number of faded words and the hardly intelligible cursive writing. Even though there was a transcribed, typed version of the letter with an explanation set adjacent to the original in the same frame, I was determined to make out the words of the original. I was in the presence of greatness, in a very real way, by just standing in front of the letter. My veneration of the words written in this correspondence had everything to do with their author.

The letter was from the eminent twentieth-century novelist and Christian apologist C. S. Lewis. The correspondence, addressed to the Reverend Dr. F. Morgan Roberts, was dated July 31, 1954, just as Lewis was in the middle of authoring the acclaimed Chronicles of Narnia. I felt as if Lewis had stepped out of Narnia and into Louisville when I realized that he had penned this letter during that time period.

As I distinguished C. S. Lewis's handwriting, I was able to observe—in a limited sense—the result of how his mind commanded his hand to form the characters, how those characters created words that had meaning, and how Lewis used those words together in order to communicate the exact message that he wanted Dr. Roberts to receive. Lewis's masterful use of words for the purpose of moving the reader to action is evidenced by the final phrase of the letter addressed to Dr. Roberts. The letter concludes with the humble, touching petition, "Perhaps you will sometimes pray for me?" Lewis invited Dr. Roberts into fellowship with him by situating these simple, yet compelling, words in the right location at the end of his brief composition. To behold the writings of Lewis—especially the words of privileged communication that come by way of personal correspondence—is to behold C. S. Lewis, whose presence continues among us through his words decades after they were penned.

Likewise, God invites people into fellowship with him through written words. These words also genuinely bear the presence of God insofar as they disclose what God desires to communicate, thereby disclosing the divine character and plan. To engage with the words that God left behind is—in a very real way—to behold the presence of God, millennia after those words were penned.[1] The Torah tells the story of how God reaches out in fellowship to people through various media that relate God's verbal communication. God uses the divine audible voice to demonstrate his closeness to humankind. God's proximity demonstrates his care and imparts the responsibility to appropriately respond to him.

Nevertheless, God's audible voice is not the only way God communicates with people. God increasingly turns to written correspondence in the Torah in order to leave a lasting word for his people, especially after the patriarchal period. The written text itself serves as a continuous reminder that God has a unique relationship with human beings, and humans have the ability to enjoy fellowship with God through words. God's written Word testifies to God's closeness and desire for fellowship with people. The very presence of the written Word of God provokes a response to the contents of the text. This fact calls us to engage with the Old Testament deliberately, regardless of how distant it may feel.

---

1. I am deeply influenced by John Frame's personal-word model of communication, through which he stresses that God's communication to human beings in the Scriptures is essentially a personal word from God—just as if one person were talking to another. See Frame, *Doctrine of the Word of God*, especially pp. 3–7, but this point is repeated throughout the book. God's written Word implies God's desire for communion with humankind and invokes a response from the recipients of the divine Word.

From Voice to Text

God's closeness through the divine Word is thematically and literarily at the core of Exodus. This is particularly evident in the scene in which God meets the people of Israel at Mount Sinai and gives them his law (Exod. 19–24). The divine encounter at Sinai formalizes the relationship between God and the covenant people, Israel (19:1–6), and highlights two additional ways God communicates with them. First, Moses further emerges as a divinely sanctioned mediator between God and humankind, passing along God's audible commands to the community. In other words, Moses functions as God's prophet. Second, God uses Moses's mediation to eventually communicate through the written Word.

Sinai is where the movement from voice to text begins. At Sinai, God authorizes written words as divine communication given to the people of Israel for their instruction. The community is subsequently able to access God's instruction in future situations in which they require guidance or simply need to be reminded of the character of their God, his promises, and his fellowship with them. Moses plays a monumental role by relating audible and written correspondence from God to the people, thereby serving as the facilitator of voice to text. This is particularly evident in the scenes in which God calls Israel to Sinai and gives the covenant people his good word through various media: the audible voice, Moses the messenger, and the written word.

In Exodus 19, God commissions Israel as his holy nation (vv. 1–6) and instructs them to gather at the base of Mount Sinai, where God plans to descend in a thick cloud to speak to Moses (vv. 7–15). While gathered, the people of Israel hear thunder and blasts of the trumpet; they see lightning and smoke as God descends upon Sinai and calls Moses to meet him (vv. 16–20). The first time Moses ascends Mount Sinai to meet God, God commands Moses to return to the camp and communicate with the people the seriousness of the situation; they were not to come up the mountain, or there would be grave consequences. Moses descends the mountain, communicates God's word to the people, and then ascends again, presumably with his brother, Aaron (vv. 21–25).

God reveals the Ten Commandments to Moses in the hearing of all the people during the next scene (Exod. 20:1–17). At this point in the narrative, the people have seen enough and heard enough; they can no longer bear the awesomeness of God's presence. The Sinai spectacle truly scares the people almost to death, so they conclude that they will not live if they experience such an overwhelming wonder again. Their disposition toward God's word is one of obedience, but, because of their dread, they categorically require a change in the medium of communication. Thus the congregation approaches Moses and demands: "Speak to us yourself and we will listen. But do not have God speak to us or we will die" (v. 19; cf. Deut. 5:28–31). The spirit of this unified declaration of the people after observing the awesome scene at Sinai is essentially a reiteration of what the Israelite elders communicated to Moses prior to God's descent upon Sinai. The leaders of Israel were already favorably inclined to Moses's mediation (Exod. 19:7–8; 20:18–21). God essentially accepts the arrangement proposed by the people[2] and begins to increasingly use intermediaries like Moses to communicate his word. Moses had certainly spoken on behalf of God before (e.g., 6:1–9) and had already been commanded by God to write prior to the episode at Sinai (17:14–16). However, from this point on, Moses is more than simply an intermediary; Moses is the herald of God's audible and written word as well as a divinely appointed author.

A notable move in the direction of God using written texts to communicate his word comes to pass when God commissions a divinely authored text to Moses: "Come up to me on the mountain and stay here, and I will give you the tablets of stone with the law and commandments I have written for their instruction" (Exod. 24:12). God's claim to have written the texts that he delegates to Moses indicates God's complete authority and responsibility for the written texts. These texts were a practical way for generations of the community of God to learn from the Scriptures that bore divine authority. The closeness that Israel experienced with God was no longer exclusively contingent upon hearing God's audible voice, which they dreaded. The people of Israel could now experience God's fellowship through the proclamation of a divinely ordained, written text. This was to be a lasting pattern for the people of Israel and for subsequent readers of the texts through which the God of Israel revealed himself.

After Moses receives further instructions at the top of Sinai, God eventually hands over the tablets to him. In this scene, the narrator specifically indicates that the tablets were inscribed with God's own finger: "When the LORD finished speaking to Moses on Mount Sinai, he gave him the two tablets of the covenant law, the tablets of stone inscribed by the finger of God" (Exod. 31:18). Why is it important that the narrator include this anthropomorphism (i.e., "the finger of God") in 31:18, when 24:12 already clearly indicates that the tablets originated from God?

The reason for the additional information is to emphasize a theological point regarding God's previous word: Exodus 31:18 reiterates the fact that the written word, which was to be used for instruction among the community,

---

2. Frame, *Doctrine of the Word of God*, 83.

came with God's authority—God was the ultimate author. But this is not a sheer reiteration of the facts; it also expands on what was previously mentioned. The striking imagery used to relate that God wrote this instruction with the divine finger makes absolutely clear that God is in the very midst of the people wherever that text is proclaimed. These same points are echoed in what seems to be an unnecessary parenthetical repetition of similar information in 32:15–16: "Moses turned and went down the mountain with the two tablets of the covenant law in his hands. They were inscribed on both sides, front and back. The tablets were the work of God; the writing was the writing of God, engraved on the tablets."

The shelf life of the tablets is, unfortunately, exceptionally brief. After being tipped off by God concerning Israel's unfaithfulness, Moses descends Sinai and observes that the people of Israel have become unfaithful to their God by making a golden calf. This treachery was led by none other than Moses's brother, Israel's first high priest, Aaron. Viewing the people dancing about a mute idol proves to be too much for Moses, who burns with anger and heaves the tablets at the base of the mountain, shattering them (Exod. 32:7–19). The destruction of the tablets illustrates the community's condition at that moment: they are not particularly interested in submitting to the authority of the Word of God, which explicitly forbids casting idols (20:3–6); and their absorption with the presence of their golden calf clearly indicates that they are uninterested in fellowship with the true God.

Nevertheless, God reaches out to the people of Israel again by taking the initiative to rewrite the tablets: "The Lord said to Moses, 'Chisel out two stone tablets like the first ones, and I will write on them the words that were on the first tablets, which you broke'" (Exod. 34:1). Why does God insist on providing the people with a written text (presumably, at least partially) inscribed with the divine finger once again (Deut. 4:13; 9:10)?[3] It seems as if these two tablets were to serve as an authoritative, tangible, and proximate reminder of God's word among the people, which reflected his care for them. The provision of the written word to the people of Israel was an act of divine fellowship, since it was through the two tablets that God provided the covenant people a permanent reminder of his truthful and dependable word as well as his constant presence with them.

Moses's ministry expands into one more area essential to our study. Moses is the herald of God's spoken word, and Moses introduces the community to the written word of God (Exod. 31:18; 34:1; Deut. 4:13), but Moses also functions as writer of the word of God. From the perspective of the community,

---

3. It seems as if Moses also wrote on these same tablets (cf. Exod. 34:27–28).

Moses begins as a transmitter of dictated material, progresses into being a distributer of God's written word, and, finally, develops into a writer of received data. This whole process comes to pass by way of God's divine order. Two examples of Moses's writing will be helpful at this point:

> Then the LORD said to Moses, "Write down these words, for in accordance with these words I have made a covenant with you and with Israel." Moses was there with the Lord forty days and forty nights without eating bread or drinking water. And he wrote on the tablets the words of the covenant—the Ten Commandments. (Exod. 34:27–28)

> At the Lord's command Moses recorded the stages in their journey. This is their journey by stages. . . . (Num. 33:2)

In both passages, the narrator establishes that Moses wrote by virtue of God's command, which reflects the conformity of Moses's word to God's word. In this, the process of God's voice to Moses's text is complete: God's audible voice demonstrating God's presence among the people became God's finger at Sinai; God's finger became Moses's hand throughout the wilderness wanderings.[4]

From Moses to Tabernacle

Moses's writings, which were in the course of time identified as "the Book of the Law of Moses" (Josh. 8:31; 23:6; 2 Kings 14:6; Neh. 8:1) or just "the Book of the Law," were revered by the community during Moses's lifetime.[5] Toward the end of his life, Moses is depicted as instructing the Levites concerning practices intended to ensure that the Word of God remain the central component of the community's spiritual life (Deut. 31:9–13, 24–29). While providing these directions, Moses commands the Levites, "Take this **Book of the Law** and place it beside the ark of the covenant of the LORD your God. There it will remain as a witness against you" (31:26). Moses's request to place his writings not just in the tabernacle but in the most holy place beside the ark of the covenant in the same chamber in which God's glory dwelled, might strike the reader as

---

4. For other verses in the Torah that depict Moses writing, see Deut. 31:9, 22, 24.

5. It is admittedly not possible to demonstrate that the collection of writings referred to as the Book of the Law and the Book of the Law of Moses is the entirety of the Pentateuch as it was passed down in the Masoretic tradition. The point of this section is to point out that Moses is straightforwardly depicted as writing and that his writings were promptly revered as the word of God by the community.

presumptuous, absurd, unwarranted, and even a death wish. This is unless, of course, the Levites identified Moses's written text as God's communication to the community. Then Moses's request is a demonstration of the community's recognition that Moses's writings essentially bear the divine authority. Beholding Moses's writings was like standing in front of a letter written with the divine finger, and, thereby, was like being in the presence of God.

Moses includes a critical addendum to his instruction. He specifically states the reason for placing the Book of the Law next to the ark by adding the words "there it will remain as a witness against you" (Deut. 31:26). How is it that an inanimate composition can serve as a witness? Scrolls do not "witness"; they do not actively provide knowledge of an event or testify to an observed situation. Only a personal being can do such a thing. The fact that the word of God is to serve as a witness against the people suggests that Moses's writings are to be a demonstration of God's very presence with the people, encouraging them to take heed of the word.[6] The proximity of the written word to God's presence in the tabernacle is an indication of God's approval of those words, their authority among the people, and the unique manner in which God is manifestly present with and cares for the people.

Ultimately, as the herald of the audible voice, the mediator of God's written word, and the writer of divine correspondence, Moses repeatedly calls the people back to the word of God for provision in every aspect of their lives. This is particularly noted in Moses's encouragement for the people of Israel to obey God's word since they learned the fickleness of their hearts through their struggles in the wilderness. Moses emphasizes that God's fellowship through his word is the primary demonstration of God's goodness to the people, despite their distress. Take, for example, Moses's words in Deuteronomy 8:1–3:

> Be careful to follow every command I am giving you today, so that you may live and increase and may enter and possess the land the Lord promised on oath to your ancestors. Remember how the Lord your God led you all the way in the wilderness these forty years, to humble and test you in order to know what was in your heart, whether or not you would keep his commands. He humbled you,

6. This same idea is portrayed in the preceding verses (Deut. 31:19–22). God commands Moses to write down a song that will serve as a witness against the people of Israel. Yet how can a song serve as a witness? The saying appears to suggest that the word originates with a personal being who testifies to the people's compliance or noncompliance with that word. God gives the song and tells Moses to teach it to the people and to write it down. In this sense, God's presence will perpetually be present through these words, assessing the reverence of the community toward the divine correspondence. This same idea of God's Word being animate is evident in Heb. 4:12: "For the word of God is **alive** and **active**. Sharper than any double-edged sword, it **penetrates** even to dividing soul and spirit, joints and marrow; it **judges** the thoughts and attitudes of the heart."

causing you to hunger and then feeding you with manna, which neither you nor
your ancestors had known, to teach you that man does not live on bread alone
but on **every word that comes from the mouth of the** Lord [literally: "every
going forth (i.e., utterance) of the mouth of the Lord"].

The people of Israel depended completely on God's verbal communication
for their sustenance. There would have been no manna, quail, or water from
the rock if God did not speak. Without words from Sinai, the people would
not have known the condition of their hearts and their need to walk with
their God. Israel would have been defeated by her enemies and decimated in
the desert if it were not for divine instruction (Num. 21:31–35; Deut. 3:1–11).
Most significantly, the people would not have known their God at all if he
had remained silent.

There is an enduring lesson for readers through these select texts related to
placing the written word next to the ark, in the tabernacle, in the middle of
the camp. This act was another means by which God showed Israel his eager-
ness for fellowship with them: he wanted to be at the geographical center of
their camp and at the spiritual heart of their community. In the Torah, God's
word is depicted as the source of physical and spiritual life and of provision
for the people.[7] The physical provision was extremely important to preserve
the people during their wilderness wanderings. Nevertheless, the abiding,
spiritual lessons learned by the people of Israel and by modern readers come
by way of perpetually returning to the written word and devoutly feeding on
"every going forth" of the mouth of God.

From Moses to Joshua

The journey of Israel toward the promised land concludes with a transition
of leadership toward the end of the Torah. Moses, the messenger of God's
word, is not permitted to enter the land because of an incident in which he
and his brother Aaron, ironically, fail to properly represent God to the covenant community (Num. 20:10–13).[8] Joshua is commissioned to lead the

7. The fact that God's Word is the source of physical and spiritual life seems to be what
Jesus is getting at in his reference to Deut. 8:3 in Matt. 4:4 and Luke 4:4. In these passages,
Jesus is tempted to sacrifice his spiritual provision in favor of accepting physical provision. By
referring to Israel's wilderness wanderings, Jesus prioritizes God's spiritual provision over accepting much needed physical provision combined with disobedience.

8. The text that communicates why Moses is not permitted to enter into the promised land
is vague. My conclusion that the issue had to do with Moses misrepresenting God is based on a
comparison between what God tells Moses, his special representative, to do in order to provide
the community with water and what Moses *actually* does (Num. 20:6–11). It is reasonable to

people just prior to Moses's death. The promise that God made to Abraham hundreds of years earlier concerning the innumerable quantity of his descendants possessing the land is on the brink of being fulfilled under Joshua's leadership.

As the Torah's story continues in the book of Joshua, the author leaves no doubt that God expects the community to revere and appropriately respond to the divine Word just as they were expected to during the time of Joshua's predecessor, Moses. Early in the book, the Lord appears to Joshua and, by way of the audible voice, assures Israel's new leader of the divine promise that the people of Israel will inherit the land: "Be strong and very courageous. Be careful to obey all the law my servant Moses gave you; do not turn from it to the right or to the left, that you may be successful wherever you go. Keep this Book of the Law always on your lips; meditate on it day and night, so that you may be careful to do everything written in it. Then you will be prosperous and successful" (Josh. 1:7–8).

God's command for Joshua to be strong and courageous is coupled with multiple iterations of encouragements for Joshua to adhere to the written word:

"Be careful to obey all the law."

"Do not turn from it."

"Keep this Book of the Law always on your lips."

"Meditate on it."

"Be careful to do everything written in it."

The allusions to the Book of the Law at the beginning and end of Joshua (1:8; 23:6) are particularly important as they relate to God's communication through the written Word. God's speech to Joshua at the beginning of the book seems to associate the Book of the Law with Moses's book that is mentioned in Deuteronomy 31:24–26, which was placed next to the ark of the covenant to serve as a witness.[9] In Joshua 1:7–8, God appears to consider this "book" to be his very word. It must always be on Joshua's mind, heart, and lips and should always guide his action. This reverent response to the Book of the Law is what will give Joshua success in carrying out the mission

---

suggest that the differences between God's commands and Moses's actions portray a different illustration than that which God wanted to portray through the event.

9. This may also be the law that Moses is depicted as writing and then giving to the Levites in Deut. 31:9. These texts suggest that *at least* the core of the teaching that subsequent generations relied on for instruction was written by Moses.

God has given him. Moses's written word to the people of Israel is received as God's written Word; this book is a means by which the people are able to know that God is with them, empowering them to carry out their mission.[10]

Toward the end of his ministry as their leader, Joshua applies this message to the entire people of Israel. In doing so, Joshua uses language similar to that of 1:7–8 to remind the people that God is with them. Obedience to the Book of the Law of Moses is instrumental to the people's remembrance of their God and to their being empowered to carry out the mission that God has given them:

> Remember how I have allotted as an inheritance for your tribes all the land of the nations that remain. . . . The LORD your God himself will push them out for your sake. He will drive them out before you, and you will take possession of their land, as the LORD your God promised you. Be very strong; be careful to obey all that is written in the Book of the Law of Moses, without turning aside to the right or to the left. . . . But you are to hold fast to the LORD your God, as you have until now. (Josh. 23:4–6, 8)

God's Word is a way by which the community can be assured that God is going to be with them all of the time. The written Word is evidence that God desires to have fellowship with the people, bringing them success and prosperity as he promised their ancestors. The community will be successful in their God-given mission insofar as they recognize that reverence to the written Word is indispensable to their existence. The community was able to cling to the Lord by way of clinging to the written Word.

The instructions concerning the writings of Moses that serve as bookends to Joshua are particularly important since the book of Joshua reflects a continuation of a transition begun during the time of Moses. The people go from hearing the authoritative word from God's audible voice to receiving the divine word through the written text. In the post-Mosaic period, the people of Israel are able to learn from the written Word and to reflect on how God had previously communicated with the people and manifested himself in their midst.[11]

10. The identification of Moses's commands with God's words seems further corroborated in Joshua when he builds an altar to the Lord "as Moses the servant of the LORD had commanded the Israelites. He builds it according to what is written in the Book of the Law of Moses" (Josh. 8:31). Moses's law reflects God's commands concerning the very important issue of building an altar, and Joshua follows what Moses had to say about this. After sacrificing peace offerings on that altar, Joshua makes his own copy of the Law of Moses, evidently in obedience to the command reflected in Deut. 27:2–4.

11. Moses's writings are surely revered as the very Word of God by the community later in the history of the people of Israel. For example, note King Josiah's reaction to hearing the words

From the Torah to Today's Reader

This survey of selected portions of the Torah and Joshua illustrate that God's close proximity to his people is evidenced by divine verbal communication. Throughout the initial books of the Bible, God transitions from primarily communicating his word audibly to using a combination of the audible word and the written word. At this point we have to ask, How should the fact that God communicated to ancient Israel through written texts affect the contemporary reader's disposition toward the Old Testament?

The Book of Moses and the other Old Testament texts have been passed down to us as the written Word of God. Reading the Bible as written correspondence from God is similar to staring at C. S. Lewis's letter in the library of Louisville Seminary: we behold the very presence of the author through his words. God is present in his written Word, demonstrating that he still desires fellowship, he is still making good on his promises, and he continues to be in the midst of his community when his Word is proclaimed. Thus our disposition toward the Old Testament should be one of reverence, since we are to some degree in the presence of God when we engage with these texts.

Our awe of God compels us to read his communication in a deliberate manner and to explore that which God desires to teach us through these ancient, yet ever-so-applicable, words. All of God's verbal communication demonstrates that God desires fellowship with humankind and creates an obligation for the recipient of the divine Word to properly respond. Our contemporary way of revering the Word of God is to deliberately engage with all of the written texts, while honoring them like we would honor the divine voice from Sinai, and striving to apply the enduring messages that are taught throughout the Bible to our lives. John Frame states, "Unlike any other ancient book, Scripture is written with the purpose of instructing those who would live many centuries into the future, to give them instruction, endurance, encouragement, and hope."[12] Scripture was written for those who were not in Sinai, and it demonstrates that the God who spoke

---

of the Book of the Law during his reign: "Go and inquire of the LORD for me and for the people and for all Judah about what is written in this book that has been found. Great is the LORD's anger that burns against us because those who have gone before us have not obeyed the words of this book; they have not acted in accordance with all that is written there concerning us" (2 Kings 22:13). The king recognized that past irreverence for the Book of the Law put them under the wrath of the Lord. In other words, not following Moses's writing was contempt for the Word of God. Consider the reaction of Josiah in light of the requirements laid out for Israel's future king (in relation to the Law) in Deut. 17:18–20.

12. Frame, *Doctrine of the Word of God*, 230.

in specific locations throughout the Old Testament still desires fellowship with humanity.

Our conversation up to this juncture has predominantly focused on *why* Christians are compelled to read the Old Testament as the divine Word, and thus we have dedicated little space to *how* Christians should read these texts deliberately. This is the hermeneutical question to which we now turn.

FOUR

Reading from Today
Back to the Text

The Bible speaks in Hebrew.

—Edward L. Greenstein,
Essays on Biblical Method and Translation

It is by the grace of . . . the Bible's foolproof composition that such extreme under-readers yet manage to grasp the essentials of plot and judgment, without suffering anything worse than boredom.

—Meir Sternberg, *The Poetics of Biblical Narrative*

It is safe to say that many interpersonal problems are rooted in misunderstandings of simple language. This is why, of course, it is always good to know exactly what someone is communicating before we respond. There is an element of humility inherent in pausing and making sure we understand what is being said by our conversation partner, or the author we are reading, before reacting. Natural human instinct is a really good thing in many areas of life, but it is rarely a good tool when considering a response to important words.

For example, consider how Spanish speakers from different areas of the world must occasionally freeze and contemplate what others who speak the same language are *actually* trying to communicate. To illustrate, let's take ten words commonly used in Puerto Rico and observe how they might be understood in Mexico. As you can see in the following chart, some of the Puerto Rican Spanish-language words have completely different meanings in Mexico, while other words are unintelligible.

English Word/Phrase	Puerto Rican Word	Word/Phrase Commonly Used in Mexico	Meaning of Puerto Rican Term in Mexico
bus	guagua	autobús	unintelligible term
in a while/a while ago	ahorita	al rato	immediately
orange (fruit)	china	naranja	China (country)
money	chavo	dinero	young boy
cheap (insult)	maceta	avaro	flowerpot
bean	habichuela	frijol	unintelligible term
jeans	mahones	pantalones de mezclilla	unintelligible term

All is fun and games until someone from Puerto Rico tries to talk in Mexico using some of these basic words to communicate everyday speech. Below, I have used these Spanish-language words in three sentences that someone who speaks Puerto Rican Spanish might say in a normal conversation with a friend. In the English translations, note the differences between what the Puerto Rican Spanish speaker is trying to convey and how a Spanish speaker from Mexico would likely understand (or *not* understand) the same exact Spanish-language phrase.

1. Ahorita, voy a subirme a la guagua y voy a comerme la china.

   Puerto Rico: In a little while, I am going to get on the bus, and I am going to eat the orange.

   Mexico: Right now, I am going to go up on the (unintelligible word), and I am going to eat myself the China (i.e., the country).

2. Le pedí chavo a Miguel para comprar habichuelas, pero no me dio nada porque es una maceta. Había gastado todo su chavo en sus nuevos mahones.

   Puerto Rico: I asked Miguel for money to buy beans, but he did not give me anything because he is cheap. He had spent all of his money on his new jeans.

   Mexico: I asked Miguel for a young boy to buy (unintelligible word), but he did not give me anything because he is a flowerpot. He spent all of his boy on his new (unintelligible word).

This type of humorous comparison is not unique to Puerto Rican and Mexican Spanish; it can be made by juxtaposing various Spanish-language terms from other countries around the world as well. When we compare just these two examples that contain common words for a Puerto Rican Spanish speaker, the main point is clear: it is generally not prudent for Spanish speakers to use just their intuition when trying to figure out what other Spanish speakers from different areas of the world might be trying to communicate. We do not inherently have the capacity to understand each other without using other faculties and asking the right questions. Sometimes we cannot use our instinct to figure out language that we think *should* be intuitive to us. Being overconfident in our ability to quickly and easily understand what someone is saying can lead to embarrassment or have serious ramifications in a situation in which the communication is of great importance.

The written text of the Bible is how God continues to communicate verbally with readers today. We must therefore be conscious to avoid pitfalls of interpretation when we read the Old Testament, since practical distances (far greater than those between regional Spanish dialects) exist between us and those who originally received the biblical text. Just as two Spanish speakers from different areas of the world lack the intuition to understand exactly what the other is saying all of the time, so we are compelled to slow down in our Old Testament readings and ask questions concerning the meaning of nuances in the text.

In any setting, asking questions about verbal communication is the best way to avoid confusion. All questions must be asked with the understanding that language does not always conform to the expectations of the hearer or reader. Rather, the recipient of the communication must conform his or her expectations to how the words, phrases, and idioms at hand are structured to communicate. Likewise, reasonable interpretation of the Old Testament is contingent upon recognizing that we are distant from the text and understanding that the biblical text does not conform to our expectations. Our interpretations should conform to how the text presents itself to us. It is our responsibility as modern readers to "work our way back to the text" as much as possible from where we stand today. Reading back to the text entails the somewhat humiliating exercise of curbing our intuition for the sake of reading deliberately and learning from the ancient author.

Intuition versus Humility

Reading the Old Testament is about "reading" and about the "Old Testament." In order to understand the message(s) of the Old Testament and apply its teachings to our lives, we must judiciously engage with the words of any given passage as well as the whole Old Testament. Reading individual Old Testament texts as well as observing where they fit in view of the whole is an exhilarating task and one that comes with considerable responsibility for students of the Old Testament.

Words do not simply rest on a page; readers listen to how words speak through the creative genius of an author. Words have the ability to provide information, provoke vivid imagery, induce a wide range of feelings, and afford glimpses into worlds otherwise inaccessible to us. Authors enliven words by weaving them together in a way that communicates more profoundly, and is more aesthetically pleasing, than the straightforward sum of the component parts. Yet in order for authors to have the greatest impact through their words, readers (i.e., those who are able to properly decipher and render aloud the words on a page) must be humble conversation partners who are willing to sensitively perceive what the author wants to communicate to the audience.

Reading the Old Testament begins by recognizing the words on the pages of Scripture and then progresses to understanding the message(s) communicated through the rhetoric in these compositions. An inherent irony associated with reading is the possibility of correctly reading the words but not comprehending the message they construct. Furthermore, it is possible to understand words, phrases, and sections of a literary work while misinterpreting the significance of the work as a whole.

We frequently use intuition to make immediate judgments about texts we read. Sometimes we subconsciously develop interpretations of what we read without being aware of what we *actually* have accomplished. In this sense, intuition can be our best friend when we are engaging with literature that is straightforward and familiar to us. Intuition can help us quickly apprehend the meaning of words, phrases, and even whole works that harmonize with our proclivities and are intended for an audience that shares characteristics with us (our preferred language, cultural customs, etc.).

Nevertheless, intuition is *not* a judicious means by which to develop a responsible interpretation of the Old Testament if it is the primary instrument we use when reading the text. The ability to quickly understand words and phrases without, perhaps, deliberately considering all that they might communicate within a composition could, ironically, become our worst enemy. One brief, well-known example from the book of Job should suffice at this point to demonstrate that a text's language cannot always be interpreted as we might initially perceive.

Job 13:15 begins, "Though he slay me, yet will I hope in him."[1] Given the tremendous sufferings of Job, many contemporary readers understand Job's

1. See the comparable translations in the ESV ("Though he slay me, I will hope in him "), the KJV ("Though he slay me, yet will I trust in him"), and the NASB ("Though He slay me, I will hope in Him").

words to mean something like, "I will trust in God no matter what happens to me—even to the point of death." Along these lines, the enduring message of this verse might be understood as an encouragement to trust in God during trying times. This is certainly an invaluable message that is extremely applicable to those who experience inexplicable trials, and especially ones that lead to acute physical distress.

The prevailing question is not so much whether this encouraging reading of Job 13:15 applies to our contemporary lives but whether the text is actually communicating hope. A couple of issues challenge this understanding of Job's words:

- First, the next line of the same verse states, "I will surely defend my ways to his face" (13:15b). The immediate context suggests that Job is determined to argue with God. If Job trusts in God so much that he is okay with God slaying him, then why would he argue with God to his face? Reading successively helps uncover this inconsistency.

- Second, Job has previously demonstrated serious contempt for God. For example, in Job 9:20–24, Job calls God an unjust judge and asserts that "he mocks the despair of the innocent" (9:23). Does this sound like a guy who is going to turn around in his very next speech and say, "I trust him so much that I believe whatever he is doing to me is fine"? Reading the book of Job entirely helps us understand his speeches in light of one another and reveals this disparity.

- Third, this is a tricky verse, not only in English but also in Hebrew.[2] The traditional text does not actually have the prepositional phrase "in him" in the phrase "though he slay me, yet will I hope in him." Rather, the text has the similarly sounding Hebrew word "no/not" instead of the phrase "in him." How should this textual issue affect how contemporary readers understand the text? Well, another acceptable translation of this verse could be, "Behold! He will slay me. I will not hope [i.e., I have no hope]."[3] Job *actually* might be expressing his lack of hope because of his perception that God is killing him!

2. To mention the Hebrew-language issue is certainly not to suggest that the opinions of people who know the biblical languages are always correct in their interpretations. Rather, I am asserting that it is strictly unacceptable to maintain and promote misguided interpretations about Old Testament passages that are developed by intuitively understanding the translated language or as a result of accepting common interpretive traditions with minimal or no examination of the passage in its context(s).

3. The NRSV translates this verse along these lines: "See, he will kill me; I have no hope; but I will defend my ways to his face." The JPS version is similar: "He may well slay me; I may have no hope; Yet I will argue my case before him."

Considering these three points, Job is potentially communicating the exact opposite of the message that some might pick up and run with based on the words used in the English translation. Given the immediate context of the verse, the framework of the book of Job as a whole, and the textual issue in this verse, Job might be conveying a pessimistic view toward his future because the divine hand has brought about his ruin. These issues cast doubt on the prudence of quickly glancing at the words of Job the sufferer and promptly writing them on a get-well-soon card. Our commitment to slowing down and reading the whole text in its context provokes us to ask effective questions regarding the passage's interpretation.

Job 13:15 adequately illustrates why we need to deliberately consider what the Old Testament text is truly saying and, thereby, what the biblical writers are "doing."[4] Striving to set aside our instincts as much as possible in order to read slowly might seem counterintuitive, especially given the prevailing assumption that academic prowess is partially established by the ability to read quickly. Reading the Old Testament is different. An interpreter's aptitude is not determined by how fast they can read but, rather, by how they answer the questions that the text inspires.

Many of the questions that modern readers ask about the Old Testament relate to the nature of the compilation of the Old Testament books, how we have received the text, and the gaps that exist because of our distance from the text. These issues warrant further explanation. In order to learn more, we will begin by reviewing the structure of the Old Testament and considering how we received the text we currently have.

Terminology Matters

Concise names and titles have the potential to communicate a great deal concerning identities and beliefs. As Christians, we make a statement about who we are and what we believe by using the compact title "Old Testament"[5] to refer to the initial section of the Christian Bible. The traditional Christian designation "Old Testament" is not a completely interchangeable term for the Hebrew Bible. Even though the Old Testament in the Protestant tradition is by and large the same text as the Hebrew Bible, we make a statement

4. In the next chapter we will discuss further what the biblical writers are "doing" and how that relates to meaning.

5. By the term "Old Testament," I specifically refer to the traditional Protestant canon, which coincides with the historical Jewish canon. The debate concerning which books should be included in the Old Testament canon is neither a contemporary nor an exclusively Western debate between Catholics and Protestants.

concerning how we read the Bible by postulating that the "New Testament" continues the literary and theological trajectories that were established in what we call the "Old Testament."

The fact that the term "Old Testament" is inherently theological and signifies belief in a "New Testament" requires us to acknowledge the degrees of separation between ourselves (who have access to the New Testament) and the original implied audience(s) of the text of the Old Testament. On the one hand, the distinctions between the audiences of the Old and New Testaments could easily be exaggerated. The New Testament writers imply that they are writing for the benefit of the community of faith and that they are continuing the trajectory set out by the Old Testament authors.[6] On the other hand, there are clearly considerable degrees of separation between us and the mostly ancient Israelite/Jewish audience(s) of the Old Testament. These degrees of separation lead to gaps in familiarity with the text of the Old Testament that we must strive to traverse as much as possible.

Created Equal? The Old Testament and the Hebrew Bible

The Old Testament consists of a compilation of twenty-four books according to the traditional Jewish counting of books in the Hebrew Bible.[7] But in the Christian Bible, the Old Testament is divided into thirty-nine books. Here are some differences in how the books are divided:

- The sequential books of 1–2 Samuel, 1–2 Kings, and 1–2 Chronicles in the Old Testament are only one book each in the Hebrew Bible.
- Ezra and Nehemiah are regarded as one composition in the Hebrew Bible.
- The twelve prophetic writings that Christians frequently refer to as the "Minor Prophets" count as only one book in the Hebrew Bible.

Furthermore, the books appear in a different order in the Old Testament and in the Hebrew Bible. The Old Testament essentially follows a historical arrangement of the biblical books by placing the Pentateuch first, followed by the historical books, the poetic literature, and, last, the major and the minor prophets. The arrangement of the Hebrew Bible consists of three major

6. See, for example, 1 Cor. 14:37, 2 Pet. 3:15–16 (where Peter refers to Paul's writings alongside the "other Scriptures"), and Heb. 1:1–2.
7. This counting of books is explicitly mentioned in the noncanonical book of 2 Esdras 14:45–46.

sections that are called by their Hebrew titles: the Torah (Law), Nevi'im (Prophets), and Ketuvim (Writings). The first letter of the words naming each section of the Hebrew Bible form the acronym TaNaK (*Tanakh*). Jewish people commonly refer to the Hebrew Bible by this epithet, though it is also frequently used by Christians to reflect the division of the biblical books accepted by early believers in Jesus, who were mostly Jewish.[8]

Despite differences in the order and division of books in the Old Testament and the *Tanakh*, wide-ranging modern translations read by diverse groups of Christians and Jewish people alike are, by and large, derived from the same primary Hebrew-language manuscript: the Leningrad Codex. The Leningrad Codex inherited the first part of its name as a result of its current location in Saint Petersburg, Russia, formerly known as Leningrad. The word "Codex" conveys that this famous manuscript exists in the form of a book that includes all the compositions of the Hebrew Bible.[9]

The Leningrad Codex was penned in Cairo, Egypt, in about AD 1008 by a Jewish scribe named Shmuel Ben-Yaakov and was copied from the manuscripts associated with Aaron ben Moshe ben Asher, which means that the manuscript represents the scribal tradition of the ben Asher family. The ben Asher family was part of a group of scribes called Masoretes, who were medieval-period Jewish scholars that assumed the responsibility of preserving the tradition (*masoret*) of the Hebrew text of the Bible as faithfully as possible through their traditional annotations (*masorah*).[10] This Masoretic tradition is exemplified in the Leningrad Codex, which is the oldest complete version of the Hebrew Bible. This codex serves as the master document for the modern critical edition titled *Biblia Hebraica Stuttgartensia* (BHS), which is frequently referred to as the Masoretic Text (MT). The contemporary critical version bears the name *Biblia Hebraica Stuttgartensia* because

8. Similar divisions are represented in New Testament passages. See, for example, Matt. 5:17; 7:12; 22:40; Luke 24:27, 44; John 1:45.

9. The codex was a post–Second Temple period development that proved to be a method of writing and transmitting the text of the Bible that was superior to the use of scrolls. Codices used fewer writing materials than scrolls did, since it was possible to write on both sides of the page; codices were more practical than scrolls because multiple biblical books could be compiled and transported in one codex instead of distributed through and transported in multiple scrolls.

10. The Masoretic Text, which serves as the base text for our contemporary English-language translations, evidently stems from a tradition of copying that precedes the time of Jesus. See Gentry, "Text of the Old Testament." Based on an analysis of the transmission of the ancient versions of the Old Testament (i.e., the Samaritan Pentateuch, Old Greek versions, and Latin versions), Gentry suggests that "the text of the OT in arrangement, content, and stability was fixed by the time of Ben Sira or more probably, at the end of the fifth century BC" (19). This claim is contrary to the commonly held opinion that the biblical text and canon was fluid (i.e., not standardized) until the end of the first century AD.

it was published by the German Bible Society, headquartered in Stuttgart, Germany.[11]

This concise sketch of the shared provenance and diverse characteristics of the Old Testament and the *Tanakh* was selectively told with the purpose of highlighting a few specific points. This summary brings to light the basic fact that modern translations of the Old Testament are effectively based on the *Tanakh*'s textual tradition. In other words, the Masoretic Text of the Leningrad Codex—printed in the critical edition as the *Biblia Hebraica Stuttgartensia*—is the composition from which the Old Testament is predominantly translated, even though the canonical books are divided and numbered differently. In this sense, translations of the Old Testament and the *Tanakh* are created equal. Whether the text is referred to as the Old Testament or the *Tanakh* tends to say more about the tradition and commitments of the person reading the text than about the actual contents of the volume.

However, the Old Testament and the *Tanakh* maintain diverse traditions that are reflected in their internal structure. Additionally, modern translations of the Old Testament/Hebrew Bible primarily depend on the textual traditions of medieval Jewish scribes. These facts prompt readers to pause and reflect on the enduring gaps between the modern Christian readership of the Old Testament and the ancient Israelite/Jewish audience(s) of the *Tanakh*. Recognizing that we read at a distance facilitates a self-awareness that is necessary for responsible interpretation.

Reading at a Distance

Reading at a distance is not inherently defective; it does not necessarily cause inaccurate or unreasonable readings. Conversely, not admitting gaps in understanding caused by lengthy intervals of language evolution, differences in space (i.e., culture), and the passage of time is an act of negligence on our behalf and can potentially facilitate misguided confidence in our interpretation of ancient texts. Reading at a distance increases our responsibility as readers to be careful interpreters and to be sensitive as we approach the text, recognizing the potential for misinterpretation due to our own unfamiliarity with ancient writing conventions and nuances in language, among other customs.

We are not abandoned to wallow in the mire of hermeneutical despair upon admitting our distance from the ancient texts. To a certain extent, we are

11. Several parts of the next generation of the Hebrew Bible, titled *Biblia Hebraica Quinta* (BHQ), have already been published. For more information on the text and the transmission of the Old Testament, see Würthwein, *Text of the Old Testament*, 15–43.

forced to work through gaps in knowledge caused by the extensive interval of time that has passed since the composition of the original text, among other factors. Reading at a distance cannot only be "worked with"; it can actually work to our advantage. Interpretation is developed by struggling through our distances from the ancient texts. Let's discuss three examples of how we read the Old Testament at a distance. Hopefully, pointing out these gaps in language, space, and time will increase our self-awareness and encourage us to slow down in the process of reading.

The Distance in Language

The Old Testament was predominantly written in Hebrew, with a small portion written in a related Semitic language, Aramaic (Gen. 31:47; Ezra 4:8–6:18; 7:12–26; Jer. 10:11; Dan. 2:4–7:28). The Old Testament texts were written in Hebrew and Aramaic because these were the primary languages of the original intended audiences. There are no contemporary native Biblical Hebrew or Biblical Aramaic speakers in the entire world. This does not mean that all related derivations of Hebrew and Aramaic are dead and useless. Modern Hebrew and Neo-Aramaic dialects certainly provide insight into the linguistic world of the Bible and contribute to understanding these languages at earlier stages. However, given that Modern Hebrew and Neo-Aramaic speakers are more than two millennia removed from the latest Old Testament writings, even speakers of modern branches of these ancient languages must be circumspect when using intuition in their interpretation of the biblical texts.

Relatedly, a glaringly conspicuous example of our distance from the ancient audience relates to the modern languages in which we read the Scriptures today. Most Christians read a translation of the Old Testament in a modern, native language. This is not a criticism per se. The discussion of how to read the Bible well should not put forth, or even camouflage, academic elitism that privileges the interpretations of scholars with language training as intrinsically more reasonable than, and thereby superior to, those of readers without this type of education.[12] Contemporary translations of the Old Testament are produced by highly educated scholars who, without a doubt, strive to accurately render the Hebrew and Aramaic into the target language. They accomplish the task of translation by using their linguistic training in both

---

12. The ability to engage with data from multiple fields related to the study of the Old Testament (e.g., linguistic, historical, literary) can certainly be helpful in the process of interpretation, but it does not *necessarily* lead to a reasonable interpretation, since all additional information is itself subject to interpretation. Access to more material does not *necessarily* indicate a proper assessment or use of the information at hand.

the source language and the target language. Scholars use diverse language styles in the translations that reflect the makeup of the intended audience in addition to the translation philosophy of those responsible for the work. Translators sometimes even attempt to reflect the layout of the biblical text on the pages of the translations in order to portray the Hebrew and Aramaic texts as closely as possible.

Be that as it may, the reality is that most modern students of the Bible are not Semitic-language experts and therefore do not consider the potential nuances of style and meaning that might be introduced by way of a linguistic analysis of the Old Testament. Meir Sternberg points out that "the interpreter of the Bible must double as a linguist far more often than the interpreter of modern literature need do."[13] Readers of translations of the Bible realize that they do not have the technical skills to participate in original-language analyses of the straightforward or, especially frustratingly, the baffling texts. The awareness that we read translations of the Bible (in fact, no one reads the original texts in his or her native language) should curb our instincts to progress through texts as quickly as possible and to heavily depend on intuition in interpreting words that are as supremely important as the Scriptures.

The Distances in Space and Time

The Old Testament consists of mostly originally independent compositions that were primarily written in Western Asia from the middle of the second millennium through the middle of the first millennium BC. The time interval of over two thousand years that has passed since these texts were written sometimes means that the literary world of the Bible's authors is at least partially concealed from us.

This distance in space and time is particularly evident in Hebrew poetry, which is replete with metaphors and imagery that were presumably once comprehensible to the ancient, Middle Eastern audience but, in some cases, are now difficult for us to decipher. In order to grasp many of the metaphors used in the Bible[14] and to picture the vivid imagery found in the Old Testament, we must be familiar with the prevailing concepts that circulated in ancient Near Eastern languages (e.g., Aramaic, Akkadian, Ugaritic) and literature. Since we find ourselves so far removed from the literary world of the Old Testament, it is helpful for us to delve into compositions written in similar languages during the same time period, and in the general vicinity of one another. These texts help us gain insight from the ancient literary environment and give us deeper

---

13. Sternberg, *Poetics of Biblical Narrative*, 21.
14. I will further discuss metaphors in chapter 15 of this book.

knowledge of the backgrounds and language of the Old Testament. Even after we study related works, the distances between us and the ancient audiences will often prove to be too broad for a quick and easy understanding of what the ancient Israelite writer was striving to communicate.

Our distances from the original audience(s) of the Old Testament prohibit us from engaging with these texts in the same way we read modern books written in familiar languages in close geographical vicinities within the past few generations. As mentioned above, closeness to texts permits readers to effectively depend on intuition in ways that are not always advisable in reading ancient texts. Recognizing this fact ironically turns out to benefit us, because self-awareness establishes the foundation for deliberate interpretation of the biblical text. When we are honest about being prone to injudicious readings, we take a difficult and colossal first step in developing interpretive methods that are particularly attentive to detail.

The further the distances and the bigger the gaps, the more intentional our contemporary readings must be for us to grasp what the writers of old were saying in their context, and what the text means to us now. A calculated and methodical reading of the Old Testament guards us from ushering the Old Testament into our world too quickly. Our responsibility is to read from where we are today back to the text, while working through and with the natural gaps in knowledge that exist because of our distance.

The Discomfort of Reading

These gaps do not make contemporary readings of the Old Testament texts inaccessible. John Frame rightly emphasizes that we human beings have to work with our finiteness in the process of reading: "Our finitude . . . bars us from an exhaustive knowledge of God's world, of the course of nature and history. It is difficult for us to understand cultures such as those described in the Bible, far removed from ours in space and time. It is not easy for us to understand the social working of tribal and monarchical cultures, the customs underlying biblical stories, the nature of biblical poetry, the ways in which the meaning of text is affected by literary practices."[15] We cannot completely overcome human finitude in interpreting the Old Testament, but we can recognize it and use it as an impetus to drive us to a closer and deeper study of the Old Testament. Human finitude drives humble, close readers to constantly ask questions of the text with the aspiration of bridging the gaps caused by reading at a distance.

15. Frame, *Doctrine of the Word of God*, 180–81.

Admitting our distances from the Old Testament leaves us with the great responsibility of interpreting it well in order to apply its teachings to our lives. This awareness is just the beginning of improving as readers. It provides what seems to be an incongruous start to a learning process, because it invokes discomfort. Being called to what feels like unnatural and hard work is inherently uncomfortable. Reading the Old Testament well includes time and again recognizing and traversing the distances from the texts while studying them in order to apply the enduring message that God has for us. Reading at a distance should bring about a discomfort that motivates us to improve in the art of reading the Old Testament. Simply by having the written Word, we know of God's desire to fellowship with us. By reading these texts well, we experience God's fellowship.

Being candid about gaps in our understanding that we cannot quite fill compels us to consider several more admissions concerning what we as Christians believe about the text of the Old Testament. Being transparent in our interpretations necessitates admitting who we are and what we believe about the text we encounter on the pages of the Old Testament. In the next chapter, we will review the organic inspiration of the Old Testament and discuss why it is so important that we understand what it has to say to us today.

FIVE

The Confessions of a Close Reader

With a convulsive motion, he tore away the ministerial band from before his breast. It was revealed! But it were irreverent to describe that revelation.
—Nathaniel Hawthorne, *The Scarlet Letter*

While we are responsible for engaging deeply with the Old Testament, we must interpret it with care. An important step at the beginning of the process of reading is recognizing that we stand at a distance from the ancient texts. Christian interpretation of the Old Testament entails more than recognizing *where we stand* in light of the original audience (as discussed in the last chapter); it also incorporates *who we are* in light of the text. In order to be good readers of the Old Testament—that is to say, responsibly interpreting the message(s) of the texts—we must begin by admitting, as much as possible, that our reading is affected by who we are, how we look at the text, and how we perceive these things.

In Anticipation of Reading

Everyone comes to literature with a set of assumptions. Readers assume *something* about what they read before engaging in the process of interpreting the actual text. We might assume that what we are reading expresses opinions that are right or wrong; that it will be enjoyable or dull; that it will be accessible or difficult—in any case, we do not come to any literature as a completely blank slate.

This discussion is particularly significant as it relates to the Old Testament because certain assumptions play into major disagreements about how we should understand the claims of the text. For instance, some of us assume that the miraculous cannot and did not happen. Those who approach the text in this manner are more likely to understand the Old Testament as an anthology of Israel's version of ancient Near Eastern myths, fanciful history turned political propaganda, and prophecy told after the fact.

Others of us who are less antagonistic toward the supernatural are likely to conclude that the Old Testament purposefully retells the history of ancient Israel and collects its religious writings from the distant past to the early Second Temple period. Christians, as testified to by our title, believe that some components of the Old Testament were ultimately realized in the person and the work of Jesus. Therefore, we are more likely to search out how the Old Testament texts are part of the redemptive plan that is ultimately fulfilled through Jesus. Regardless of whether one holds these views, a combination of these views, or entirely different perspectives, the point remains the same: we all assume something about the Old Testament when we read it, and our assumptions influence our readings. Edward L. Greenstein correctly states, "Our very observations, and not only our interpretations, are necessarily shaped by whatever presuppositions, hypotheses, and funds of knowledge we possess."[1]

It is not possible to be aware of everything we assume about a text, but it is possible to admit the assumptions we are aware of. In fact, it is our responsibility to admit them—not just to our conversation partners but also to ourselves. When we admit our assumptions about the Old Testament, it becomes possible to critique those assumptions and to reevaluate our dependence on them. Refining assumptions helps us interpret written texts, since it enables us to nuance and improve on the foundational beliefs that go into our reading of them.[2] If we don't confess what we believe about the Old Testament, we minimize the chance of being fair in our readings and eliminate a crucial part of the conversations relating to interpretation.

The Scandal of Confession

Toward the end of Nathaniel Hawthorne's classic book *The Scarlet Letter*, Reverend Dimmesdale is prepared to finally make his confession. Overwhelmed

---

1. Greenstein, *Essays on Biblical Method and Translation*, 54.
2. Greenstein states, "It is useful to become aware of our assumptions so that we may subject them to criticism and reconsider our reliance on them. But even when we do not notice them, they are there." Greenstein, *Essays on Biblical Method and Translation*, 57.

with the guilt of an adulterous affair he engaged in years earlier, Dimmesdale ascends to a platform with his daughter, Pearl, and Hester Prynne, the accomplice in his wrongdoing, and there confesses his participation in the great scandal that has captivated the town for years. As Dimmesdale collapses after his confession, he rips open his ministerial garments and reveals that he too has a sign of his act of impropriety, just like Hester's scarlet letter. After years of posing as a righteous and chaste clergyman, Dimmesdale fully exposes himself by uncovering the proof of his misdeeds, permitting the crowd that once held him in high regard to realize who he *really* is.

There is a common perception that admitting one's presuppositions about the Old Testament is akin to Dimmesdale's final act. In this sense, confessing presuppositions is a scandal; it is analogous to ripping open the honorable garments of open-minded, fair readers and revealing who they really are, subjecting them to public embarrassment. This is based on common perceptions of scholarly methods—namely, that it is possible to evaluate data in a neutral manner and, consequently, to essentially make evenhanded, unbiased conclusions based on impartially analyzing information.

This is not at all the case when we read the Old Testament. Our readings do not simply reflect the product of data that is examined in an impartial manner. There is no shame for us in admitting that we are supernaturalists and that this affects how we read the numerous miraculous events recorded in the Old Testament. There is no dishonor in admitting that our belief in Jesus as the culmination of God's revelation to humanity affects how we view certain passages as we read the Old Testament successively toward the apex of God's redemptive activity. There is great integrity in revealing who *we really are* despite potential dissent by those who do not share our presuppositions. At least by revealing our assumptions about the Old Testament, we will be able to challenge them and to have open conversations about what is really at stake in our readings. It is precisely because of what we believe about the Old Testament that we are on a quest to read it well and to locate its maximum applicability to our lives as contemporary readers.

Organic Inspiration

Our perspective on scriptural inspiration sets the trajectory for our reading of the Old Testament. In the Old Testament, narrators frequently claim to be talking for God; prophets allege that they speak on behalf of God; and writers assert that they write for God. Whether or not contemporary readers identify these words as God's words determines whether the Old Testament texts are read as inspired literature or on other terms.

Much ink has been spilled on the important theological topic of biblical inspiration. John Frame's concise definition is fitting for the sake of our conversation. Frame explains that inspiration is the "identity between God's words and human words."[3] The implication of this definition related to the writing of the Old Testament is summarized by asserting that "what the human words say, God says."[4] Yet inspiration was not brought about in such a way that the human writers turned into idling drones that waited for the divine finger to move the quill on the scroll. Rather, inspiration came to pass organically in such a way that "God used all the distinct personal qualities of each writer, . . . and the final result is exactly what he wanted to say to us."[5]

Inspiration is organic in the sense that God's Word is harmoniously expressed in human words, authentically incorporating not just the styles but also the ingenuity of the human authors as they wrote. Since human authors of the Bible naturally articulate God's Word to humankind, the better we understand their rhetorical artistry, the better we understand the enduring message for the community of God. Our view of inspiration is nothing to be ashamed of; rather, the opinion that biblical inspiration came about organically is precisely why we are compelled to read even the most challenging Old Testament texts conscientiously.

A further aspect to this concept of organic inspiration can be illustrated by how the word "organic" is commonly used. It is frequently associated with food and generally designates items that are grown without any artificial agents. This food is unadulterated and to a certain extent considered ultra-beneficial to the human body. The purity of the food is one of the main reasons people are willing to pay more when buying organic food; its purity assures customers that they are consuming a better product than food with artificial additives. Likewise, the organic inspiration of the Scriptures relates the conviction that God identifies divine words with human words in such a way that no human agent has added any artificial additives to the word, despite writing it while fully employing their own faculties. Organic inspiration implies that readers engage with an organic text in the sense that there is nothing unnatural about it; it is the fully synthesized Word of God and writing of the authors. The resulting product is a text that is ultra-beneficial for reading and application.

Organic inspiration naturally implies that God communicated through the pages of the Old Testament in language that the original readers (or hearers)

---

3. Frame, *Doctrine of the Word of God*, 82.
4. Frame, *Doctrine of the Word of God*, 82.
5. Frame, *Doctrine of the Word of God*, 142–43. Frame borrows from Abraham Kuyper and Herman Bavinck here.

would have understood—even if that language is sometimes difficult for us today. Therefore, it should not shock us that some of the Old Testament's rhetoric, imagery, stories, poetry, proverbs, and the like sound strikingly similar to other ancient Near Eastern documents from the same time period. It is reasonable to expect the Bible to have the same texture, language, and even structure as some of these other ancient Near Eastern compositions (e.g., Enuma Elish, Atrahasis, Gilgamesh, Hammurabi's Law Code, Instructions of Amenemope). These ancient documents, among others, reveal to modern readers matters that the inhabitants of the ancient Near East were thinking about and how the contemporaries of ancient Israel evaluated these issues (e.g., the creation of the cosmos, a major flood, regulating a society, poverty).

Organic inspiration is unique to the Bible, yet the concept notably facilitates an understanding that the inspiration of the Old Testament text does not always imply the uniqueness of all its contents. Equating inspiration and uniqueness can cause unnecessary theological quandaries; especially when one encounters other ancient Near Eastern documents that sound similar to the Old Testament. Proponents of the organic view of inspiration anticipate similarities between the Bible and ancient Near Eastern compositions that address similar issues, and they embrace the biblical text as God's written Word, even in light of its correspondence to extrabiblical texts. Again, Frame's comments are helpful: "To demand that Scripture be absolutely unique in its context over against the traditions of other nations is confusion. Nothing in the biblical doctrine of Scripture requires uniqueness of that kind. . . . To go 'outside of the Bible' is not to go outside of God's revelation. It is rather to move from the sphere of special revelation to the sphere of general revelation."[6]

What, then, does organic inspiration mean, as far as reading the Old Testament is concerned? God communicates his word to modern readers through the Old Testament like he communicated his word to the people of Israel at Sinai in a language that they could understand—in fully human language. That word flows from the pages of the Old Testament into our minds and hearts by way of reading. Our view of inspiration drives us to realize that the communication of God is inextricably linked with the creativity of the biblical author in the ancient Near Eastern literary context. The artistry of the author in its context is integral to the meaning of the text. Organic inspiration pushes modern readers of the Old Testament to appreciate the ingenuity of the authors, which is frequently on display through their usage of aesthetic devices. Our deliberate readings of these meticulously crafted texts should be conducted responsibly and in a balanced manner, in order to

6. Frame, *Doctrine of the Word of God*, 195, 232.

grasp the teachings of the Bible and to apply them within the contemporary
believing community.

Reading in Balance

Organic inspiration implies the obligation to be a balanced reader. On the
one hand, this view fully endorses the Scriptures as the Word of God. The
enduring principles that contemporary readers learn from the written Word
are just as authoritative as the commands of the divine word that were spoken to the people of Israel at Sinai. On the other hand, organic inspiration
compels readers to strongly consider how the human writers crafted their
compositions in order to carry out their literary and theological objectives.

This organic fusion of the divine and human word places an obligation
on the reader to carefully interpret the words in order to take heed of them,
permitting the divine message to affect the life of the reader. It is not sufficient
to merely understand what the words of the Old Testament signify and leave
it at that. Any good reader is capable of developing reasonable interpretations of the Old Testament, regardless of their presuppositions or religious
convictions; Christian readers can learn a great deal from good readers of
the Old Testament who do not share the same presuppositions. However, it
is not sufficient for us to simply read well. The Old Testament, as the written
Word of God, demands a faithful response to the words contained therein.
This response, however, cannot be given to just *any* form of reading of the
biblical text, since it is irresponsible to subject oneself to words that are not
effectively understood. The abiding principles that are relevant for all ages
of believers emerge through a balanced engagement with the texts of the
Old Testament.

Balance in the process of reading the Old Testament can be elusive. When
we are reading these Scriptures, our presuppositions generally lead us toward
either "underreading" or "overreading" the text. Both are problematic and
do not do justice to the written Word of God as a holistic medium of divine
communication with human beings.

Underreading is a problem for those with a more fundamentalistic hermeneutic as well as for some critical biblical scholars. One might wonder,
"How could both fundamentalists and critical scholars read in similar ways,
since their views of the Bible are so divergent?" Underreading the Bible is
frequently characterized by muting the author and not permitting the writer
to speak through literary techniques that the reader might not expect. Some
fundamentalist readers and critical scholars tend to stifle the biblical author's
voice when it does not correspond to what they expect from the text. In this

sense, fundamentalists and critical scholars are liable to read similarly, despite differing in what they ultimately believe the Bible to be.

Fundamentalist readings tend to view the Bible as an *exclusively* divine product and can unintentionally neglect, or intentionally disregard, the ingenious techniques that the sometimes shrewd, and other times subtle, human authors use to engage their audiences. For some, even the idea of examining how the human authors might have crafted their writing in order to engage and, ultimately, shape their readership seems irreverent, an exertion of human authority or reason over the biblical text. Fundamentalist readers approach the Bible as if they are with the people of Israel at the base of Sinai, expectantly waiting for the divine voice to speak without any human agency.

However, that is not how the written Word was either composed or transmitted into the hands of contemporary readers. The Old Testament was creatively authored using all types of aesthetic devices that we might expect—as well as adopting unexpected methods—in order to communicate the intentions of the ancient authors. The Old Testament was crafted, compiled, and transmitted to subsequent generations to be read as a compilation of well-thought-out compositions. A reading that takes this into consideration is not at all irreverent; in fact, it can be reasonably argued that readers do not give the Bible its proper due when they deny it the type of analysis it beckons. There is nothing pious about intentionally underanalyzing the Old Testament, whose human writers' cleverness organically aligns with the divine intentions. Since the text is a fusion of the divine and human words, neglecting the human authors' genius is a detriment to hearing the divine voice.

Critical scholars patently differ from fundamentalists. Some critical scholars read portions of the Old Testament as such a fragmented human product that the ingenuity of the human authors—or even compilers and redactors (i.e., editors)—can be overlooked.[7] Discounting the resourcefulness of the biblical authors can lead to perceiving issues that might not be problematic for those who are inclined to observe authorial creativity. Frequently, resolutions proposed by critical scholars to unexpected rhetoric, changes in scenery,

---

7. Admittedly, aspects of the ultimate processes of the compositions of individual books, and of the Old Testament as a whole, remain a mystery. Nevertheless, a key to reading portions of the Old Testament as well as the full composition is assuming a sense of coherence despite some of the unknown factors related to composition. For example, multiple sources were indeed drawn on in the writing of various books in the Bible, such as the books of Proverbs and the Psalms. Yet the compilers of these psalms and proverbs were anything but novice scribes who disjointedly assembled texts; rather, they were creative authors who crafted documents for a particular readership. By the term "author," I refer both to singular authors of books (e.g., Nehemiah) and to the redactor(s) of books that were ultimately compilations of texts (e.g., Psalms, Proverbs).

and other points in question end up being the attestation of an additional source document, another author, or a sweeping redaction.[8] At variance, other scholars might consider the same supposed problems to be literary maneuvers by the biblical author and, therefore, are prone to investigate the purposes for these devices through the process of reading. In reality, the fundamentalist and the critic end up with a similar type of Bible—one that meets their expectations.

Yet great authors never meet readers' expectations; they exceed them. The biblical writers captivate their audiences and move them toward the theological truth they endeavor to teach, but only if their readers are humble and open to being instructed. That same readership has the ability to overlook the call of the authors by turning them into divine puppets or confused scribes. Either way, the problem is the same: the underreader establishes expectations and explains the Old Testament in ways that do not adequately consider the aesthetic nature of the biblical authors' writing and how they used their rhetoric to influence their audiences. Frequently, these expectations go without saying or maybe even without knowing. The end result is that losing sight of writing conventions can turn the biblical texts into fanciful fiction and pious religious ideas, on the one hand, or into a fundamentalist weapon, on the other.

Some readers fully recognize the fact that the biblical compositions were intended to be read in a deliberate manner, and they strive to honor the genuine authorial objectives of the compositions. Yet in a search for meaning in the text, it is possible to commit the error of overreading. Overreading is the attribution of significance to aspects of the composition that were not, perhaps, intended to convey meaning. For example, sometimes readers strive to unearth exegetical significance in how Hebrew letters were shaped or even in the numerical value of words by using the Hebrew system of gematria (i.e., the numeric value of Hebrew words). These methods rarely produce convincing readings for contemporary audiences since they generally promote searching for latent meaning that was likely not intended by the original authors.

Overreading might also take the form of placing undue emphasis on analyzing the literary techniques used in the Bible, while stripping them of any

8. Frequently, the proposal of additional source documents and arguments for multiple authors are not reactionary but a presuppositional and fundamental component to a methodology of analyzing Old Testament texts. Adele Berlin's comments are helpful here: "It has been noticed by many scholars that the problem with traditional source criticism is that it begins with the assumption that the text is composed of a number of sources, and then proceeds to find them. Methodologically speaking, it is more correct to begin with the text, and find sources only if a careful reading so indicates." Berlin, *Poetics and Interpretation*, 116.

practical spiritual merits. This manner of reading elevates the reader's literary analysis to utmost importance, and thus the reading of the text becomes more important than what might be learned from the text and applied to the lives of people in the believing community. If readers prioritize their own creativity and imagination, they can sometimes add meaning to a text that may not have been intended by the author(s).[9] Those who hold to the organic inspiration view of the Scriptures do not fancy elevating our creative readings above the writer's goals, since meaning is bound to a real author's intention. It is the responsibility of the reader to walk the tightrope of paying close attention to, and reveling in, the genius of the writer, while simultaneously hearing and heeding the divine voice.

Reading on Purpose

We must strive to approach the Bible as it is: both as literature that God inspired and superintended for his divine purposes and as creative human literature. Having this attitude permits us to approach the Bible expecting to hear from God while also engaging in a serious analysis of the human genius demonstrated through the text. The better we understand what the human writers were saying, the better we will learn what God is communicating, and the better we can learn contemporary lessons from the ancient Word. Holding to organic inspiration does away with the model of reading the Bible as holy, religious literature that is desecrated if it is analyzed in a critical manner. It is precisely because of the belief that the words of the human authors are also God's words that we are compelled to critically engage with these holy documents, examining the rhetoric, style, and devices that the authors used to move their readers. This type of analysis is what leads to the lasting application of those compositions that is still relevant today.

Figuring out what these authors were doing with their readership is not always an easy task. As previously discussed, there are distances that separate us from the Old Testament that do not permit us to intuitively understand parts of the text. These gaps sometimes cause textual, linguistic, historical,

9. Much insight concerning what the biblical authors communicate through their rhetorical techniques can be gained from those who primarily analyze the Bible as literature. Thus it is possible for people who hold different assumptions about the Bible to come to similar readings of the same biblical text since their methods of analysis (at least partially) overlap. Similar readings by scholars of different convictions rarely have the same implications for their respective communities. Nevertheless, exclusively studying the Bible for the sake of analyzing a work of literary art facilitates a method of reading that can overemphasize the literary aspects of a text, since one's reading is of utmost importance, without the divine component.

archaeological, and even theological difficulties. Those who hold to the organic inspiration of the Scriptures expect these types of issues, since the real human component is emphasized in the analysis of the text.[10] Nevertheless, despite the possible difficulties, our default position is to read the text with a hermeneutic of trust as opposed to one of suspicion. This hermeneutic of trust permits us to see some of the potential discontinuities in the texts as reflecting intentional creative activity by the author.[11]

The decision to read the text with a hermeneutic of trust is not the same as turning a blind eye to legitimately difficult issues; it does, however, direct us to search for design instead of discord in the biblical text. This disposition affects our reading of individual biblical compositions as well as the whole Bible. The Bible's design as a whole transcends the individual books and authors, who wrote with goals that were superintended by God and naturally aligned with the divine purposes.

The writers of the Old Testament wrote with a purpose.

The way they wrote was on purpose.

We then have to read the Old Testament with purpose, determined to put the ancient written Word into practice in our day and age. We are now the reading audience to whom the ancient writer is communicating through the narratives, poetry, and prophecy of the Old Testament.

---

10. The Bible is not comprehensive concerning the topics it broaches. Sometimes we encounter difficulties in the texts because writers do not tell us all the information that we would like to have as contemporary readers. The biblical writers communicated what the readers needed to know in conformity with their purposes for writing. More on this in chapter 6.

11. Frequently, perceived incongruities—such as the location of Judah and Tamar's narrative in Gen. 38 supposedly interpolated into the "Joseph Narrative"—cause us to slow down and read in a deliberate manner. As we abate our pace, we are able to pick up on the poetics of any given text. These incongruities help us evaluate how the story of the Old Testament is being told.

SIX

How the Old Testament Is Told

Narrative

Except for a veto on graven images, God does not appear a critic of art.
—Meir Sternberg, *The Poetics of Biblical Narrative*

The year is AD 3522, and excavators have come across a thin sheet of fibrous substance, apparently made out of wood pulp, during an excavation of ruins dating back about fifteen hundred years. After a close inspection, analysts realize that words were written on this material with a stylus of sorts that permitted ink to be released and stain the sheet. As researchers endeavor to discern the writing, it becomes apparent that they have come across what seems to be a grocery list. The items on the list are recorded as follows: "Apples, Bananas, Cherries, Donuts, Eggplants, French Fries, Green Beans." Just below the list, there is another statement that reads: "First thing Friday, fly to find food; for your family is famished."

At first glance, it appears as if the excavators have simply encountered an unexceptional ancient fragment with no distinct features about which to become excited. However, as scientists pore over the piece of paper, they begin to perceive the very intentional manner in which it was crafted. The grocery items are listed in alphabetical order and are all in the plural. Additionally, there are seven items on the list that are organized in a symmetric manner; the first three are sweet fruits, the last three are non-sweet foods that come from plants. The middle item in the list serves as the axis and is a completely different type of food item—sweet junk food. Last, the message at the bottom of the page exhibits alliteration using the consonant "f," to a T.

Even though excavators come across this document hundreds of years after it was originally written, they are forced to recognize the extremely slim chances of this fragment being fortuitously arranged in such an organized manner. This compels them to ask the ensuing logical question: *Why* was this text written in such a noticeably stylistic manner? After all, if the list were *only* making a note of groceries, it did not have to be alphabetized or symmetrically arranged. If the comment at the bottom of the list were *only* a directive to go to the supermarket, then there was no need to feature alliteration so prominently. Reading this highly stylized document and asking the questions it evokes leads to the reasonable conclusion that the author of the fragment was striving to be artistic in the writing of the list. Yet to what end was the author being artistic?

Stylization is inherent to all different types of writing. When authors write documents ranging from grocery lists to stories to poetry, they tend to consider how they will design that particular composition in order to give it a distinctive appearance, and how specific words will carry out their intended effect on their readers. Considering the grocery list above, we can see that the aesthetic devices used by the author make it impossible to classify this fragment as *just* a grocery list. At the same time, the creativity of the writer does not necessarily call into question the reality behind the grocery list and the command. Artistic style and the communication of truth are not mutually exclusive. The fragment is, at bare minimum, a grocery list, but it was intentionally crafted so as to encourage the reader's participation. For example, if the fragment were composed by a parent for their children, then perhaps the alphabetization of the grocery list was a device intended as a catchy reminder for forgetful teenagers to ensure they would purchase all the items. Perhaps the alliteration of the final command was a playful gesture intended to soften the blow of the directive to complete this chore with excellence.

The Old Testament shows this type of intentional design on every page. The ancient writers used techniques that continue to persuade us to recognize that we are participating in something more profound than simply reading ancient fragments. Through deliberately reading the biblical text, we can pick up on the author's intentions. They variously sought to guide and instruct readers, to influence their way of thinking about a particular matter, to move them to physical action, and sometimes even to play on their emotions. The biblical writers used their cleverness, ingenuity, and resourcefulness both to communicate in an aesthetically pleasing manner and to influence their readers.

Inspired Artists

Meir Sternberg's statement used in the epigraph of this chapter rings true in light of the fact that the biblical writers never demonstrated a dichotomy between communicating God's word and being creative. They certainly believed they were writing on behalf of God.[1] At the same time, they were inspired writers who creatively engaged the reader by using aesthetic devices to add beauty to their compositions, while simultaneously leading the reader to their literary and theological destinations.[2]

Reading the Old Testament, therefore, is active, not passive. The adventure of reading is guided by the inspired author, but the reader is not *just* along for the journey any more than young children are *just* along for a long car ride. Young children generally have difficulty being in the dark with regard to the destination point of long journeys. It is not uncommon for them to repeatedly ask, "Where are we going?" "Why are we here right now?" and, most famously, "Are we there yet?" When answers to these questions do not satisfy their curiosity, exhausted parents might find their children staring out the car window trying to make sense of everything the car passes and repeatedly guessing at the destination based on the observable clues. Children certainly do not set the course for the journey, but they participate in the trek—and perhaps even enjoy it more—by actively seeking out information about where they are being taken, why they are being taken there, and when they will arrive.

Similarly, readers of the Old Testament recognize that the creative, inspired writers lead them on a journey with an ultimate destination. During this adventure, active readers ask, "Where are we headed in this text?" "Why is the author taking me here?" and "Are we there yet?" as they travel along. Additionally, readers search for clues to their questions by looking at their surroundings and striving to make sense out of what they pass in their reading. These

---

1. It is always the prerogative of the readers to reject what writers assert, to think they are crazy and to disbelieve every point. It is never the right of the reader to change what the writer has endeavored to communicate, which at bare minimum would violate the creative genius of the author. In the case of inspiration and the Bible, honest readers can reject the veracity of Old Testament authors' identification of their words with God's words, but they cannot deny that the writers actually indicated that they were writing on behalf of God. In many cases throughout the Old Testament, the concept of inspiration was assumed by the authors as they spoke on behalf of God, though it may not have been explicitly stated.

2. Edwin Good states that "we have been so concerned (and properly concerned) with its [i.e., the Bible's] truth, both factual and religious, that we have not investigated the literary means the Biblical writers use to convey their truth. . . . We have, in other words, been so eager to *interpret* the Bible that we have sometimes forgotten to *read* it." Good, *Irony in the Old Testament*, 9.

observations are based on clues that the writer left for readers to explore as they read. Readers do not set the course for the text, but they are able to enjoy the experience and understand the text as they actively seek out information concerning where they are being led. This is how readers are able to discern the purpose of the journey and to reflect on what they have learned when arriving at the final destination. Passivity on this journey could be likened to falling asleep on the subway—you might miss your stop and end up lost.

Generally speaking, the Old Testament authors carry readers toward the ultimate destination in three ways: (1) the authors fashion narrators who tell stories, (2) the authors write poetry that captivates the audience through overt artistic splendor, or (3) the authors recount prophecy in writing. Narrative, poetry, and prophecy are means by which biblical authors communicate meaning to the reader, using rhetorical devices that are somewhat distinct to each category. Sometimes a mix of narrative, poetry, and prophecy appear within the same composition, and other times it is not always clear how to classify the text.[3] Nevertheless, distinctions between narrative, poetry, and prophecy are generally apparent, and readers observe meaning in the text by following the nuances of how writers use features that are common to the literature they write.

Narrative, poetry, and prophecy of the Old Testament were designed to relay important information in a manner that invites the reader to participate in the text, to enjoy it, and to apply it. Narratives relate the major stories of numerous Old Testament characters; but through subtleties in how the story is told, the author can also provoke the reader's participation in the lessons being taught. Poetry in the Old Testament expresses the ideas and feelings of the biblical authors but does so in a way that invites the reader to share the writer's emotional experience. Prophecy tells of the oracles and visions of the prophets of ancient Israel, but, in many cases, the author recounts the prophet's words so that their messages transcend the immediate historical context and work their way directly into the world of the reader.

The more we can discover about the ways the biblical authors invite us as readers into their writings, the more we will find ourselves engaging with their art and understanding their intended meanings. As we try to figure out how the authors influence their audiences, we actively go along for the ride to the

---

3. It is not reasonable to suggest that entire Old Testament books can always be cleanly broken up into genres. It is clear that different kinds of writing sometimes appear within the same compositions. For example, large portions of biblical prophecy consist of poetry and should be analyzed as such. However, these sections are also prophecy, because they generally share other characteristics employed by the prophets—such as oracles, typology, and parables—that are less common in poetry that is not prophecy.

authors' destinations. In the following section, I will briefly summarize how the authors of narrative invite readers to participate in their texts.[4]

How Old Testament Narrators Narrate Narrative

Much of the Old Testament from Genesis to Esther (in the traditional Christian arrangement of the books) consists of interconnected stories relating to the emergence, development, and eventual destiny of the people of Israel. The individual books in this section are generally composed of select accounts of events, artistically crafted by the authors in order to pursue their particular objectives. The individual sections of biblical books that tell stories are frequently referred to as "narrative."[5]

One of the major characteristics of biblical narrative is the introduction of the character that tells the story—the narrator. Sometimes the narrator is unintentionally ignored by the reader, is overlooked as a character, or becomes an expendable part of the story because of our concern for what the author is trying to communicate through the entirety of the narrative. However, the narrator is an actual character that is developed by the author to tell the story in a particular way throughout the narrative.

Overlooking the function of the narrator would not be a big deal if it were the author's goal to neutrally retell any given story. But in biblical narrative there is no neutrality in recounting the events of the past—especially since those events relate to how God has intervened in history to bring about divine purposes. The writer crafts the narrator to have his own personality and way of telling the story so that the author can lead readers toward the narrative's main goals. So following the author's depiction of the narrator—and thereby the narrator's selective and artistic depiction of the events in the narrative—is crucial to grasping the author's main points.

Several characteristics of biblical narrators are helpful for observing how authors use them to lead readers toward their objectives.

4. I will discuss how poets write poetry and prophets prophesy in chapters 14–19 of this book. Furthermore, it is important to note a couple of important points here: (1) The following summary of techniques that the biblical narrators used in order to invite their readers to participate in the act of reading is not at all comprehensive. The authors used rhetoric to influence their audience(s) in many other ways. (2) Several of the characteristics pointed out below are shared between different types of literature. The issue relates not to whether certain literary devices are used in different types of writing but to *how* literary devices are used in diverse compositions.

5. The term "narrative" can refer to one of the individual stories or to the overall metanarrative of an entire literary work. It is common to hear the term "narrative" employed as it relates to the storyline of the Bible, since the entirety of the Bible is interconnected. In this book, I generally use the term "narrative" to refer to individual stories unless otherwise noted.

1. The narrator tends to be *anonymous*.[6]
2. The narrator is depicted as *omniscient* (i.e., all-knowing). The narrator frequently provides the reader insight that normal human beings would not have.
3. The narrator is *selective* with respect to the quantity and timing of the information shared. For example, narrators sometimes intentionally withhold information to leave gaps or judiciously add information to create foreshadowing or suspense.

Let's briefly expound on these general features of biblical narration and discuss how paying attention to them is helpful in reading.

The Anonymous Narrator

In the world of biblical narrative, the anonymity of the person telling the story (the narrator) rarely fascinates the readership; rather, it frequently goes unnoticed. Readers hardly pay attention to the fact that when they read narrative they are being told a story by a character *in* the story. Sternberg states that "the Bible's verbal artistry, without precedent in literary history and unrivaled since, operates by passing off its art for artlessness."[7] The retelling of narrative by an anonymous narrator is one of the reasons that certain sections of biblical stories might appear inconsequential at first glance. On further review a reader will frequently discover that the author is using the narrator to elicit a response from the audience and to establish his authority through serving as a literary proxy of God.

Designing the narrator as an anonymous character who relates the story is a creative and productive literary maneuver. In biblical narrative, the author writes on behalf of God. In most cases, the author is reluctant to retell the story in the first person, even if the writer is featured in the story. Thus the author develops a narrator, who rarely self-identifies, in order to communicate on behalf of the author, who writes on behalf of God. The narrator plays the ambassador of the author, who functions as the spokesperson for God.[8] Through the narrator, the author is able to cleverly express opinions and

6. Anonymity of the narrator is clearly not the case in the first-person accounts of Ezra and Nehemiah, in which the writers appeal to their personal experiences and observations in order to recount their stories.

7. Sternberg, *Poetics of Biblical Narrative*, 53.

8. See Sternberg again, who states, "The biblical narrator is a plenipotentiary [i.e., ambassador] of the author, holding the same views, enjoying the same authority, addressing the same audience, pursuing the same strategy, self-effacement included." Sternberg, *Poetics of Biblical Narrative*, 75.

lead the reader toward the significant principles of the stories. This manner
of telling stories provokes reader participation more effectively than if the
author directly stated historical facts and recited unbiased details in direct,
first-person speech. As readers are told a story by an anonymous narrator,
they are able to dedicate their attention to the divine purpose of the account.
Narrators are able to highlight the characters without diverting any attention
to themselves as storytellers. In this manner, a broad group of subsequent
readers are able to read the same texts and discern how the principles of the
narrative might apply to future generations.

As an example of this, we briefly return to the "Book of Moses." In chapter 3, we discussed that the Torah depicts Moses as authoring a "book" that
was subsequently placed in the tabernacle next to the ark of the covenant
(Deut. 31:9, 26). Taken at face value, the scene appears to indicate that Moses's book, in some measure, relates some of the previous sections of the
Torah—especially, the book of Deuteronomy. If this is the case, the question that remains from the reader's perspective is, Why is Moses repeatedly
referred to in the third person if the Torah identifies him as the author of
(at least) some of those sections? Surely the identification of the book with
Moses provided the text with authority among its early audience. Yet there is
a literary function for refraining from explicitly identifying Moses as the narrator, even though he is depicted in the narrative as the source of some of the
text: the portrayal of Moses in the third person functionally takes the reader
from the text directly to God's abiding message for the community without
the intervention of the well-known author. The mediator of the narrative is
the anonymous narrator who, in many cases, is barely noticed by the reader.

It might seem inconsequential, or even unreasonable, to *not* depict Moses
as the narrator of sections of the Torah, since he is indeed portrayed as the
mouthpiece of God. However, the Torah ultimately portrays itself as having divine origins, not just Mosaic origins. Moses is a crucial personage in
communicating the word of God to the people, yet the anonymous narrator
brings the reader one step closer to the divine origins of the narrative and
expands its applicability to a broader community after the time of Moses.
This is precisely what is reflected during the period of Ezra by the Judean
exiles who have returned to Israel: "And when the seventh month came and
the Israelites had settled in their towns, all the people came together as one
in the square before the Water Gate. They told Ezra the teacher of the Law
to bring out the Book of the Law of Moses, which the LORD had commanded
for Israel" (Neh. 7:73–8:1).

Notice that this passage from Nehemiah specifically communicates that the
Book of the Law of Moses was commanded from the *Lord* to Israel. The book

is not identified as the report that Moses gave to Israel, which would have necessarily been inferred if the Torah's narratives were exclusively told by Moses in the first person. The passage from Nehemiah identifies the book with Moses, but the content of the book was from the Lord and thus was continually applicable to the entire community. The Book of the Law of Moses was still relevant hundreds of years after Moses, at least in part, because of the anonymity of the narrator in the Torah. The Book of the Law of Moses is not just about Moses telling the people stories of their ancestors or giving the people divinely ordained laws in the original, historical context. Rather, the anonymity of the narrator includes Moses in a much bigger and broader story and relates the importance of the abiding messages of the texts to future generations.

There are many other sections of biblical narrative in which readers have no idea who is actually telling the story they are reading (e.g., Judges, 1–2 Samuel, 1–2 Kings). While reading these texts, we must remember that the author is using the storyteller character as a tool to draw the reader into the narrative. Irrespective of whether or not that narrator should be identified with the historical author, anonymous narration focuses the reader on the text, gets them asking questions, and eventually, leads them to the author's divinely motivated lesson(s).

The Know-It-All Narrator

The moniker "know-it-all" carries quite a negative connotation, since it generally refers to someone who feigns the possession of information that he or she does not actually have. Know-it-alls generally tend to be nuisances, not just because they are impostors but because they insist on letting other people know how much they assume that they know. On the contrary, people who actually know significantly more information than they divulge are generally respected for their intellectual prowess once their genius is discovered. The clandestine nature of bona fide know-it-alls in any given discipline increases one's appreciation of their genius, since these savants have the ability to reveal previously unforeseen information.

The biblical narrators are presented as bona fide know-it-alls—no negativity implied. The narrator possesses privileged knowledge that transcends what the reader—or any human being, for that matter—could have without God's authorization. For example, the biblical narrator has access to information about scenes in the divine council (Gen. 1:26–27; Job 1–2), provides detailed accounts of stories that came to pass many years prior to them being documented (e.g., Gen. 6–9; compare 1 Chron. 9–10), is a bystander in the most private interactions (e.g., Onan and Tamar in Gen. 38:9), and even knows the thoughts of the characters without them speaking (Exod. 3:3).[9] Like the characteristic of anonymity, the omniscience of the narrator is not explicitly stated and is only perceptible by reading, rereading, and observing how the narrator provides readers insight into narratives by sharing what he knows.

The narrator's omniscience naturally establishes the author's authority by connecting the narrator's character to one of God's most fundamental characteristics—his all-knowingness. As readers we are compelled to believe the given account of events upon realizing that the storyteller is privy to information that only God should know. In this way, the inspired author is able to use his knowledge to influence how we should think, feel, and/or react to the events narrated in the story.

Take, for example, the well-known story of King David's mistreatment of Bathsheba, his murder of Uriah, and the rebuke he received from Nathan the prophet, which are masterfully narrated in 2 Samuel 11–12. This is a complex story meriting a great deal of discussion.[10] Yet for the sake of illustration, I would like to draw our attention to a concise section in the middle of the narrative, in which the storyteller exhibits his omniscience and provokes the reader to action.

In 1 Samuel 11, the narrator succinctly relates the account of King David pressuring Bathsheba to come to the royal residence. King David has inappropriate relations with Bathsheba; murders Bathsheba's husband, Uriah; and conspires with his military commander, Joab, to cover his tracks. Just when King David thinks that he has literally gotten away with murder (not to mention adultery, bearing false witness, and pride), the anonymous and omniscient narrator makes a half-verse declaration that serves as an axis on which the narrative rotates in order to disclose the gravity of King David's actions and to evoke a reaction from the readers: "But the thing that David had done was evil in the eyes of the Lord" (2 Sam. 11:27, my translation).

In this short and eminently powerful statement, the narrator speaks for God, claiming to know God's extremely negative assessment of what David had done. Clearly, David's actions are wicked according to the Torah (Exod. 20:14; Lev. 18:20; Deut. 5:18; 22:22), but the narrator does not specifically point that out. The narrator is focused on providing the reader with God's opinion concerning King David's actions: God considers David's behavior to be wicked. The narrator provides the reader insight into the divine mind by expressing God's view of the situation at hand, even before the protagonist, King David, is told God's official opinion on the matter. By

---

9. Some of these ideas are adapted from Sternberg, *Poetics of Biblical Narrative*, 12, 83.
10. We will return to this narrative and further analyze it in chapter 12 of this book.

simply communicating God's assessment of the circumstances, the narrator elicits certain thoughts, sentiments, and practical reactions from the reader.[11] For example, readers should agree with God and think that what King David did was wicked; they should feel terrible for and empathize with those that King David has abused; and they should react by expecting King David's day of reckoning to come.

On a more personal level, the fact that the narrator alludes to King David's day of reckoning moves all readers to consider whether they are using their own authority and influence to abuse those in weaker positions in society. Through this half-verse remark, ancient and contemporary readers are urged to avoid the type of immorality that led King David to his terrible predicament and negatively affected many others around him. The fact that the narrator knows and communicates what God thinks creates an obligation on the reader to agree with God and act accordingly.

Maintaining the biblical narrators' anonymity and presenting them as omniscient are ingenious literary moves by the biblical authors. A simple retelling of events from the perspective of a common human might cause the reader to question the validity of the story. Additionally, all human beings are finite, meaning that eyewitness stories can only relay natural accounts of any given narrative. Through concealing the identity of the narrator and characterizing the storyteller as omniscient, the biblical authors teach the lessons of their compositions while demonstrating their divine authority. These shrewd maneuvers by the author promote the divine nature of the message of narrative texts.[12]

The Selective Narrator

A blank canvas propped up on an easel invites the deep contemplation of the painter who stands in front of it. As the artist envisions the piece that will

11. When the narrator provides information that the readers know they should not have, readers occasionally question how the historical writer learned that information. Finding out how the biblical authors obtained their information is certainly a valuable endeavor. However, in most cases, this is not what the author is trying to get us to ask by offering privileged information. If the author wanted readers to be privy to that information, he would have provided it. Instead, in many cases, the author simply provides information through the narrator that fortifies the authority of the author since, from the reader's perspective, the information must have come from God. The biblical authors of narrative frequently provoke their readership to ask *why* certain information is revealed and not necessarily *how* it was obtained.

12. Sternberg mentions how anonymity and omniscience work together, asserting that "anonymity in ancient culture validates supernatural powers of narration." He goes on to state that "omniscience in modern narrative attends and signals fictionality, while in the ancient tradition it not only accommodates but also guarantees authenticity." Sternberg, *Poetics of Biblical Narrative*, 33, 34.

shortly be created, she mulls over the colors that will be added to the canvas and the sequence in which they will be used in order to realize her vision. Every time she adds a particular color to the canvas, she measures the paint on her brush and applies it in a manner that produces the stroke and design she desires. Every stroke of the brush matters, since it is part of a larger panoramic, a broader expression of what she wants to communicate. Artists generally finish their paintings with leftover paint on their palette, meaning that they possess more material than what they needed to realize their vision. Painters use their resources selectively in order to design a work that represents what they wanted to communicate to art enthusiasts.

Similar principles of selectivity apply to how narrators artistically recount biblical narrative. The omniscient narrator has more than enough information about each story with which to bombard the reader. Yet narrators refrain from overloading their stories with details, which would be akin to an artist painting with all the colors on the palette at the same time. Instead, the narrators selectively choose what they share. This creates strokes of information communicated at just the right time. These strokes combine with the other movements of the brush in order to represent the panorama that the author envisioned. The authors of biblical narratives were artists who, just like painters, had to discern the type, quantity, and timing of the materials they used. They included and excluded substance from their stories in order to carry the reader along to their ultimate purpose(s).[13]

Even though the biblical narrators are depicted as omniscient, they are hardly omni-communicative as they recount their stories. Much of what they could have told us has been intentionally excluded so that they can tell stories that not only have their own lesson(s) but also function within the broader scope of the biblical storyline. Old Testament narratives reflect important aspects of the history of redemption. God's acts are selectively and creatively recorded in Old Testament stories that bear witness to God's activity in time and space—by way of both mighty deeds and the mundane—with the ultimate goal of progressively directing readers toward the culmination of the redemptive plan.[14]

The narration of these stories is necessarily bound by time. All the information is not released at once, since reading takes time. When we look at a

---

13. Adele Berlin states, "Narrative is a product of *selective* representation. Not every scene or event need be presented in full; some may be summarized, and some may be omitted altogether." Berlin, *Poetics and Interpretation*, 97.

14. John Frame defines redemptive history as "that series of events by which God redeems people from sin, a narrative fulfilled by Jesus. . . . Redemptive history constitutes the mighty acts of God that he performs for the sake of his people, those acts by which people come to know that he is Lord (Ex. 7:5; 14:18)." Frame, *Doctrine of the Word of God*, 79.

finished work of art, we cannot tell when the artist made each stroke. But if
we read biblical narratives successively, we can perceive and appreciate how
the narrator releases information in a timely manner in order to move the
audience while creating an artistic masterpiece. In this sense, reading narrative
can be likened to Bob Ross's famous television show *The Joy of Painting*. An
attraction of this show was that Ross would discuss his painting techniques
while demonstrating how to paint on canvas in front of the camera. One of
the reasons Ross's modest setup and calm demeanor fascinated viewers was
because the show added the element of time to the creation of artwork. The
show began with the camera pointed at a blank canvas; yet stroke after stroke
the viewer was able to observe how the piece of art developed and how the
artist brought the individual movements together. By the end of the show, the
canvas bore a painting. Time was a crucial component to viewer experience
and was used in the show to keep viewers' attention by creating expectations
about the final work of art.

Likewise, biblical narrators do not reveal the entire panorama that they are
creating at one time; in fact, they cannot do this, since narration takes time
to unfold, just as Ross's work took time to be painted. Narrators take advantage of the fact that stories gradually unfold.[15] Time is a crucial component
to the reader's experience because authors reveal information on a temporal
continuum, which grasps the readers' attention, keeps them engaged, and
creates expectations concerning the artist's handiwork.[16] The gradual unfold-
ing of stories also heightens the effect of rhetorical devices. For example, the
biblical narrator might

- withhold information, intentionally producing gaps in the narrative
  that readers are forced to interpret;
- provide dribs and drabs of information that create tension to be pro-
  cessed by the readers;
- provide what might seem to be a surplus of information in order to
  foreshadow a future event;
- tell a story out of order to surprise and move readers to action; or

15. This does not necessarily mean that all biblical narratives recount events in the exact
order in which they historically came to pass. As Adele Berlin states, "It is much more effective
to give information to the reader when it is most useful or significant, to link it with other relevant information, rather than present it in the form of an annal or chronicle." Berlin, *Poetics
and Interpretation*, 95–96.

16. Sternberg states, "The Bible exploits the fact that literature is a time art, in which the
textual continuum is apprehended in a temporal continuum and things unfold sequentially
rather than simultaneously." Sternberg, *Poetics of Biblical Narrative*, 198.

- offer or withhold information in order to cast ambiguity into narratives to bring about a greater impact on readers than could have been possible if the narrator had simply told the narrative straightforwardly.

There are surely other techniques narrators might use and reasons they might offer or withhold information and craft the timing of its release.[17] What is important to note at this juncture is that selectivity is one of the primary ways the narrators wield influence over their audiences.

The book of Jonah provides an example of how the narrator withholds information in order to influence how readers view God and to move them to action. At the beginning of the story, the narrator reports God's commands to Jonah to go to Nineveh and to confront its inhabitants: "Go to the great city of Nineveh and preach against it, because its wickedness has come up before me" (Jon. 1:2). In the next verse, the narrator surprisingly relates Jonah's utter disobedience to God's command to go to Nineveh, stating, "But Jonah ran away from the LORD and headed for Tarshish . . . to flee from the LORD" (1:3). Nineveh was inland and to the northeast of Israel; any ship leaving from Joppa would have likely sailed west. Jonah is absolutely set on not doing what God has commanded him to do.

Readers observe Jonah's curious reaction to God's directives and wonder, "Why in the world would Jonah flee from God after explicitly hearing his command?" This question is provoked over and over again as readers progress through chapter 2 and consider the terrible circumstances in which Jonah finds himself—in the belly of a large fish. Finally, in chapter 3, Jonah receives the command to go to Nineveh once again, but this time he obeys. Still, as Jonah cries out to the Ninevites, "Forty more days and Nineveh will be overthrown!" (Jon. 3:4), readers naturally wonder, "Why didn't Jonah just do this the first time he was called?" Then the Ninevites respond favorably to Jonah's message, in what might seem to be an unexpected twist in the story. The king of Nineveh also repents and issues a proclamation for all to refrain from food and water, dress in sackcloth, and turn from their evil ways (3:5–8). God sees the Ninevites' repentance and relents from "the destruction he had threatened" (3:10).

Then, there is another surprise in the story: Jonah grows resentful because of the outcome of his ministry. The Ninevites' repentance should be an occasion of great excitement and rejoicing for a messenger of the God of Israel. However, readers encounter Jonah pouting, even though there was an

17. This is simply a representative list of some of the techniques that narrators employ in order to bring readers toward their main points. Other techniques will be brought up and addressed in subsequent chapters when we discuss specific biblical narratives.

overwhelmingly positive response to his message: "But to Jonah this seemed very wrong, and he became angry" (Jon. 4:1). This depiction of Jonah evokes the memory of the disobedient prophet at the beginning of the book and forces the reader to ask, "What is this guy's problem?" It is at this point that the author *finally* reveals information crucial to understanding the prophet's anger and rebellious behavior. The narrator puts his omniscience on display and reveals the content of a private prayer that Jonah made to the Lord, which discloses the reason for his behavior: "Isn't this what I said, LORD, when I was at home? That is what I tried to forestall by fleeing to Tarshish. I knew that you are a gracious and compassionate God, slow to anger and abounding in love, and a God who relents from sending calamity" (4:2).[18] Jonah was deeply entrenched in ancient Israelite tradition, which is evident in that his assessment of God's character is extremely similar to Moses's words in Exodus 34:6–7: "The LORD, the LORD, the compassionate and gracious God, slow to anger, and abounding in love and faithfulness, maintaining love to thousands, and forgiving wickedness, rebellion and sin." Jonah knew the character of the God of Israel and trusted that he would be who Moses revealed him to be, even to the wicked inhabitants of Nineveh, if they repented. When the Ninevites do repent, Jonah becomes indignant because he had known that God would forgive them from the moment that God summoned him to go. Jonah is evidently not interested at all in seeing the Ninevites come to repentance.

We, as readers, are grateful that the narrator finally told us what was happening with Jonah, since it explains some of his behavior and provides clarity to the preceding events. However, satisfying the readers' curiosity is not the only effect that releasing this information has. Revealing Jonah's reason for disobedience after the Ninevites' repentance teaches one of the profound theological points of the book: the God of Israel, who called Jonah from the land of Israel, is not only the God of the relatively small people group and land of Israel but also the God of the Ninevites—the inhabitants of the city that eventually became the capital of the mighty Assyrian Empire, which conquered almost the entirety of the Fertile Crescent (i.e., Mesopotamia, through the Levant, and into Egypt).

Jonah teaches that the one, true God of Israel is willing to forgive all people insofar as they turn to him in repentance. This message would not have been so clear if the reason for Jonah's fleeing was explained at the beginning of the book, since the reader does not yet know whether the Ninevites will respond

18. Of omniscient narrators, Meir Sternberg states, "The narrator's disclosures put us [the readers] in a position to fathom their secret thoughts and designs, or trace or even foreknow their acts, to jeer or grieve at their misguided attempts at concealment, plotting, interpretation." Sternberg, *Poetics of Biblical Narrative*, 164.

to God's message. Upon observing the striking response of the Ninevites to the God of Israel, and subsequently seeing Jonah become upset, readers are able to understand what Jonah knew all along: the God of (tiny) Israel is the God of the greatest empires and is willing to forgive all—regardless of ethnicity—who turn to him.[19]

Narrators Facilitate Application

As contemporary readers delve into Old Testament narrative, our attention can sometimes be diverted to considering the historical events behind the narrative and the people responsible for the writing of a particular story. These are legitimate interests that have their place in exploring the background of texts and facilitating an understanding of the world around the Old Testament narratives. However, some of our modern concerns were not a priority for the narrators. Answering the reader's potential questions concerning all that historically came to pass, who wrote about it, and who told the story was not what narrators considered most important as they recounted, in many cases, extremely abbreviated versions of their stories. In Old Testament narrative, the narrators recount stylized versions of the events that ultimately fit into redemptive history. Readers dedicated to reading the Bible entirely are best able to see the ultimate purpose for the selectivity of the Old Testament authors, since their reading considers the fullness of salvation history.

Biblical narratives are communicated in historiographic portraits that touch on many topics and make many theological points, but they also direct the reader toward the work God is doing to redeem humankind. By following the information the narrators give us, we are able to track the divine hand guiding the human hand and teaching us the timeless lessons that are set in the text. In this sense, narrators facilitate the application of biblical narratives.

We shall now delve into a number of Old Testament narratives and examine how they speak to us today. We will begin by looking at the legal sections of the Torah and discussing how to read the biblical laws as essential parts of the overall story.

---

19. The position of the book of Jonah in the Hebrew Bible is particularly important as it relates to the overall message of the Twelve (i.e., the Minor Prophets). The prophecy of Nahum comes after Jonah in the Hebrew Bible, and Nahum pronounces judgment on the city of Nineveh. By reading Nahum, successive readers are able to observe that the gracious and forgiving God of Israel also enacts judgment upon those who presume upon his kindness.

SEVEN

Learning to Love the *Law*?

It is helpful to think of the Torah as one very big narrative, from the
creation of the universe to Moses's death on Mt. Nebo.
—Seth Postell, Eitan Bar, and Erez Soref,
Reading Moses, Seeing Jesus

The well-known Israeli children's book *Abba Oseh Bushot* (*My Father Always
Embarrasses Me*) poetically yet humorously relates little-boy Ephraim's first-
person account of the ways his father perpetually embarrasses him. Ephraim
perceives his father as childish and constantly needing to be parented by
Ephraim himself. The father's immaturity especially relates to his lack of
social consciousness; he sings loudly in public and shows affection for his
son in front of his classmates. Ephraim sometimes ignores his father out of
humiliation, merely because he does not know how to deal with the uneasiness his father's behavior brings. Ephraim wishes that his father would be
more like his mother, who works as a news reporter, keeps a daily schedule,
and is more civil than his father is.

One day, there is a baking competition at Ephraim's school. Ephraim's
responsible mother is too occupied with her work to participate in the bake-
off, leaving the young boy to reluctantly trust his father to bake a cake.
Ephraim's father stays up all night baking and, by morning, fashions an
unattractive brown circular object that looks more like a tire than anything
edible. Naturally, Ephraim is embarrassed upon viewing the exquisite treats
that other students' mothers have created. Ephraim's humiliation persists
until Ephraim's father slices the cake and the inside parts emerge from the

core like a blooming flower, turning the plain block of cooked batter into the most beautiful culinary creation at the contest. Needless to say, Ephraim is no longer embarrassed.

Christians have a tendency to view legal sections of the Torah[1] much like Ephraim views his father in this story; modern readers have an affection for the Torah, but we are sometimes embarrassed by its peculiarities and, therefore, occasionally ignore it or simply do not know what to do with it. Just like Ephraim considers himself to be more grown up than his father, so we might consider ourselves and contemporary societal norms to be more mature than a collection of three-and-a-half-millennia-old laws. Consequently, just like Ephraim wishes his father would be more sophisticated like his mother, so modern readers tend to view the Torah's laws as uncultured and struggle to develop readings that are applicable to our contemporary, progressive societies.

Completing an applicable reading of the Torah[2] is a challenging task because these laws communicate values that, quite frankly, embarrass and perplex most of us. For instance, God commands the death penalty for a person working on the Sabbath (Num. 15:32–36); God is strangely concerned about unruly oxen being put to death (Exod. 21:28–29, 32); and God permits a law that orders a dead man's brother to have a child with his sister-in-law (Deut. 25:5–10). The peculiarity of these laws is inextricably linked with our modern penchant to consider the legal texts as antiquated and irrelevant. Modern

1. It is easy to be confused by terminology relating to the "Law." This confusion is generally based on how Christians and Jews have traditionally used this terminology. As mentioned in chapter 4, the first five books of the Bible are frequently called the "Torah" by Jews and the "Pentateuch" by Christians. The difference in name can be ascribed to the fact that the Torah was translated into Greek during the middle of the Second Temple period and consequently became known as the "five" (*penta*) "scrolls" or "cases for papyrus scrolls" (*teuchos*). Sometimes, the entirety of the Torah (a.k.a. the Pentateuch) is referred to as simply the "Law," since it consists of large sections of laws. Defining the "Law" is also complicated a bit by New Testament passages like Rom. 3:21, in which the Greek word for law (*nomos*) is seemingly used to refer to the individual laws of the Torah as well as the entire book: "But now apart from the law (*nomou*) the righteousness of God has been made known, to which the Law and the Prophets testify." In this book, I refer to the entirety of the first five books of the Bible using the terms "Torah" and "Pentateuch," and the individual precepts that are a part of this five-book composition as (lowercase) "law(s)" (cf. Gal. 3:17) or "legal texts." Understood in this manner, the Torah (a.k.a. the Pentateuch) is the five-book, unified story that partially consists of laws given to the community of Israel as part of this narrative. More on this below.

2. According to Jewish tradition, God gave the people of Israel a separate Oral Torah (a.k.a. "Oral Law") at Sinai along with the written Torah. This Oral Torah was not recorded in writing until much later, probably beginning in the early second century AD by the famous Rabbi Akiva and becoming formalized in the Mishnah (third century AD). This Oral Torah, which is generally uncharted territory for Christian readers of the written Torah, is also often simply referred to as "Torah" by Jewish people. To distinguish the two "Torahs," Jewish people refer to the books of the Bible as the "Torah in writing." I use the terms "Law" and "Torah" in order to exclusively refer to the written Torah and not the Oral Law.

readers, we assume, *really* know how a mature, developed, and refined society should run; modern readers know how cultured citizens should behave. These laws do not seem to fit into any enlightened contemporary paradigm.

How, then, do we read these ancient biblical legal texts in a way that permits us to consider how they speak to a contemporary audience, granting the recognizable differences between modern societies and those of the second millennium BC?[3] To answer this question, we return to Ephraim. Upon seeing the cake cut open, Ephraim realizes that he had been viewing his father in terms of how his father made him feel, and not in terms of what he could learn from his father. Also, Ephraim learns that appearances are a shallow way to judge people; his father is truly talented, which could only be observed by permitting his father to express himself. Ephraim grows to openly identify with his father by the end of the book and recognizes that his father, though sometimes peculiar, is an invaluable part of his life.

As we spend more and more time with the legal sections of the Torah, we may come to see beauty there if we are willing to let the text speak for itself. Like Ephraim, we should adopt a disposition toward the text that prioritizes hearing the teaching of the text as opposed to focusing on the weirdness that we might feel because of our distance from the laws therein. Just like Ephraim's father (and like the cake), the legal sections of the Torah are beautiful, not in how they appear at first glance but in their rich content as we carefully read. Loving the law (i.e., the legal sections of the Torah) is not an automatic result of the text being canonical any more than truly loving a family member is contingent upon sharing a house. Rather, readers develop a true affection for, and identity with, the biblical laws by reading them humbly, successively, entirely, and deliberately.

The Embarrassment of the Law: Reading Humbly

At the outset, it is important to be completely honest as modern Christian readers of the biblical laws: some laws can seem very strange to our sensibilities. Maintaining self-awareness in this regard is critical to studying these legal

3. This question is a bit ironic since the legal texts of the Bible are not just ancient literature to us. These legal texts have been part of the Scriptures of the Jewish and Christian communities for thousands of years, meaning that multiple communities have worked through their relevance for themselves many years after they were originally written. Many readers before us may have also sensed that these sections of the Torah felt "primitive" in light of contemporary advancements in practical life. Thus trying to make sense of the biblical laws is not exclusive to any generation of readers. Hopefully, in what follows, I will be able to provide practical encouragement for the Christian community to read the Torah's laws in a way that highlights their importance to our present-day lives.

sections, because it helps us pinpoint and then actually work through one of the main issues in reading—namely, the expectation that the text should meet the norms of contemporary societies, churches, and other interpretive communities. We become flustered when we perceive that the biblical text does not meet modern standards of conduct or, even more seriously, does not reflect our expectations of who God is and how God should behave. Modern readers' distances from the text can sometimes cause such a gap in knowledge that we feel a sense of embarrassment about the Bible being the foundational text of our faith. We cannot fathom how God could permit, and even command, such "primitive" laws.

The type of self-awareness displayed by admitting the uneasiness caused by some biblical laws prevents hubris from developing. Self-awareness facilitates an appropriate understanding of our place in the course of interpretation. By admitting that certain biblical laws are bizarre to us, we are reminded that we are not responsible for creating a comfortable text or for devising a God of whom moderns would more easily approve. Instead, uneasiness evokes our responsibility to evaluate what the text may have been saying to the community that received it and how that message corresponds to contemporary situations. Receiving from the text—as opposed to imposing present-day expectations on difficult passages—takes a certain level of humility; this humility compels us to resist the temptation to become discouraged when the strangeness of biblical laws *feels* like an affront to our emotions and even to our intellect.

Reading humbly encourages us to effectively close some of the gaps in knowledge because it leads us to read successively, entirely, and deliberately. Slowing down and reading the biblical laws in this manner alleviates the burden we might feel of having to hastily propose solutions to the embarrassments that emerge from the laws or to conform the text into our contemporary image and likeness upon encountering perplexing verses. There is no sense in reading and analyzing the biblical laws unless we are willing to admit the vanity of imposing our modern norms and assumptions on what the laws *should* communicate and how the laws *should* represent our perception of God. Humility is needed in order to approach the difficult laws of the Torah expecting to learn more from and about God—especially if we feel like we should correct these laws.

If we prioritize learning about God in reading the biblical laws, then we will be compelled to consider what it *actually* means to be a modern recipient of the Torah. This may, of course, sound counterintuitive, since most Christians profess that the entire Bible is eminently relevant for modern life. We do not simply read the Bible to get more information; we read it because we believe that God's Word still speaks to our lives. Accordingly, many of us are inclined to quickly apply the biblical text by substituting ourselves as God's (or Moses's) interlocutors, instead of recognizing that the biblical laws had a primary audience (i.e., the people of Israel). Promptly replacing the original audience with a modern one is an almost surefire way to misread biblical texts. By doing this, we are bound to ask questions that the text was not written to answer, thereby developing misguided applications for our community. Recognizing and consequently resisting the temptation to embed our modern Christian community into the Torah as if we were the original recipients is a characteristic of reading humbly.

Nevertheless, the question remains: If we should refrain from embedding ourselves into the Torah, then how should we go about studying the laws in it? This question leads to another positive result of reading the Torah's laws humbly: reading humbly pushes us to understand the various contexts in which the laws were written (e.g., historical, literary, sociological). This point calls for a bit of explanation.

Upon engaging with the legal sections of the Torah, we will quickly notice that these sections read very much like straight commands. Given our tendency to overlook the fact that narratives are narrated (see chap. 6) and that the Torah's laws are given within the context of a narrative (see below), we are inclined to exclusively view the law sections as divinely sanctioned commands or to think that these sections were written only to regulate people's behavior. This manner of reading, which primarily strives to understand the normative practice of the ancient biblical laws, naturally leads us to question modern Christian behavior relating to these same topics. For instance, questions such as "Should Christians eat only biblically kosher food?" or "Should Christian men wear tassels?" are ordinary results of reading the biblical laws while being exclusively focused on how they should regulate the behavior of the community of faith.

Nevertheless, this type of reading diminishes the fact that specific laws were given and then *written down* in a variety of contexts (e.g., literary, historical, sociological, religious). The Torah's laws fit into these contexts, and thus we should refrain from gauging the laws' sophistication or their modern application(s) relative to any community's contemporary expectations. This means that, on the one hand, we should not do away with the laws because they do not meet our expectations. On the other hand, we must refrain from advocating that the strict, direct application of specific biblical laws within the modern community of faith was the ultimate reason for them being written. Humility avoids the extremes of either disregarding the biblical laws or excessively amplifying our own importance in the Torah's narrative. To the degree that we can find a balanced position between these extremes, we will be humble readers who proudly identify with the entirety of the biblical text as the Word of God.

Bizarre Laws: Reading Successively

Reading humbly is just the first step for us to proudly identify with all the laws of the Torah as our Scriptures. Once we embrace the fact that we cannot impose expectations on the laws to make us feel more comfortable about them, we are ready to deal with the next issue: there are *still* some weird laws in the Torah. Reading the biblical laws successively and within their contexts facilitates an understanding of their meanings and can help clarify some of the issues that strike us as peculiar.

As mentioned above, reading the laws of ancient Israel and immediately applying them to our contemporary life or any given society without contemplating what they might have communicated in their original contexts is not a particularly wise reading of the texts. The laws were not intended to be read in that manner, since they are embedded in a larger narrative (see below). Even if some laws could directly transfer to a modern society, others would never be accepted by a contemporary community as part of any modern system of law in the way they are presented in the Torah. This is particularly true for those laws that give relatively harsh consequences for what seem to be comparably minor offenses. The laws that relate to the Sabbath fit into this category, since, according to the Torah, violating the Sabbath was punishable by death.

Numbers 15:32–36 relates an occasion in which a man violated the Sabbath law by gathering sticks. He was subsequently put to death for his transgression: "While the Israelites were in the wilderness, a man was found gathering wood on the Sabbath day. Those who found him gathering wood brought him to Moses and Aaron and the whole assembly, and they kept him in custody, because it was not clear what should be done to him. Then the LORD said to Moses, 'The man must die. The whole assembly must stone him outside the camp.' So the assembly took him outside the camp and stoned him to death, as the LORD commanded Moses."

At first glance, the fact that the man who broke the Sabbath is punished with a divinely commanded death penalty appears to be the definition of the use of excessive force. The prohibition of refraining from labor one day of the week may seem reasonable enough to some modern readers, but this rarely prohibits people from conducting activities that most would consider mundane, such as gathering sticks. How are modern readers supposed to make sense of the Sabbath law that leads to God commanding the death penalty? A commitment to reading the Bible successively helps us work through this issue.

The death penalty for picking up sticks was not decided on the whim of divine capriciousness but results from a series of laws and events that are recorded in the immediate and broader contexts of the Torah. Let's start at the beginning of the Old Testament and successively read several passages that will shed light on the consequences of violating the Sabbath. In Genesis 1:2–4, God is depicted as creating the world in six days. Instead of conveniently ending the week after day six, God added another day in which he rested (Hebrew: *Shabbat* [Sabbath]; see Gen. 2:3). Those who have read up to this point of the creation narrative in Genesis know that there is no need for the omnipotent (i.e., "all-powerful") creator God to rest in order to regain strength. Thus the question emerges: What is God accomplishing by refraining from further creative activity on this apparently superfluous seventh day?

There are varying opinions about the purpose and function of the Sabbath as it is depicted in the creation narrative. At minimum, it appears that God's rest on the seventh day provides an example for ancient readers to emulate; if God rests, so should they. Additionally, the Sabbath day was particularly unique because, along with resting, God is explicitly portrayed as specially blessing and setting apart the Sabbath from all of the other days of the week. God's overt blessing of the Sabbath upon the completion of his creative activity necessarily makes it one of the highlights of the creation story. The reader moves on from the creation narrative knowing that the Sabbath is eminently important, but with no knowledge of why God has expressly appointed a day entirely for rest.

Further clarification for the purpose of the Sabbath is provided when the people of Israel receive the Ten Commandments at Sinai. In this narrative, God explicitly invokes creation order as the reason he was calling his community to rest on one day: "The seventh day is a sabbath to the LORD your God. On it you shall not do any work. . . . For in six days the LORD made the heavens and the earth, the sea, and all that is in them, but he rested on the seventh day. Therefore the LORD blessed the Sabbath day and made it holy" (Exod. 20:10–11).[4] Upon arriving at this passage, the reader learns information not available in Genesis. God did not create a day for rest because he was tired and expected humans to be tired. Instead, God established a pattern fundamental to the creation narrative that included a day of rest, and he commanded his people to emulate this model as a way of representing him.

---

4. The Sabbath command of Deut. 5:13–14 expands to include another reason: the people are prohibited from working on the Sabbath because they had been slaves in Egypt. God delivered the people of Israel from lives of constant servitude, and they are to remember this by taking one day a week to rest from their work.

God wanted the people to be like him. He wanted their activity—and lack of activity—to reflect his. The fact that God called the people of Israel to represent him in some manner through observing the Sabbath is an important element of the Sabbath laws, and it coincides with God's expectations of Israel elsewhere in the Bible. Israel was called to be holy as their God was holy, and observing the Sabbath was inextricably linked to this call (Lev. 11:44; 19:2–3; see also 1 Pet. 1:14–16). Israel was to identify with and represent the one true God by way of observing his statutes (Lev. 18:1–5, 24–25), particularly those like the Sabbath laws that expressly portray the creator God's unparalleled character. By doing this, Israel was able to benefit from God's perfect plan for them established in creation, as well as serve as God's witness to the polytheistic nations around them.[5]

Being designated as the representatives of the one true God among the other ancient Near Eastern gods was no small matter. Thus the laws like those governing Sabbath that were specific to representing God's order were a very big deal, though contemporary readers may not intuitively perceive them as such.[6] An intentional violation of this brought about severe consequences for those who were especially set apart by God for his purposes (Exod. 31:13). This severe judgment for violating the Sabbath is precisely what we observe by continuing to read the legal sections in Exodus:

> For six days, work is to be done, but the seventh day is a day of sabbath rest, holy to the Lord. Whoever does any work on the Sabbath day is to be put to death. (31:15)

> For six days, work is to be done, but the seventh day shall be your holy day, a day of sabbath rest, holy to the Lord. Whoever does any work on it is to be put to death. (35:2)

Reading successively allows us both to consider passages on the same topic as the section under consideration and to take notice of the context of the

---

5. Isaiah subsequently states that Israel will be a "light for the Gentiles" (Isa. 42:6; cf. 60:3). This later terminology represents what the people were supposed to be from the beginning of their existence as the covenant people of God. See the discussion concerning the phrase in chapter 19.

6. It is possible to argue that the Law was never intended to be kept by anyone except for the people of Israel in the normative sense. It was given to Israel for Israel with a unique purpose—to set Israel apart as God's people, to make Israel a light to the nations. Postell, Bar, and Soref briefly clarify that though God's Word is eternal, the Torah's laws were not intended to be the ultimate standard for any community forever. "These laws aren't the permanent, divine ideal for all peoples everywhere at all times. They are specific to a people with their specific need in that ancient era." Postell, Bar, and Soref, *Reading Moses, Seeing Jesus*, 101.

passage. Numbers 15:12–16 must be understood in light of the verses that come just before it. In this context, God says through Moses, "But anyone who sins defiantly, whether native-born or foreigner, blasphemes the Lord and must be cut off from the people of Israel. Because they have despised the Lord's word and broken his commands, they must surely be cut off; their guilt remains on them" (15:30–31).

These verses provide a clear situation in which one of the people of Israel would suffer extreme consequences (i.e., be cut off)—namely, intentionally committing an act of transgression by willfully disobeying the word of the Lord. The harsh ramifications built into these verses coincide with the broader framework surrounding the commands related to the Sabbath (see Exod. 31:15; 35:2 above). The statement in Numbers 15:30–31 provides the context for the narrative of the Sabbath violator's punishment. What might at first seem to us to be a tiny peccadillo should be understood as an intentional and direct affront to God's creation order and a rejection of the divine purpose for the people of Israel. The text explicitly states that a person who despises the word of the Lord utterly disrespects God and can no longer remain in the camp. Reading successively helps the reader understand that the Sabbath laws were perhaps not as bizarre, or as indiscriminate, as they may have initially seemed.

Oxen and the Image of God: Reading Entirely

Reading humbly and successively facilitates an improved understanding of the biblical laws because it encourages us to continue reading—especially after encountering a difficult text—without imposing our own, present-day expectations on the Scriptures. As we continue to read with a disposition open to instruction, we encounter relevant and useful information concerning the biblical laws that makes them more intelligible to us as modern readers. Additionally, the biblical laws were not given in a vacuum, and thus it is important to consider them in their entire biblical context. As we read the entirety of the Scriptures, we will discover that even some of the most peculiar laws communicate more theologically in their biblical context than initially meets the eye.

Let's take, for example, the Bible's anti-goring laws, outlined in Exodus 21:28–32. It is safe to say that these laws are far more unconventional to our modern communities than they were to ancient Near Eastern people groups, including Israel. The Torah records that God provides the people of Israel with specific standards concerning the conduct of their oxen and the ramifications for their animals hurting human beings. Many contemporary communities simply *cannot* insert themselves into this story as the interlocutors; pet oxen goring people is hardly an issue for many of us. However, similar ancient Mesopotamian laws lend insight into the biblical precepts and allow modern readers to observe several important nuances in ancient Israelite thought. A short section from the ancient Laws of Hammurabi (eighteenth century BC) relating to oxen serves as a backdrop to the comparable biblical laws.

Exodus 21:28–29, 32	Laws of Hammurabi, 250–52
[28]When an ox gores a man or a woman to death, the ox shall be stoned, and its flesh shall not be eaten, but the owner of the ox shall not be liable.	250. If an ox gores to death a man while it is passing through the streets, that case has no basis for a claim.
[29]But if the ox has been accustomed to gore in the past, and its owner has been warned but has not kept it in, and it kills a man or a woman, the ox shall be stoned, and its owner also shall be put to death.	251. If a man's ox is a known gorer, and the authorities of his city quarter notify him that it is a known gorer, but he does not blunt its horns or control his ox, and that ox gores to death a member of the *awīlu* (privileged) class, he (the owner) shall give thirty shekels of silver.
[32]If the ox gores a slave, male or female, the owner shall give to their master thirty shekels of silver, and the ox shall be stoned.	252. If it is a man's slave (who is fatally gored), he shall give twenty shekels of silver.

Note: Citations from the Laws of Hammurabi are adapted from Roth, *Law Collections*, 128.

The laws in Exodus 21 are straightforward enough, but some modern readers might not intuitively understand the implications of these laws for our present-day communities. As we can see by reading the biblical laws side by side with the Laws of Hammurabi, God's verbal communication came to the people of Israel in language that would have been intelligible and applicable to them. As weird as it might sound to some of us, oxen goring people was evidently an issue that surfaced in the ancient Near East. Therefore, the owners of oxen needed to be held accountable for the behavior of their animals and to make restitution for the animals' vicious conduct, especially if an attack was foreseeable. Accountability consisted of the execution of the animal—and potentially its owner—in the biblical laws, and a financial penalty in the Laws of Hammurabi.

These differences between the consequences for the oxen and their owner depicted in the two sets of laws tip the reader off to an extremely important aspect of the biblical laws about oxen. A major difference between the two sets of laws relates to the fact that monetary compensation was permitted for the death of a human being in the Laws of Hammurabi, but the animal responsible for the goring was to be put to death in the biblical laws. According to the Torah, the death of the animal was the only appropriate penalty for taking the life of a human being. If the animal was known to have violent tendencies in the past, the biblical law is even more extreme: Exodus 21:29 declares the death penalty for the animal's owner as a consequence of the beast's actions.

This raises the question, Why did the ancient Israelite laws require the death of the guilty party instead of permitting the animal's owner to make financial restitution for a death caused by his oxen, as is the case of the Laws of Hammurabi? It appears as though the biblical law regarding oxen endeavors to illustrate a more profound teaching, unique to the values of Israel: Human beings were created in the image of God, and thus the senseless killing of a human is an assault on the divine image that would be met with the severest of consequences (Gen. 1:26–27; 9:6). The Torah expounds on this ideal by emphasizing the significance of blood from the divine perspective: Human blood is considered precious to God since it represents life. God is ultimately responsible for life, and so human beings are forbidden from eating blood (Lev. 3:17; 7:26; 17:10–14; 1 Sam. 14:32–35). Greenstein summarizes by stating, "Because blood, symbolizing life, is the element of God, and the human is a mortal clone of God, the Torah places the highest penalty on the shedding of human blood. . . . While the allegedly more 'advanced' Mesopotamian codes allow for monetary compensations, the Torah cannot place a price tag on life or limb."[7]

Understanding the divergences between the biblical and Mesopotamian laws in this manner, we see that the Bible's oxen-goring laws are not so much about restitution. Rather, they reflect a much more important theological picture that runs throughout the entirety of the Bible concerning the sanctity of human lives, since humans are made in the image of God (Gen. 5:1–2; James 3:9). Relatedly, Scripture consistently regards taking a human life with the utmost seriousness because all human beings bear the divine image (Exod. 20:13; Deut. 5:17; Matt. 5:21; 19:18; Luke 18:20; Rom. 13:9; James 2:11; 1 John 3:15). Reading the Bible entirely helps us understand the immediate applicability of the oxen laws to present-day communities: human beings are made in the image of God, and, therefore, the loss of life is an utter tragedy—especially if it is preventable.

Reading the Law as Narrative: Reading Deliberately

Reading the biblical laws within the context of the entire Bible facilitates readers understanding how certain precepts fit into a broader theological motif that runs throughout the Bible. Yet even when reading the Torah's laws

7. Greenstein, "Biblical Law," 92.

humbly, successively, and entirely, readers might still wonder, How can we take every single word of the biblical laws as God's very word and as ultimately applicable to our contemporary believing communities despite the distances that inevitably hinder a complete understanding of all of the nuances of individual laws? Intuitively, we tend to recognize that, as important as every single one of the Torah's laws were in their historical context, there may have been more profound principles at play in the overall giving of the individual laws. So how do we read the legal sections of the Torah in a way that permits us to learn from them without meaninglessly striving to "keep our oxen in check"?

The answer to these questions is one and the same: we read deliberately. As we slow down and ask questions of the text, we realize that the Torah as a whole as well as the biblical laws within are ultimately presented to the reader as narrative in two senses: (1) the entirety of the Torah functions as one extended story spanning from the creation to the threshold of the conquest of Canaan, and (2) many of the individual laws are actually written as embedded narratives within the literary context of the Torah.[8] Let's consider the law as narrative in these two senses in turn.

Narrative Times Two

The Torah consists of a series of connected stories that depict the creative activity of the God of Israel, the emergence of the people of Israel, and their commissioning as God's covenant people. Various types of literature are represented in the first five books of the Bible (e.g., poetic music in Exod. 15:1–18, 21). Yet given the interrelation of the historical accounts, the appearance of similar motifs, the development of characters, and the shared overarching goals of the individual textual units, the Torah as a whole can be referred to as a narrative. The Torah (i.e., the entire, continuous narrative) includes a section in which the people of Israel receive specific laws relating to a multitude of issues (e.g., the tabernacle, holy days, sacrifices, purity and impurity, etc.). Israel was commanded to obey these laws for the purpose of being set apart as the community that would represent their God among the other peoples of their time and in their region. All these individual laws were part of a much larger story that spans the entire Torah and, ultimately, the whole Bible.

Viewing the Torah as a narrative, and the individual laws as a part of the overall story, is crucial in terms of the application of the entirety of the

---

8. See Bartor, *Reading Law as Narrative*, 18, for the concept of an embedded story. An embedded story is a story told by the characters themselves, taking the narrative to a level deeper than the "frame story" that is retold by the narrator.

Torah to modern readers. An appropriate application of the individual laws for Christians today is based on grasping how they set the people of Israel apart in their religious, social, and historical contexts. We as contemporary readers must deliberately ask how the heart of a law given to ancient Israel can be carried out in our contexts.[9] This is only possible insofar as we can properly bridge some of the distances between the original audiences and ourselves. Despite our gaps in knowledge, this manner of reading facilitates an appreciation of every single word of every single law as God-given Scriptures, since it takes all of the words of the law as indispensable components to the Torah's story.

The Law Is Literature

Another way to read law as narrative emerges when we slow down and pay close attention to how the Torah is told. There are short sections of text within the Torah that appear to simply be law at first glance but are actually narratives in which the author uses a narrator and—albeit briefly—develops characters. These laws function, essentially, as narratives within narratives, and we should read them as such. The laws of the Torah, read as narrative, communicate more than the standardization of practices in ancient Israel. Many biblical laws are portrayed so the readers can perceive how the authors create scenarios to carry out theological purposes.[10] In this sense, there is a good bit of overlap between how traditional narratives are narrated and how certain sections of biblical law are presented.

Before continuing, we should set aside a couple of potential misconceptions. First, it is misguided to extract the legal sections out of the overall narrative of the Torah and label them as the "Law" irrespective of where they are actually located. Surely, the legal sections reverberate differently than narrative throughout the course of reading since they typically consist of terse instructional statements that primarily communicate behavior that is expected of the community of Israel. However, the biblical laws were given in a narrative framework and cannot be properly understood without their literary contexts. Bluntly stated, there is no "legal genre" in the Torah that can be analyzed outside of the greater narrative within which it is told. Thus it is an inexact literary distinction to create a complete dichotomy between the

9. This manner of reading the biblical laws as narrative is particularly helpful when we are considering "apodictic laws," through which precepts are depicted as being explicitly commanded by God.

10. This manner of reading the biblical laws as narrative is particularly helpful in the cases of "casuistic laws" in which statutes are established by cases and there is a conditional element to the law (a.k.a. "case law"). See more below.

legal and narrative genres in the Torah—as if it were possible to disentangle the laws therein and make them their own type of literature.

Additionally, it is important to recognize that since the biblical laws were communicated in written form as part of a broader narrative, the authors who penned them used the types of aesthetic devices that they might employ elsewhere in their writing. There is no reason to expect the Torah's legal sections to be completely devoid of the literary toolkit that authors put to work in other areas of the Bible. The legal sections of the Torah were also written down with the intent of engaging readers and moving them to proper action. We are able to read the entirety of the Torah as relevant biblical literature upon recognizing that biblical laws cannot be extracted from the narratives in which they are told, and that the legal sections of the Torah also employ the aesthetic devices apparent elsewhere in biblical literature. Read in this manner, laws no longer form embarrassing antiquated sections of the Torah that interrupt the stories of the matriarchs and the patriarchs of Israel. Rather, we are able to see how they are fundamental to God's story that is recounted in the Torah.

Not only were the biblical laws given within the context of a story, but many (especially casuistic) laws are actually portrayed as stories themselves. Assnat Bartor helpfully defines casuistic law as "the type of law that describes a hypothetical case, in which a certain problem is described and to which the law provides a solution."[11] When the casuistic laws are presented in the Torah, they wind up functioning like miniature stories, in contrast to apodictic laws (divine commands), which are much less inviting of a narrative reading.[12]

Reading casuistic laws as mini narratives is helpful to modern readers since some of those cases are particularly odd in light of modern conventions. Take, for example, the seemingly bizarre situation relating to what is known as "levirate marriage":

> If brothers are living together and one of them dies without a son, his widow
> must not marry outside the family. Her husband's brother shall take her and
> marry her and fulfill the duty of a brother-in-law to her. The first son she bears

11. Bartor, *Reading Law as Narrative*, 6.
12. Be that as it may, apodictic laws are still part of the larger narrative of the Torah, as well as the entirety of the Bible, and should also be understood as small sections of a broader story. Assnat Bartor helpfully points out that the "laws play a role in advancing the main story, as they constitute a necessary condition for the realization of the divine plan. The laws themselves, even if we ignore their content, motivate the story plot, since the continued survival of the nation is dependent on receiving and observing them. . . . The reader of the biblical narrative scrutinize[s] how the acceptance and (non)observance of the laws affect the destiny of the children of Israel." Bartor, *Reading Law as Narrative*, 20.

shall carry on the name of the dead brother so that his name will not be blotted out from Israel.

However, if a man does not want to marry his brother's wife, she shall go
to the elders at the town gate and say, "My husband's brother refuses to carry
on his brother's name in Israel. He will not fulfill the duty of a brother-in-law
to me." Then the elders of his town shall summon him and talk to him. If he
persists in saying, "I do not want to marry her," his brother's widow shall go up
to him in the presence of the elders, take off one of his sandals, spit in his face
and say, "This is what is done to the man who will not build up his brother's
family line." That man's line shall be known in Israel as The Family of the
Unsandaled. (Deut. 25:5–10)

Readers observe the fact that this is quite a drawn-out solution to an issue
that could have been settled by a concise divine command with consequences
for those who violate it. Something like "If a brother dies without children,
then the dead man's brother must have a child with the dead man's wife or
his face will receive spit" would have worked perfectly fine to discourage men
from defaulting on this law. This being the case, why is an exemplary scenario
presented with a dialogue when all that is needed is the legal solution? Bartor
provides a reason: "The only thing that is missing [with just the legal solution]
is the attitude of the parties to their new position, regarding the difficult situation that has transpired following the death of the husband or brother, and
regarding one another. This attitude can only be found within their speech."[13]
In other words, the hypothetical case is presented in order for the narrator
to demonstrate the potential feelings of people toward one another who find
themselves in this type of situation. The way that the levirate marriage custom
is regulated in Deuteronomy 25:5–10 serves the narrator's overall purpose
of striving to engage the reader's emotions in order to move them to action.

Here is how the narrator goes about doing this: The narrator indicates
that the man does not want to raise up children for his brother. He then gives
the hypothetically wronged woman a voice in order to demonstrate how a
woman in that scenario might perceive the actions of a man who does not
want to perform the duty of the husband's brother. The man is then given
a chance to change his behavior, but, instead, he reaffirms his lack of desire
to take the woman. The woman condemns his actions, only after taking his
sandal and spitting in his face. She then declares, "This is what is done to the
man who will not build up his brother's family line." The narrator concludes
this section by stating that the whole community will call the violator by an
unpleasant, lengthy moniker, "The Family of the Unsandaled."

13. Bartor, *Reading Law as Narrative*, 107.

By providing insight into the attitudes and emotions of the characters, the narrator vividly portrays a situation in which a woman who has no family is intentionally denied the claim that she has within her community. Notice that the ancient Israelite law gives the woman in this scenario the license to request that her brother-in-law provide a descendant for his deceased brother.[14] In this type of situation, the man involved still maintains the prerogative to reject participation in the community's practice. Nevertheless, by providing insight into the feelings of the characters in such a situation, the narrator illustrates two major points. First, in ancient Israel, the woman was not to blame or to be shamed for remaining childless in this scenario. Contrarily, the humiliation was to fall on her brother-in-law, who refused to participate in the community's practice at the woman's expense. Second, it was completely detestable for a man to willingly leave this woman in such a precarious situation, with no husband, no child, and perhaps not able to be given in marriage again by her family, since she had already been married. The man's behavior that causes this situation is perceived as reprehensible by the woman but also looked upon with extreme disfavor by the elders, everyone else in his community, the narrator, and, ultimately, God.

Levirate marriage may *still* seem odd to our modern senses, even after this brief analysis. However, reading this law as a mini narrative provides the narrator the space to illustrate principles that are exceedingly applicable to all people, everywhere, at all times. In this situation, he depicts a woman who is intentionally left wanting by a person in her community who should be concerned about her well-being. Viewed in that manner, some of the weirdness that hinges on the cultural context of the law is stripped away, and this text can then be considered as a mini narrative about justice and the importance of caring for those dispossessed of family. The relevance of these lessons transcends time, space, cultures, and individual people groups.

Embracing the Torah

At the end of *My Father Always Embarrasses Me*, Ephraim's attitude toward his father changes. The scene in which the inside of the cake demonstrates its beauty illustrates how Ephraim should view his father; that is to say, if Ephraim only focused on his father's appearance, he would have never been

---

14. The fact that the woman has the right to make this demand on her dead husband's family sets the biblical iteration of levirate marriage apart from other comparable laws in the ancient Near East. Other ancient Near Eastern laws depict the woman as passive, and the responsibility of raising up offspring for the dead man falls upon the dead husband's family.

able to realize the beauty of who his father actually was and the benefit of learning from him. By observing his father's culinary aptitude, Ephraim not only learned to appreciate his father's creativity but also stopped wishing that his father would become someone else in order to make Ephraim feel better about himself. Ephraim finally saw who his father really was, and he was no longer embarrassed; in fact, Ephraim became proud of his relationship to him and became eager to identify with him.

Feeling uneasy when reading some of the Torah's laws is completely natural, given our distances from the text. Yet if we impose our modern expectations on biblical law (and on God), wishing that it were something that it is not, we will inevitably be embarrassed. This embarrassment stems from the same issue that Ephraim had—namely, the problem of imposing expectations that cannot be met on something from which we are intended to learn and which we are meant to embrace. It takes humility to honestly assess one's disposition toward the biblical laws and to change that disposition if we find room for improvement. In the case of biblical laws, it serves us well to read them with eyes that focus on their purposeful literary arrangement and their unique teachings in their contexts instead of considering them as an affront to our modern sensibilities. Just as Ephraim eventually changed how he viewed his father, realizing his father's artistic brilliance and discovering a need to learn from him, so we can choose to read all the laws as the divinely inspired Scriptures. We can decide to appreciate them as component parts that are adroitly compiled to form Israel's larger narrative, from which we can learn about how God has reached out to humankind. Once we begin looking at the Torah's laws with the right lenses, we will learn to love all of them, just like Ephraim learned to embrace all of who his father was.

EIGHT

Seeds of Remembrance

The control of the past depends above all on the training of the memory.
—Emmanuel Goldstein, in George Orwell, *1984*

One of the most brilliant components of George Orwell's classic dystopian novel, *1984*, is the contrivance of the "Newspeak" language. Newspeak is an ingenious creation by the Party, while at the same time being egregious for its citizens, since it provides terminology that relates only orthodox Party dogma. In this manner, the Party is able to control the people's thoughts by regulating their language. "Doublethink" is a Newspeak term that relates the ability to wittingly accept contradictory information while, at the same time, unconsciously ignoring the fact that conflicting data should bring about the recognition of falsehood. The language used by the Party and adopted by the masses inevitably leads to doublethink as a way in which people are willing to accept each and every claim of the Party, whether they are coherent or not.

Mass doublethink is the primary way the Party is able to rewrite the past and, ultimately, control the memory of the inhabitants of Oceania, the homeland of *1984*'s protagonist, Winston Smith. The Party is especially concerned with manipulating the historical narrative as a way of demonstrating that it has consistently made the right decisions and perfectly foreseen the future. The Party radiates an aura of perfection, when, in reality, the primary goal is to coerce the people and realize one of the Party's main slogans: "Who controls the past controls the future; who controls the present controls the past."

The Temptation toward Doublethink

Unlike the Party in *1984*, the God of Israel is not at all an advocate of doublethink. God is all-powerful and yet does not assert his authority by coercion or by manipulating the narrative of the past. The fact that the people of Israel were not coerced into obeying God is inherent in the laws God gave to Israel, since Israel had the genuine options of obeying or disobeying God's commands (Deut. 28:1, 15). Additionally, Israel's relationship to and with God was fundamentally rooted in the truths of the past, and therefore, an accurate recollection of history was key to the relationship between God and the people. For example, the Passover and the exodus are alluded to in the Sinai narrative when God sanctifies the people of Israel and gives them his word: "I am the LORD your God, who brought you out of Egypt, out of the land of slavery" (Exod. 20:2). Recognizing God's character and obeying him based on past realities were eminently important for ancient Israel.

God's activity in Israel's past also demonstrated who God would be for them in the future. The people of Israel were to trust that God's character would be consistent with his distinctive nature, which had been exhibited through, for example, the major salvific events, such as the Passover and the exodus. Israel's ongoing, everyday relationship with God, and their future hope in him, were based in the reality of who he had formerly been for them. For these reasons, the people of Israel were not at liberty to rewrite their past. In fact, it was by actively recollecting their past that they were able to remember who their God was, who he continued to be, and who he would be for them in future times.

The legal sections of the Torah outline God's strategy for protecting Israel from cutting itself off from the past and inevitably rewriting history. If the people of Israel were disconnected from memories of God providing for and protecting them, they might eventually wonder whether these events actually happened or whether they were fanciful legends circulated in their community. This evolution of the awareness of God would be especially problematic as it relates to major, community-forming events such as the Passover and the exodus. It would be equally unsettling for Israel to let the recollection of God's provision in the desert slip from their collective memory. It would be highly troubling if the community somehow forgot that God repeatedly established a connection with them, despite their major transgressions (e.g., the golden calf in Exod. 32), and established a divinely ordained system through which the community would recognize and respond to God's holiness (e.g., Lev. 16).

If Israel were to forget its past, it would inevitably forget its God. To prevent this from happening, God planted "seeds" of remembrance—markers in the Torah referring to his actions on behalf of the people of Israel.[1] These seeds not only would become a part of Israel's daily communal life and practice but also would be preserved and further developed in later sections of the Bible, becoming foundational aspects of faith even for modern Christians.

The Feasts as Commemorations

Practices that symbolized the community's relationship to their God were embedded in the laws of ancient Israel. Implicit in these reminders is the idea that the people of Israel would be prone to rewrite their past and inclined to forget their God, if left to their own devices. With the passing of time, the people might employ doublethink on themselves, trying to hold to the traditions of their past while simultaneously replacing them with their conflicting, present-day whims. The laws of the Torah were intended to develop into rhythms of life for the community; they were to form habits by which the people of Israel would actively recall who their God was to them and who they were in light of their God.[2] Israel was to remember everything from God's mighty feats to his day-to-day provision, while all along looking forward to how he would continue to work in and through them in the future. By obeying the precepts that God had given them, the people of Israel established a way of life that would prohibit them from rewriting the past.

God was absolutely inimical to the people of Israel relating a narrative of their past any differently than it had actually occurred. God was jealous for his covenant people (Exod. 20:5), and therefore, God delineated in the Torah "appointed" times (i.e., the feasts of Israel; Lev. 23:2) throughout the year that would serve as tangible ways in which Israel would recall their past and consciously remember their God. During the feasts, the community acknowledged that God had cared for them in the past and would care for them in the future, regardless of the present situation (e.g., the Feasts of Tabernacles, Trumpets, First Fruits, and Weeks); the people recognized their distance from God and the gravity of their sin, and they demonstrated gratefulness for

1. This idea is adapted from Kaiser, *Old Testament Documents.* Kaiser states that "the message of the Pentateuch is more than merely the beginning of the narrative of the nation of Israel and the people of God. . . . It often contains in seed form the idea of what will later be developed in the organized wholeness of the message of the Bible" (131–32).

2. For example, the Sabbath is technically considered a feast of Israel and was practiced weekly in view of the creation narrative (Lev. 23:3). See comments relating to the Sabbath in chapter 7.

God's redemption and steadfast love toward them (e.g., the Passover and the Day of Atonement).[3]

The feasts not only were replete with reminders of what God had done in the past but also incorporated signs pointing toward what God would do in the future—how God was going to use the people of Israel in unique ways to fulfill his promises to Abraham, Isaac, and Jacob to give them a land, multiply them, and make them a blessing to all the nations (Gen. 12:3; 18:18; 22:18; 26:4; 28:14). If the people of Israel were to observe the feasts properly and genuinely, then neglecting God and accepting a narrative contradictory to the realities of their past relationship with him would simply be impossible.

In the rest of this chapter, we will briefly discuss one of the major feasts that Israel was commanded to perpetually observe: the Passover. We will begin with a review of the history leading up to the event, the symbolism embedded into the observance of the day, and the progression and materialization of some of these signs, which are noticeable when we read the text successively and entirely. The Passover narrative manifests principles in seed form that are cultivated by later biblical writers and that eventually blossom throughout the whole Bible.

The Passover Predicament

From the perspective of the reader, God's promises to Abraham (Gen. 12:1–7; 15:5–7) fall into jeopardy almost immediately after they are declared. The rollercoaster of following the jeopardization of God's promises to Israel reaches an all-time low with the departure of Moses from Egypt. There appears to be no earthly hope for the people of Israel. Their only hope is unmediated divine intervention.

Now God has the people of Israel, and the reader, exactly where he wants them.

By way of effective narration up to this point in the Torah, all readers are compelled to recognize Israel's utter powerlessness in bringing about the divine purposes. Moses is exiled; Israel is enslaved; God is Israel's only hope. Extraordinary feats will have to come to pass in order to bring about the salvation of the people—so much so that all will be forced to recognize God as the ultimate liberator and promise keeper. The initial phase of deliverance and assurance comes by way of God yanking Israel from the grips of its putative destroyer in the event known as "the Passover."

3. The Passover and the Feast of Unleavened Bread are technically two feasts celebrated as one eight-day event. See Exod. 12:14–20; 13:1–16; Lev. 23:4–8; Num. 28:17; Deut. 16:3.

With the purpose of fulfilling the land promise that he gave to Israel's ancestors (Exod. 13:11), God calls Moses to return to Egypt to be an instrument of liberation (3:7–8). Moses is initially reluctant,[4] but God shows Moses his authority over natural laws, performing signs and miracles to demonstrate that Israel will be saved by divine power and not through any other means (4:2–9). The fact that God enables Moses to perform miracles is crucial to providing Moses, Israel, and, of course, the readers hope that Israel's salvation will indeed come to pass. This hope is necessary because another issue almost immediately arises in the narrative that endangers the fulfillment of God's promises: the Egyptians, as they are represented by their Pharaoh, refuse to let the people of Israel leave Egypt. Even after a series of nine devastating plagues, Pharaoh remains obstinate (7:15–10:29). The fact that God is directly involved and using Moses to carry out his wonderous deeds predicts a successful outcome. Nevertheless, Pharaoh will not budge, meaning that God alone must supernaturally intervene in order to save Israel and set them on the trajectory toward the fulfillment of his promise.

Moses makes direct, divine intervention explicitly known to all in Egypt by announcing that God's final plague will result in the death of all the firstborn in Egypt (including animals! [Exod. 11:1–8]). Though the death of the firstborn will be carried out by their God, the people of Israel are commanded to mark their homes to keep them safe from the tenth plague. The community is instructed to kill a spotless lamb and place its blood on the two doorposts and the lintel of the house in which they eat the animal. It seems as if the lamb is to be killed at the threshold of the house,[5] which is a vivid image: the entrance of every Israelite dwelling is completely covered in the animal's blood. This grotesque scene strikingly illustrates that obedience to God's command is lifesaving (see more below). God promises to see the blood and "pass over"—that is, not inflict death on that household (12:1–7, 12–13, 22). Those who do not have the sign of the blood are subject to the horrific tenth plague on the night of the Passover: "At midnight the LORD struck down all the firstborn in Egypt, from the firstborn of Pharaoh, who sat on the throne, to the firstborn of the prisoner, who was in the dungeon, and the firstborn of all the livestock as well. Pharaoh and all his officials and all the Egyptians got up during the night, and there was loud wailing in Egypt, for there was not a house without someone dead" (12:29–30).

4. Other biblical prophets are also portrayed as reluctant to accept God's call. See, for example, Isa. 6:5; Jer. 1:6; Jon. 1:3.

5. The Hebrew word that is translated "basin" (saph) in some translations (ESV, KJV, NASB, NIV, NJPS, NRSV) can also refer to the "threshold" at the bottom of an entranceway.

Perhaps the most conspicuously disturbing aspect of the Passover story is that the God of Israel—who made humankind in his image and according to his likeness—is now emphatically depicted as completely responsible for the death of Egypt's firstborn children. This detail is repeatedly emphasized throughout the Passover narrative: It begins with God declaring, in the first person, that he will bring the grisly final plague on Pharaoh and Egypt (11:1); Moses then likewise asserts that the firstborn will die because God will go out into Egypt (Exod. 11:4–5; 12:12–13, 23, 27). God then discloses a reason for the plague that emphasizes his responsibility: Pharaoh would not listen, and so God brings about the death of the firstborn as another "wonder" in Egypt (11:9). After the event, the narrator conclusively states that God struck down all the firstborn in Egypt on the night of the Passover (12:29; 13:15). Only as a result of God's heavy hand falling on the Egyptians—God's direct intervention resulting in the death of the firstborn—are the Egyptians finally willing to let the people of Israel go.

Reading the Passover Account

Contemporary readers do not have access to the ancients' minds, and therefore we are not privy to what the people of Israel were thinking upon hearing Moses's command to slaughter a lamb, smear blood all over the entryways of their houses, and wait things out while all of the firstborn of Egypt were killed by divine order. We do, however, have access to the words that were used in the narrator's selective account of the Passover story. The narrative relays specific details that were retold to emphasize important aspects of the story for future generations of readers. At least two aspects of this story are accentuated for us: (1) the Passover was to be perpetually celebrated by the community from then on, and (2) symbolism is embedded in the killing of the lamb and the smearing of its blood.

Israel's First Memorial Day

Many countries in the world annually set apart time to honor fallen soldiers and others lost in military conflicts. This time is frequently called "Memorial Day" or something similar. For the people of Israel, the Passover was to be a sort of Memorial Day that they were instructed to continually celebrate (Exod. 12:14; Lev. 23:3–4; Deut. 16:1). However, instead of honoring fallen soldiers, Israel was to remember that none of their own had died in Egypt. God had clashed with the Egyptians and their gods on Israel's behalf (Exod. 12:12). Therefore Israel was to set aside a period of remembrance so that they would never forget that they were once helpless slaves in a foreign land, but God alone defeated their oppressor and moved them toward the fulfillment of all his promises to them.

While the reader might expect some emphasis on Israel's need to remember what God did on their behalf in Egypt, the way the narrator highlights commemorating the Passover makes it all the more important for the reader. At two distinct points in the retelling of the Passover story, the narrator abruptly changes the tone of communication in order to command the people of Israel to observe the Passover in the future.

The first time this happens is when Moses provides Israel with the initial instructions concerning the night of the Passover. Moses calls for the people to kill a lamb, to smear its blood on their doorposts, and to stay inside their residence in order to avoid the plague. Suddenly, Moses's speech shifts into a mandate regarding how the people are to perpetually observe the Passover upon settling in their land (Exod. 12:24–25). This is an awkward shift in the monologue, akin to a modern military leader standing among his troops before a battle and instructing the soldiers concerning how to go about celebrating Memorial Day upon returning home. The Passover has not yet happened, but Israel's campaign in Egypt is effectively over in the eyes of Moses, because God is directly involved in their affairs and ready to bring about his promises. The God of Israel unexpectedly defeats Egypt without Israel forming the army that the Pharaoh dreaded (1:10). Consequently, Israel is commanded to actively remember what God has done on their behalf.

The second time the people are called to commemorate God's activity in the Passover involves an even more abrupt shift in the narrative. After the account of the night of the Passover, the narrator briefly summarizes Israel's exodus from Egypt (Exod. 12:33–42). At this point, an extended section of divine instructions comes before the expected continuation of the story of Israel's exodus (12:43–13:16). This section almost seems out of place, since the narrative would not skip a beat if the divine instructions were absent. The first portion of God's commands specifically relates direction about how to celebrate the Passover on the actual night of the event as well as in future generations (12:43–49). It is almost as if God were saying through Moses, "Before going any further in our story, you have to understand one of the morals: Israel, you must obey my commands in order to properly remember your past!"

The call for the people of Israel to forever commemorate their history by keeping the particular commands of God had a practical and beneficial purpose for the future of their community. Remembering the past, as well as keeping the specific commands of God and the symbolism therein, was the way through which the people of Israel were to instruct their children. Observing the Passover was intended to invoke Israel's children to inquire about the reason for the signs—especially the sign of the blood on the doorposts; the children's questions about the sign of the blood were intended to provoke parental responses that retold the story of how God passed over the houses covered in the blood of the unblemished lamb; this exchange was to evoke remembrance and, ultimately, worship. The act of perpetually remembering Israel's history and how God used blood to save them would be especially important once the people of Israel had inherited the land and were situated comfortably therein (Exod. 12:25–28).[6]

Signs in the Passover Sacrifice

It is comical to suggest that the God of Israel would have needed an actual sign on the doorposts of the people of Israel in order to recall where they were located during the night of the Passover. God is indeed portrayed as demonstrating divine omniscience and omnipotence throughout this passage through his prediction of the Passover, his knowledge of exactly how Pharoah and the Egyptians will react to the plague, and then his carrying out of the event. Thus the blood of the lamb is intended to be a sign for the people of Israel in that moment, as well as for subsequent readers (Exod. 12:13–14). The question that still remains is this: Why did God command the people of Israel to stain their doorways specifically with the blood of an unblemished lamb on the night of the Passover? The answer to this question is not directly or fully answered in the Passover narrative, but reasons for this imagery emerge when we read through the Scriptures successively, entirely, and deliberately.

Israel's community tradition before the Passover included stories in which their ancestors carried out sacrifices. Noah and Abraham sacrificed animals on distinct occasions as a response to God's goodness to them (Gen. 8:20; 15:7–11). Also ingrained in the tradition of Israel was the teaching related to the sanctity of blood; blood represented life, and the control of life was exclusively God's jurisdiction. The people could eat animals but not consume their blood (9:2–6). In the event of the Passover, a spotless lamb was to be slaughtered and eaten, but the blood, which represented life, was not done away with; it stained the most conspicuous part of the residence as a sign for the people: Israel was only able to escape suffering and bloodshed by being marked with the blood of a lamb.

6. The fact that symbolism was put in place with the intent of teaching children is explicitly stated in the instructions for the observation of the Feast of Unleavened Bread (cf. 13:8–16).

In the Passover, offerings and blood were associated with preserving human life. The idea that one life would be taken in order for another to be preserved is noteworthy because it demonstrates a crucial shift in how animals are sacrificed up to this point in the tradition of Israel. The monumental event of the Passover showed the community that blood spilled on behalf of people could somehow preserve them from death—that obedience in applying the blood of the lamb to their doorposts protected them from being struck down by God. In the Passover, the lamb bore the death of the firstborn; the blood on the doorpost was a sign that a life had been taken. Israel was subsequently commanded to set apart the firstborn of every womb as a way of intentionally remembering that they were saved by the effectual application of the blood of the lamb on their doorposts, while the Egyptians' firstborn perished (Exod. 13:2). Overall, imagery emerges from this narrative that relates the notion of substitution: one living being (i.e., the lamb) dies in the place of another (i.e., the firstborn). The blood of the dead being protects the living being from the wrath of God, who brings about retribution for disobedience.

The imagery projected in the Passover offering does not simply represent substitution in a vague sense, since specific details are provided concerning the nature of the animal to be offered. The lamb that was offered needed to be without blemish (Exod. 12:5; Num. 28:19). This is an important point but not unique to the Passover, since later in ancient Israelite history God explicitly forbade offering defective animals (Lev. 22:19–21; Deut. 17:1). However, what appears to be unique about the Passover offering was that the community was not permitted to break any of its bones upon either offering it or consuming it (Exod. 12:46; Num. 9:12)—that is to say, the animal needed to be intact prior to and subsequent to the sacrifice. This is a particularly important detail to the reader that is fleshed out by continuing to read the Bible and considering this imagery in light of other, later passages.

Reception of the Passover Sacrifice

The prescribed nature and processes for offerings are significantly expounded on in the Levitical sections of the Mosaic Law. Consequently, the sacrificial system became a central part of the cultural and religious consciousness of the people of Israel (Lev. 1–7). In this way, images from the Passover functioned as seeds that developed in the context of the Law and then were uniquely adopted and expanded by later biblical writers.

For example, Isaiah portrays aspects of sacrificial imagery through the suffering servant, who is ultimately emblematic of a person who would undergo affliction on behalf of others as if he were an animal sacrifice (Isa. 53). Isaiah's illustration functions as a bridge of sorts from the sacrificial imagery used in the Torah to some of the rhetoric and imagery used in reference to Jesus in the New Testament.[7] We are finally able to see seeds that were planted in the Passover narrative flourish into a full blossom on the pages of the New Testament.

Christians tend to intuitively grasp the New Testament's "Lamb of God" imagery because it is liberally applied to Jesus within modern Christian circles. Perhaps the most well-known passage in which this image is connected to Jesus is the scene of Jesus's baptism. John the Baptist sees Jesus approaching him and exclaims, "Look, the Lamb of God, who takes away the sin of the world!" (John 1:29). Despite the fact that modern readers commonly hear and perhaps intuitively process this type of language about Jesus, deliberate readers of the Bible are still forced to ask, "Why is John calling Jesus a 'lamb'? Surely, this is a metaphor, but where does it come from, and what does it mean?" The answer seems to be that this imagery has its origins in the Passover. John the Baptist identified Jesus as a metaphorical sacrificial lamb that would die in the place of human beings so that they would not suffer the wrath of God. Implied in John the Baptist's application of this lamb metaphor to Jesus is the declaration that Jesus's sacrificial death, and the effectual application of his blood, would free human beings from slavery. Sin enslaves and, ultimately, causes death (Rom. 3:23); Jesus would protect humankind by taking away the sin of the world so that through his death many could be freed from their bondage.

John the Evangelist refers to Jesus as the Passover lamb during the crucifixion scene. John reports that the Roman governor, Pontius Pilate, is at the point of requesting that Jesus's legs be broken, at the behest of the Jewish leaders, so that Jesus will not remain on the cross during the Sabbath. The Roman soldiers break the legs of the other two people who were crucified with Jesus, but when they come to Jesus, they realize that he is already dead. To verify this, a Roman soldier pierces Jesus's side with his spear, causing blood and water to flow out. This provokes John to claim, "These things happened so that the scripture would be fulfilled: 'Not one of his bones will be broken'" (John 19:36). Though not an exact citation, John's language sounds conspicuously similar to the Torah's commands of not breaking any of the bones of the Passover offering, either before or after the sacrifice (Exod. 12:46; Num. 9:12).[8] The Torah's reference to a perfect lamb whose bones would never be

---

7. These ideas will be considerably expounded upon in our discussion of the Lord's servant passages in chapter 19 of this book.

8. It appears as if John conflates the idea of a blameless Passover lamb with the personal language relating to the righteous person depicted in Ps. 34:20. By doing this, John personalizes the illustration of the lamb as Jesus, the righteous sacrifice.

broken was a seed that ultimately blossomed in the depiction of Jesus as a lamb, dying in the stead of others at the crucifixion.

All of the Gospels make a connection between Jesus and the Passover by portraying Jesus commemorating the feast with his disciples and being crucified shortly thereafter (Matt. 26:17–35; Mark 14:12–31; Luke 22:7–13; John 13–17; 19:14, 31). The apostle Peter affirms that Jesus's blood ransoms people like the blood of the blameless Passover lamb (1 Pet. 1:18–19); the author of the letter to the Hebrews claims that Jesus's blood sanctifies and purifies his people because Jesus offered himself as a sacrifice without blemish to God (Heb. 9:14); the apostle Paul, likewise, calls the Corinthians to put away sinful behaviors because Jesus, the Passover lamb, was sacrificed on their behalf (1 Cor. 5:6–8).[9] The New Testament writers suggest that the culmination of Jesus's work on earth can only be holistically grasped when we consider it in light of the imagery depicted in the Passover scene.

Remembering Passover

God commanded the people of Israel to perpetually remember their history because Israel's past was absolutely crucial to understanding Israel's relationship to their God at any given time. Israel was to remember that their salvation was exclusively brought about by God and that their promised inheritance of land was a result of divine intervention in space and time to rescue them from their impending peril. The offering that was annually presented during the Passover commemoration illustrated the fact that the firstborn children of Israel were exempt from death—the little ones they watched grow during their time in the wilderness did not die because the blood of the lamb spared them on the night in which God passed through Egypt and all of the unmarked homes experienced death.

Furthermore, Israel's past pointed to a glorious future for their people. The past called attention to their unique relationship with their covenant God and the fulfillment of the promises that he made to them through their forefather Abraham (Gen. 12:1–3). Even though God's promises seemed like they were in jeopardy from the very beginning, he always came through. God had already turned Israel into a numerous group (Exod. 12:37); he was intending

9. The 1 Cor. 5:6–8 passage is an example of how yet another seed from the Passover narrative is received and expanded upon by later writers. The people of Israel were commanded to celebrate the Feast of Unleavened Bread for seven days after the Passover, during which time they were not permitted to consume any leaven (Exod. 12:8, 15–20; 13:3–10; cf. 12:33–34, 39). Paul uses leaven as a metaphor for sin and commands the Corinthians to rid themselves of it as a reflection of what Jesus had done for them.

to bring them into their land; and ultimately all nations would be blessed through them. Israel could not fall into doublethink, ultimately believing a false narrative that they had rescued themselves or that the blessings eventually bestowed on them were results of their own accomplishments. The Passover *is* Israel's narrative of salvation from slavery and transition into the fulfillment of God's promises. Any other narrative is fundamentally incompatible with their being the people of Israel.

Jesus came from the people of Israel and brought the message of God's love and forgiveness to all humanity (John 3:16–17). In Jesus, Israel has blessed all nations. The correlation between Jesus's sacrificial death in the New Testament and the death of the Passover lamb suggests that one's relationship with God is determined by looking back on Jesus's sacrifice. Jesus is the means by which God singlehandedly rescues people from their impending peril; Jesus's blood functions as the blood of the Passover lamb by sparing the lives of those who believe in him. God's future promises (the resurrection of the dead, eternal life, etc.) for those marked by the blood of Jesus are secure despite the fact that they might *feel* jeopardized throughout their journey. Christians cannot forget the Passover and what it illustrates, or we might be prone to doublethink and to forget the depths of despair that preceded redemption. Jesus as the Passover lamb *is* the Christian's narrative, relating a transfer from captivity as helpless and hopeless slaves of sin and death into the kingdom of God to await the fulfillment of guaranteed promises. Any other narrative is fundamentally incompatible with being a follower of Jesus.

NINE

Redeeming Rahab the Conqueror

> Nobody knew what form of intimidation Mr. Radley employed to keep
> Boo out of sight, but Jem figured that Mr. Radley kept him chained to
> the bed most of the time.
>
> —Scout Finch, in Harper Lee, *To Kill a Mockingbird*

As he is depicted in Harper Lee's novel *To Kill a Mockingbird*, Arthur "Boo"
Radley represents everything that children like Scout Finch and her older
brother, Jem, should fear. During their childhood years in the town of Maycomb, Alabama, legend had it that Boo Radley would only come out at night
to peep into neighborhood windows and mutilate people's animals. Boo was
a churchless recluse who had been confined in his house by his father for years
after committing relatively petty childhood crimes. The Radley residence,
which was adjacent to the Maycomb school grounds, was uncharted territory,
and therefore Scout and Jem became increasingly terrified by the prospects of
approaching the house as the days of their elementary school years went on.

The obsession with the Radley home dwindles from the forefront of the
narrative when Scout and Jem's father, Atticus, becomes embroiled in a fierce
legal battle. A lawyer by trade, Atticus becomes the court-appointed attorney
who defends a Black man named Tom Robinson against charges that he as-
saulted a White woman, Mayella Ewell. Mayella's father, Bob Ewell, promises
revenge on Atticus for defending Tom and for embarrassing his daughter in
the process.

One night, Scout and Jem sense that they are being followed while they walk home through the pitch-black schoolyard after an evening event at school. While pausing to verify that the sounds they heard were real, Scout and Jem are, all of a sudden, brutally attacked. The attacker incapacitates Jem and begins squeezing the breath out of Scout. Just when she is in a good deal of trouble, he unexpectantly drops her. The assailant is pulled to the ground, wheezes, and then, he falls silent.

The assailant is dead; the children have somehow been saved. At this point, an important detail in the story begins to make sense: the Radley property is adjacent to the school grounds!

Boo Radley, who Scout and Jem feared might one day attack them if they ever encountered him in person close to the school grounds, has unexpectedly saved them from their adversary and perpetrator, Bob Ewell. Scout eventually realizes that Boo has been conscious of the children's neighborhood activities for years. Boo has developed an affection for the children, which motivated him to help them when they fell into danger. Arthur "Boo" Radley, the unlikeliest of all people—the man who represents all that typical children like Scout and Jem fear throughout their youth—saved them when they were in dire need.

Like Boo, the biblical character Rahab is ta-"Boo." Rahab is not only "off-limits," analogous to the Radley residence, but also represents everything that the people of Israel should legitimately fear as a fledgling society at the beginning of their conquest of Canaan: Rahab is a Canaanite; Canaanites are idol worshipers. Rahab is a prostitute; prostitutes participate in sexual immorality as a profession. This woman clearly illustrates the dangers associated with the uncharted territory of Canaan. The people of Israel should absolutely be wary of everything that Rahab represents. She is the very last person, at this point in the early history of Israel, who might be expected to help them.

In spite of this, it is Rahab who preemptively intervenes in Israel's conflict in order to save them, thereby turning out to be the unlikely hero of the conquest narrative. Like Boo Radley's reputation, Rahab's reputation undergoes a transformation in the narrative: she goes from being a risky character to being a life saver. After Rahab saves the Israelites, her testimony unfolds, and she reveals that she has been following the story of Israel for years. Rahab had developed a devotion to Israel's God and instinctively facilitated the rescue of the covenant people when an opportunity arose. Rahab's disposition toward the God of Israel and his promises encourages the people of Israel to accomplish their mission, which is evident through the repetition of her words at the end of the narrative.

In this chapter, we will discuss Rahab's role in the conquest narrative by paying close attention to how the narrator depicts the events of Joshua 2 in light of the buildup to the conquest in the Torah. We will consider the long-standing questions that emerge from this story relating to why Israelite spies visited a prostitute and how to understand Rahab's deceptive speech to the envoys of the king of Jericho. Understood holistically, Rahab's narrative depicts an occasion in which God uses odd circumstances and an unexpected character to fulfill the divine purposes in an unforeseen manner.

On the Cusp of the Conquest

Moses, God's primary human agent of Israel's liberation and leader of the people throughout their wanderings in the wilderness, dies at the end of the Torah (Deut. 34:1–8). Prior to Moses's death, God supernaturally provides him with a glimpse of the entire expanse of the promised land. As Moses beholds Canaan from the top of Mount Nebo, God's voice emerges, reiterating the divine guarantee of that land, made to Abraham more than five hundred years prior. Yet now, God specifically includes Moses's descendants as inheritors. Irrespective of the long interval that passed between God's initial pledge to Abraham and the time of Moses, God is faithful to his word and will keep his promises. As Moses looks down from Nebo, God's guarantee that Israel would finally settle in a prosperous homeland becomes more tangible than it has ever been.

Israel is on the cusp of the conquest of Canaan.

That is the good news.

The bad news is that Moses is not going into Canaan with Israel. Since God is faithful to his word, he is compelled by his nature to maintain the appropriate consequences for disobedience. This is especially the case for God's servant Moses, who was called on to uniquely represent him by serving as his spokesperson to the people of Israel.

As Moses nears death and Deuteronomy comes to an end, God alludes to the incident that came to pass at Meribah (Num. 20:2–13). There, the people of Israel complain because of a water shortage and stubbornly insist that they would rather die than be in the wilderness. God responds to this situation by directing Moses to gather his staff, assemble the congregation, and command a rock to provide water for the people and their cattle. Moses obeys two-thirds of God's instruction: he picks up his staff and assembles the people.

But, as the old adage goes, "Partial obedience is complete disobedience."

Moses's emotions overflow prior to the water flowing. Instead of *speaking to the rock* as God had commanded, Moses *raises his voice to the people*, saying, "Listen, you rebels, must we bring you water out of this rock?" (Num. 20:10).

Instead of facilitating a miraculous scene in which he serves as God's mouth-piece and controls nature, Moses derides the people, raises his arm, and strikes the rock with his timeworn staff. Water then flows from the rock, and the hope of Moses leading Israel into the land is simultaneously carried off in the current. Moses disobeys God, does not properly represent him, and interferes with a divine wonder that would have encouraged the people to esteem the Lord for divinely administered provision.

With two blows and a bellow, Moses forfeits the privilege of leading Israel into the land. God immediately declares the consequence for Moses's misdeed: "Because you did not trust in me enough to honor me as holy in the sight of the Israelites, you will not bring this community into the land I give them" (Num. 20:12). Though still full of strength at the age of 120, Moses dies in Moab, east of the Jordan River, with the promised land in his sight—yet not within his reach (Deut. 34:6–7).

Joshua's appointment at the end of Moses's burial narrative (Deut. 34:9) and the recollection of Moses at the beginning of Joshua's assignment (Josh. 1:1) suggest that the Torah's narrative continues in the book of Joshua. Following the historical events, theological motifs, and overall storyline in Joshua is contingent upon familiarity with the contents of the Torah. The narrative continues from the books of Moses to the book of Joshua, yet the main character changes from Moses to Joshua.

Perhaps the most important fact concerning Israel's new leader relates to the last time Israel was on the cusp of conquering Canaan. In Numbers 13, Moses sent twelve spies into Canaan to explore the land and report on its inhabitants. Upon the return of the spies to Paran at Kadesh, Joshua and Caleb encourage the people to enter into the land. The other ten spies discourage the community, insisting that the survival of their people will be at risk if they attempt to settle in the land. The majority wins out, and the grumbling among the community grows to the point that a group of Israelites threaten to return to Egypt (Num. 14).

Joshua and Caleb persist in declaring that God will give the land to them and that fear is a sign of disobedience. Their boldness nearly gets them stoned—a threat that is abruptly interrupted by an appearance of God at the Tent of Meeting. God expresses extreme discontentment with the community's response and declares that they are set to wander for forty years—one year for each day that the spies were in the land. God will fulfill his divine promises through Israel's children even though the terrified adults worry that their little ones will be consumed by the inhabitants of the land. Joshua and Caleb are the only men above the age of twenty that will be permitted to witness the fulfillment of God's promises to their ancestors.

As readers turn the final page of the Torah and open the book of Joshua, Israel's new leader is presented with the opportunity to again exercise the faith he exhibited decades earlier upon his return to Moses and the community of Israel at Kadesh. Israel, with Joshua as their leader, is once again on the cusp of conquering Canaan. However, the appearance of fulfillment does not always turn out as expected. Repeatedly throughout the Torah, it seems as if God is on the verge of fulfilling a major promise, only for some complication to delay its realization.[1] At this point in the wilderness wanderings, the reader is well prepared to expect difficulties—especially related to conquering the land in light of the previous spy situation. Israel has already been wandering for forty years near the land of their inheritance, given that it is only an eleven-day journey from Mount Horeb (a.k.a. Sinai) to the border of the promised land (Deut. 1:2).

Thus even though the people of Israel are geographically close to Canaan (Josh. 2:1); *and* God explicitly identifies Joshua as the leader that will guide Israel into the land (Deut. 3:28; 31:23; see also Josh. 1:2–4, 6); *and* Joshua is filled with the spirit of wisdom (Deut. 34:9); *and* Joshua has been encouraged and approved by his predecessor, Moses (31:7–8); *and* Joshua specifically communicates to the people of Israel that they will cross the Jordan in three days (Josh. 1:11); *and* the people of Israel recognize Joshua as their new, authoritative leader (1:16–18), the reader is still completely justified in wondering whether the people of Israel will do something to somehow mess up the situation.

Additional questions emerge at the beginning of Joshua relating to how Israel will actually conquer the land. Israel is promised that the conquest will happen but is not specifically informed of *how* it will come to pass. Except for the decades-old report of Joshua and Caleb, Israel is completely oblivious to the geography of the land and ignorant about its inhabitants as Joshua begins his tenure as the main leader. The fact that there are several roadblocks ahead of the Israelites and no clear indication of how the people will be able to accomplish their mission causes readers to once again look for overt supernatural intervention. Divine intervention does materialize in due time

---

1. For example, the issue of infertility seems to endanger the divine plan for multitudinous offspring when Abraham and Sarah struggle to conceive. Then, despite the birth of their child of promise in their old age (Isaac), Abraham is commanded to sacrifice him (Gen. 22). Isaac barely escapes, only to also endure a struggle with fertility alongside his wife, Rebekah, jeopardizing God's plans once again until God provides the conception of twins, Esau and Jacob (25:19–26). Esau, the older brother, sells his birthright to Jacob in a time of great desperation (25:29–34) and is subsequently tricked out of his firstborn blessing by Jacob his brother and Rebekah their mother (Gen. 27). This is enough for Esau to plan to murder Jacob, threatening the fulfillment of God's promises through Jacob (28:10–15).

at both the parting of the Jordan River—permitting the people to cross over into Canaan (Josh. 3)—and the crumbling of the wall of Jericho (Josh. 6).

But prior to this, the people of Israel experience great uncertainty: They have a new leader, serious obstacles, and ancient promises. They do not possess a thorough knowledge of the land and the people therein, or definitive instructions pertaining to their mission. No one knows whether they actually have the confidence in their God that it will take to advance toward their inheritance. As a result of the people's past faults, and in light of the enormous task that lies ahead of them, readers are forced to wonder if the people of Israel will falter once again, given the tremendous faith needed to go into Canaan and inherit the land.

Rahab's Reception

With this uncertainty in mind, the beginning of the book of Joshua immediately informs readers that the people of Israel are camped at Shittim (Josh. 2:1; see also Num. 33:49). Joshua sends spies into Canaan from Shittim, echoing what Moses did in Numbers 13. However, in contrast to Moses, Joshua dispatches only two spies and does so without a community-wide awareness of their venture. The men are responsible for reporting directly back to Joshua (Josh. 2:23–24), effectively permitting him to lead without a sizable dissenting voice within the community. Having only two spies reporting directly back to him minimizes the chance for disunity among the tribes upon their return, unlike the ten-versus-two scenario that came to pass when Moses sent spies into Canaan. That initial foray into Canaan has evidently influenced Joshua to tweak the manner in which intelligence relating to Canaan and its inhabitants is collected in order to avoid resistance from the community.

Be that as it may, readers are instantly presented with a peculiar scene featuring the two Israelite spies upon their departure from Shittim. The nameless spies leave the Israelite camp and are promptly depicted as arriving inside the house of a Canaanite prostitute named Rahab. The residence of a prostitute seems to be a bizarre landing spot for the Israelite spies, given that prostitution would hardly be acceptable in ancient Israel (Lev. 19:29). On that account, it is intriguing that the narrator includes this story, featuring Rahab, as a necessary part of the conquest narrative. This is especially interesting given that Joshua 2 could have been omitted—along with a couple verses in chapter 6—without affecting the overall story of Joshua. Yet the narrative of Rahab is featured at the very beginning of Joshua, at the very beginning of the conquest. Why, then, would the author take pains to explicitly state that the spies left from Shittim and landed in the dwelling of a Canaanite prostitute?

In order to responsibly explore the possible explanation(s) to this question, readers must consciously dedicate themselves to striving for self-awareness in their interpretations. In this case, readers might knowingly or unknowingly be inclined to protect the integrity of the Israelite spies—especially since God's promise of giving Israel the land through the leadership of Joshua is reiterated in chapter 1. Readers might suppose and defend the rectitude of the spies' actions because it appears as if God is going to use Joshua, the noble leader of Israel, as a broker of the divine promises immediately.

Notwithstanding, the stories of the Torah demonstrate that God is not compelled to bring about the divine promises at any given time because of an increase in expectations thereof. God's promises are "put on hold" time and time again for one reason or another. Thus to read Rahab's narrative assuming that the Israelite spies make an appropriate decision by landing in the house of a Canaanite prostitute because God is going to fulfill the land promise to Israel is a quintessential example of confirmation bias. Simply stated, if readers assume that the Israelite men were upright, then their arrival at the residence of a Canaanite prostitute will somehow serve a righteous purpose in their mission; if readers assume that the agents of victory will be the Israelite spies, then they will be. The fact that they actually took up residence in the house of a Canaanite prostitute will somehow be rationalized. If this aspect of the narrative is explained away, then the story of Rahab will ultimately serve to demonstrate how righteous Israelite men saved a desperate Canaanite prostitute. Though this is a common line of interpretation, I do not think it is the best reading based on understanding Joshua in light of the Torah's narrative as well as the subsequent interpretation of Rahab in the Scriptures.

Recognizing the potential inclination toward idealizing the Israelite spies in Joshua 2 opens readers up to other, less flattering interpretations of their decision to visit Rahab. At bare minimum, conscientious readers are compelled to refrain from propagating fanciful theories concerning the reasons that the spies went to visit the Canaanite prostitute. No safe assumption can be made about the spies merely lodging in Rahab's home or about the spies settling into her residence because the loose personality of the prostitute would have been conducive to acquiring information about the city. Perhaps Rahab's house served as a hostel of sorts; perhaps she gossiped about the affairs of Jericho. However, these types of explanations are formed by one generation and transmitted from one generation to another like family holiday traditions; they seem reasonable enough to repeat but may or may not be based in anything of substance. These traditions concerning the Rahab narrative cannot supersede what the biblical narrator suggests about the men of Israel by mentioning Shittim in the same narrative that features a non-Israelite prostitute. To this we will now briefly turn.

The narrator does not expressly communicate why the Israelite spies arrive at Rahab's house, but he is not silent on the matter either. Biblical narrators tend to paint pictures with words for readers to assess instead of transcending the story to make explicit judgment calls. By mentioning Shittim in Joshua 2, the narrator brings to mind an occasion in which the people of Israel were previously on the cusp of the conquest of Canaan. Years prior to the events of Joshua 2, Israel was in the same location when disaster struck: "While Israel was staying in Shittim, the men began to indulge in sexual immorality with Moabite women, who invited them to the sacrifices to their gods. The people ate the sacrificial meal and bowed down before these gods. So Israel yoked themselves to the Baal of Peor. And the LORD's anger burned against them" (Num. 25:1–3).

Evidently, the anger of the Lord was manifested through a plague that broke out among the people of Israel. While the community's leaders wept before the Lord because of Israel's treachery, and a plague raged throughout the camp, an Israelite leader named Zimri, from the tribe of Simeon, defiantly brought the daughter of the chief of Midian, Cozbi, into his private quarters. Phineas, the grandson of the high priest Aaron, killed both Zimri and Cozbi, finally putting an end to the plague that caused the deaths of twenty-four thousand people (Num. 25:4–18). Instead of entering the promised land from Shittim in Numbers 25—despite being so geographically close—the people of Israel entered into spiritual and physical prostitution.

Meanwhile, in Joshua 2:1 the narrator depicts Israel in strikingly similar circumstances. The simple mention of the fact that Israel is at Shittim once again brings to mind the disaster brought about by worshiping the foreign gods of the land, the sexual immorality with non-Israelite women, and the deaths of twenty-four thousand Israelites.

With this memory in mind, readers encounter the two spies leaving Shittim and immediately arriving at the residence of a Canaanite prostitute. God specifically warned the people of Israel that intermingling too closely with the people of Canaan could lead to the worship of their gods (Exod. 34:11–16; Deut. 7:1–5).[2] Considering the previous incident at Shittim and the warnings related to drawing close to the Canaanites, it is almost incomprehen-

---

2. The condemnation of the Israelites' relationship with the local peoples throughout the Torah is inextricably linked with the worship of foreign gods. The major issue, for example, in Num. 25 is that sexual immorality is combined with idolatry, and not that Israel interacts with the Moabites.

sible that the Israelite spies would choose to visit the house of a Canaanite prostitute.

The conquest narrative begins with great uncertainty. The location, Shittim, coupled with the prospect of sexual immorality with a non-Israelite woman who may worship foreign gods, engenders great drama as Israel is on the verge of its inheritance. Since the intentions of the Israelite men are dubious at best after the introduction to the story, readers divert their attention to Rahab. If the men of Israel are back at immorality again, then Rahab's reaction is what might make this situation different from the earlier predicament at Shittim. Even though Rahab represents everything the people of Israel should have feared, her responses to the king's messengers and the Israelites are what will make or break Israel and determine her legacy as either the hero or the villain of the narrative.

Rahab's Deception

Drama in the narrative heightens when the king of Jericho discovers that there are Israelite spies in his city and sends envoys directly to Rahab's house to search for them (Josh. 2:2–4). This is a legitimate threat being portrayed by the narrator. Joshua's plan of sending spies into the land has utterly failed. The classified mission has somehow been detected by the king of Jericho, who figures out exactly where the Israelite spies are located. Given the sensitive nature of spy activity, the capture of the spies could have resulted in their demise and, presumably, posed a legitimate threat to the security of the entire community of Israel.

Another reasonable concern relates to the internal stability of the community waiting back at Shittim. What if news of the apprehension of the Israelite spies gets back to the people? Given the unruly situation at Meribah years earlier when the spies instilled fear into the community, would there be another uprising in Israel against the idea of entering the land of their inheritance? This reaction could seriously jeopardize the inheritance of the land of Canaan in this moment and further delay the realization of God's promises.

The envoys' knock on the door of Rahab's home solidifies the focus of the narrative on Rahab's reaction. The men of Israel are in a position of great weakness and are in need of immediate and radical assistance. As the king's servants continue to pound on Rahab's door, the entire community of Israel becomes more and more entrenched in a precarious situation—whether they are cognizant of it or not—and needs someone to help them by saving their spies. The intelligence that the spies are supposed to bring back to Joshua is essential to executing the conquest of Canaan. At a practical level, Israel has no hope of inheriting the land without these spies, meaning that all the people of Israel are, ironically, in dire need of the Canaanite prostitute to help them. If the spies are going to facilitate the conquest, Rahab has to protect the spies. If Rahab protects the spies, she turns into the true Canaanite conqueror by facilitating the salvation of the people of Israel.

Rahab anticipates a breach in security and decides to win the favor of the Israelites by protecting the spies. Somehow knowing that the king's representatives will come to her home, Rahab hides the Israelite spies on her roof (Josh. 2:4, 6). The narrator shows readers Rahab's genuine character by depicting her acting on behalf of the Israelite spies prior to her speaking in the narrative. The reader might not know exactly what to think about Rahab's subsequent speech if it were not for the narrator depicting her willingness to endanger herself for the sake of the Israelites first. The brief comment depicting Rahab's actions prior to her words communicates that she is a person of upright character, irrespective of her profession up to that point.

The portrayal of Rahab virtuously hiding the spies before speaking is particularly important because of the subsequent section of the narrative in which she converses with the king's emissaries and blatantly misleads them. Rahab's deception consists of three parts.

1. Rahab admits that the Israelite men were at her house but insists she does not know their origin. Though Rahab may not have known the Israelite spies' exact place of origin, it becomes clear that she most certainly knows they are from the people of Israel.
2. Rahab claims that the men left the city prior to the gates being shut at sundown. This is nonsense, since the men are on her roof.
3. Rahab encourages the king's emissaries to quickly pursue the Israelite spies before they have more time to flee. This is a blatant lie with the intent of deluding the king's servants into chasing abroad after men who are, in fact, within the city limits.

The king's men are convinced by Rahab's deception, leave her residence, and run into the desert to chase the figments of their imaginations. As the king's men pursue the fictional escapees, a challenge emerges for observant readers. A cursory reading of the Torah reveals that God condemns falsehood (Exod. 20:16; see also 23:1; Lev. 19:11; Deut. 5:20; 19:16–18). Truth-telling is a prerequisite to edifying one's neighbor and to avoiding a perversion of justice. Deliberately propagating false information is damaging to living in community and does not reflect the holiness of the God of Israel. Viewed in this manner, the words

Rahab uses to get the king's servants to leave have an ethical issue embedded in them: Was it acceptable for Rahab to intentionally deceive the king's servants? What if Rahab's statements reflect a case in which deception might be acceptable? Rahab's deception is not carried out with the intent of perverting justice or exploiting the weak in society. Rahab does not violate the Torah in these senses. Rather, her situation should be viewed in light of the fact that she is already at war; she has chosen sides, and she implements a preemptive maneuver. Rahab's deception is a war tactic that is employed both in self-defense and in order to protect the powerless Israelite spies.

Misleading a foe is commonplace and rarely considered immoral during a war. In fact, Rahab's technique of deceiving in order to misdirect the enemy is, more or less, the same battle technique later commanded by God in order to conquer the city of Ai. God directs Joshua, saying, "Set an ambush behind the city" (Josh. 8:2). Following God's instructions, Joshua directs a group of soldiers to hide themselves close to the city and to wait for his signal before engaging in battle. Joshua then approaches the city, feigning as if the Israelite troops are going to battle with the inhabitants of Ai. As soon as the fighters from Ai are tricked, the Israelite troops are instructed to turn and run away from the city, intentionally misdirecting the fighters of Ai. As the people from Ai run after the Israelites, Joshua is commanded by God to complete the trickery; he stretches out his javelin and the Israelite fighters who are lying in ambush run into the vulnerable city, capturing it. Israel then kills all twelve thousand inhabitants of Ai, burns the city, and hangs its king on a tree (8:3–29).

This narrative in Joshua 8 demonstrates that using deception in order to misdirect is an invaluable preemptive war tactic that is even commanded by God. In Joshua 2, Rahab is in a cold war of sorts, but she recognizes that it is a *real* war already. She knows that the people of Israel are on their way and that their God has given them the land (see Josh. 2:9–14; see below). For all intents and purposes, she is preserving her life and saving the lives of two others who have come into her house. Rahab does not have spears or javelins to fight against the king's men. Thus she takes up the only armor she has that will profit her in this situation—her shrewdness. She has to be savvy in the battle with the men who come to her door, or she and her two Israelite visitors will most assuredly become casualties in this war.

Rahab's Revelation

At this point, readers have observed *what* Rahab has done: she hid the Israelite spies and deceived the king's messengers. However, readers are still in the dark with regard to the *motive* behind Rahab's actions. Rahab reveals this information in a short monologue in which she states to the Israelite spies,

> I know that the LORD has given you this land and that a great fear of you has fallen on us, so that all who live in this country are melting in fear because of you. We have heard how the LORD dried up the water of the Red Sea for you when you came out of Egypt, and what you did to Sihon and Og, the two kings of the Amorites east of the Jordan, whom you completely destroyed. When we heard of it, our hearts melted in fear and everyone's courage failed because of you, for the LORD your God is God in heaven above and on the earth below. (Josh 2:9–11)

Rahab makes her motivations known in this concise monologue by way of repetition. On three occasions, Rahab mentions the name of the covenant God of Israel (YHWH), with three different acknowledgments: (1) the Lord gave Israel the land of Canaan, causing the people of Jericho to fear; (2) the Lord performed wonders on behalf of Israel, causing the hearts of the inhabitants of Jericho to melt; (3) the Lord is the God of all. Rahab repeats the Tetragrammaton (YHWH) three times and, ultimately, declares that she believes the God of Israel will carry out his promises.

Rahab expresses that she has become aware of events that transpired upward of forty years prior to that moment (i.e., the exodus). She has even heard about military victories that came to pass during the community's wanderings in the desert (i.e., against the Amorites). By following the Israelite newsfeed, Rahab has become convinced that there is something special about their God, and therefore, she is obligated to help them. Thus when the time comes for Rahab to live out her belief in the God of Israel, she acts before she speaks, demonstrating her commitment to the God of Israel prior to making a confession in him. Readers are able to tell that Rahab is indeed genuine because the narrator depicts her actions prior to conveying her words.

Rahab's Salvation

Given that Rahab is repeatedly called a prostitute (Josh. 2:1; 6:17, 22, 25; see also Heb. 11:31; James 2:25), it is ironic that her main proposition to the Israelite men relates to an agreement concerning her future salvation in light of how she acted toward them (Josh 2:12–14). Unlike the vague motives of the men of Israel, Rahab is patently not interested in facilitating another physically and spiritually precarious situation. This Canaanite prostitute remarkably advocates for the promises of the God of Israel and facilitates the

conquest of her very own city by compelling the spies to swear by the name
of the Lord, the God of Israel, that they will save her and her family upon
entering Canaan.

The culmination of the fall of Jericho is recorded in Joshua 6. Prior to
instructing the people of Israel to overtake the city, Joshua declares that only
Rahab and those in her house will live (6:17–20). Upon the collapse of the wall
of Jericho, Joshua specifically instructs the same Israelite spies who potentially
compromised the conquest to "go into the prostitute's house and bring her
out and all who belong to her, in accordance with your oath to her" (6:22).
In this manner, the spies personally fulfill the pact Rahab had made with
them in the name of the Lord (2:12–14). After Rahab and her family are set
outside of the camp of Israel, likely for a period of cleansing (see Lev. 13:46;
Num. 12:10, 14–16), she and her family remain among the community until
at least the writing of the book of Joshua.

Yet the story does not quite end here. The narrator makes one more comment that is particularly important in depicting Rahab's integrity. Before
moving on from her narrative to tell of the rest of Israel's military conquest
of Canaan, the narrator is sure to reiterate exactly what Rahab *did* in order
to save the people of Israel. She hid the spies; she demonstrated her faith with
more than just words (Josh. 6:25). This is one of the main reasons Rahab is
remembered in redemptive history.

Rahab in Redemptive History

In the New Testament, Rahab's hiding of the Israelite spies is interpreted as
the quintessential example of genuine faith in the God of Israel. James mentions Rahab alongside the patriarch Abraham to demonstrate that justifica-
tion before God is always accompanied by good deeds. Rahab manifested her
belief in the God of Israel not just by words but also by receiving the spies,
concocting a strategy to save them, and implementing the plan (James 2:25).
The writer of the Letter to the Hebrews spells out that Rahab did not want
to die with her own people, who were disobedient; rather, she welcomed the
spies, demonstrating her faith in the God of Israel (Heb. 11:31). The writer of
Hebrews includes Rahab in a list featuring some of the most admired ancestors and prophets of the Jewish people. Rahab makes the grade because her
faith and shrewdness facilitated the conquest of Canaan.

Being paired with the other greats in the tradition of Israel does not compare to the honor of being mentioned in the genealogy of Jesus the Messiah.
Rahab was a forebear of Jesus by way of being welcomed into the tribe of

Judah. Christians actually believe that Jesus, the God-man, bore in his humanity the blood of a Canaanite prostitute. Rahab was a prime example of being considered righteous as a result of trusting in the God of Israel—irrespective of her people group, where she was from, or what she used to do (Matt. 1:5). Matthew's mention of Rahab shows the reader that Jesus was serious when he called sinners and non-Israelites into his community (Matt. 15:21–18; Luke 5:32; John 1:11–13). Jesus's human ancestry consisted of a descendant who bore these characteristics. Before we read any of the words of Jesus in the Gospel of Matthew, there is a hint of this good news for all by the simple acknowledgment of Rahab.

Reflecting on Rahab

At the end of *To Kill a Mockingbird*, Scout walks Boo home. As Scout stands on the Radley porch, she remembers that her father once said to her, "You never really know a man until you stand in his shoes and walk around in them."[3] For Scout, standing on Boo's porch that evening was good enough for her to see the world from his perspective. Scout realizes that he had watched the children's neighborhood activity for years from that angle. He knew what was going on in their lives; he had come to care for them and had determined to help them if an opportunity arose.

After visiting Rahab, the spies have come to see their situation from Rahab's perspective. She has tracked the exploits of the God of Israel, believed in that God, and facilitated the execution of his promises when presented with the opportunity. Seeing things from Rahab's perspective deeply influences the Israelite spies' point of view on their own situation. When the spies return to Joshua at Shittim, their report to Joshua is an abbreviated yet strikingly similar version of Rahab's speech: "The LORD has surely given the whole land into our hands; all the people are melting in fear because of us" (Josh. 2:24; 2:9–11). Readers do not know exactly what the spies are thinking upon leaving Shittim to go to Canaan, but their words communicate what they are thinking upon their return to Shittim: they have come to see the conquest from Rahab's perspective.

Prior to supernatural events that facilitate the conquest of Canaan, God uses (perhaps) an even more unexpected means to carry out his promises: the unforeseen savvy of a Canaanite prostitute. This woman of exemplary faith is an agent in bringing God's promises to fruition twice—once through the conquest of Canaan and again through the advent of the Messiah.

3. Lee, *To Kill a Mockingbird*, 321.

TEN

Why Is the Book of Judges So Weird?

All animals are equal but some animals are more equal than others.
—George Orwell, *Animal Farm*

Things are not always what they appear to be, especially in literature. Writers frequently employ literary techniques that seem to project a certain meaning; in time, readers might grow to understand that something else is being communicated in the text along with the readily apparent significance. This is especially the case in narratives, since narrators tend to relay stories in a way that holds readers' interest at a superficial level while simultaneously piquing readers' deep-seated curiosities relating to the interpretation of the story. Many narratives portray legitimate stories that can be understood on their own while simultaneously relating a framework that corresponds to another reality.

Let's take, for example, *Animal Farm*, another of George Orwell's classic works. One might pick up this relatively short novel, which is normally presented with an illustrated animal on the cover, and consider it an age-appropriate read for fifth- or sixth-grade students. This suspicion might be confirmed by the straightforward and unsophisticated manner in which the story is told. Read evenhandedly, *Animal Farm* could be understood as a fictitious account of a group of animals on a farm trying to manage their community without any human beings. The moral of the story read in this manner is quite easy to discern: in real life, a diverse group of animals cannot get along well on a farm without the intervention of human beings.

However, as attentive readers spend time in *Animal Farm*, clues emerge that provoke reflection on a deeper reality that might be illustrated through the story. For example, the practice of animal equality on the farm is repeatedly changed throughout the book in order to benefit an increasingly separatist and coercive group of pigs. The members of this group of highbrow pigs become no longer compatible with one another, and Napoleon emerges as the sole leader of the rebellion of the farm animals against humans by way of violently expelling his adversary, Snowball. Napoleon's behavior is evermore sly and secretive, and the intentions at the root of his decisions are perpetually enigmatic. Eventually, it becomes obvious that the common animals work at the whim of Napoleon, who becomes increasingly like the human beings that the revolution was intended to oust. This pattern of behavior reflects countless political scenarios that have played out in a similar manner throughout world history.

From the outset of the book, *Animal Farm* hints that it is not just a children's story about animals on a farm but, rather, an allegory that corresponds to certain societies at large. Despite the fact that the meaning of the book is never explained, a number of literary prods provoke historically and socially aware readers to interpret the events and interactions in the book as a parallel account of the real world.

Like *Animal Farm*, the biblical Samson narrative—understood within the context of the book of Judges—is not simply what it *appears* to be. Samson's story ultimately epitomizes the downward spiral of Israel by depicting his personal behavior in a way that corresponds with the stages of the cyclical and wayward spiritual trajectory of his community. Samson's story functions as a microcosm of the people of Israel—though, as with *Animal Farm*, this story's correspondence to its broader reality is never plainly elucidated for the reader. Nevertheless, the way Israel's downward spiral is depicted from the beginning of Judges prods readers to wonder what the author is trying to communicate by highlighting this pattern of misbehavior in Samson's narrative.

Unlike with *Animal Farm*, a straightforward reading of Judges is not at all developmentally appropriate for the youngest of children. This book features rape, murder, dismemberment, and other bizarre behavior. In this chapter, we will observe the downward spiral of the people of Israel and pay special attention to the unique features of the major judges' narratives. Ultimately, we will discuss the literary function of highlighting so many unpleasant events in the book. The spiral of disobedience, Samson's story, and the other minor judges and events are arranged in Judges in order to demonstrate that the people of Israel are in a quickly worsening predicament without a righteous kingly leader in their midst.

The Beginning of the Spiral

Despite the genuine promises that the people of Israel made to follow the Lord their God—from their experience at Sinai (Exod. 19:8; 20:18–21) through the end of the book of Joshua (24:16–28)—for all intents and purposes, Israel forgot their God and turned away from him upon entering the promised land. Meir Sternberg candidly points out an issue, intrinsic to frail humanity, with which the people of Israel struggled throughout their early history in Canaan: "No matter how hard-earned, how deep-felt, how sincere its expression at the time, learning tends to evaporate with frightening speed and regularity."[1] In the book of Judges, Israel is portrayed as having forgotten what they learned about the Lord their God through the major events recorded in the Torah.

Inattention to the Lord's ways in Canaan is portended before the time of the judges (Josh. 24:20, 23) and ultimately comes to pass upon the death of Israel's leader Joshua. As Joshua nears the end of his life, he admonishes the congregation of Israel to only serve the Lord their God and to keep away from the false gods of the land (24:15, 23). The people, in turn, insist that they will only worship the Lord, who freed them from Egypt and set them in the land in which they were dwelling (vv. 16–28). Upon Joshua's death, the narrator's final comment about Joshua's life affirms that "Israel served the LORD throughout the lifetime of Joshua and of the elders who outlived him and who had experienced everything the LORD had done for Israel" (24:31).

This is a stark contrast to the book of Judges, which begins by asserting that the people of Israel did not drive out the inhabitants of Canaan from the portions allotted to them by Joshua (Judg. 1:20–36). This failure is explicitly condemned by the angel of the Lord (2:1–3) and foreshadows disaster since it reflects outright disobedience to a command that was repeatedly communicated in the Torah (Exod. 23:31–33; 34:11–16; Num. 33:50–56; Deut. 7:1–5, 16–26; 20:1–20). The main reason God commanded the Israelites to drive out the inhabitants of the land was directly related to the inhabitants' religious disposition: God did not want the Israelites to fall prey to worshiping the gods of Canaan. Nevertheless, God cautioned the people against despairing since the conquest would come to pass slowly (Exod. 23:29–30; Deut. 7:22–23). Obedience in pressing on in the conquest of Canaan was inextricably linked with the elimination of the Canaanite gods from the land and purity of Israel's

---

1. Sternberg, *Poetics of Biblical Narrative*, 177.

worship of God. However, Israel did not endure in their struggle for the land, and as expected, the gods of Canaan became their perpetual snare (Judg. 2:3).

The book of Judges documents the people of Israel's indefensible attraction to the local deities, as well as a self-inflicted identity crisis they undergo regarding their position as the Lord's people. This combination ultimately led to the Israelites forgetting their God. Judges 2:10 is a telling comment on how Israel turned from the Lord, despite all the feasts and symbols that God embedded in the Torah for them: "After that whole generation had been gathered to their ancestors, another generation grew up who knew neither the LORD nor what he had done for Israel." This damning accusation is indicative of Israel's trajectory toward idolatry at the time of Joshua's death.

Israel's apostasy and alienation from God depicted in Judges 2:10 precipitates a continuation of the vicious spiral depicted time and again in the book of Judges. The onset of the downward spiral is outlined in general terms at the beginning of the book (2:11–23) and is alluded to each time Israel renounces their God (e.g., 3:7, 12; 4:1; 6:1; 10:6; 13:1). Just as a spiral continuously winds in a circular manner, so the people of Israel follow a cyclical pattern of descent into idolatry and evildoing, generally by way of repeating the following six steps.

1. Forgetting: The people of Israel turn away from the Lord by not actively remembering who God has been for their community. This first step is implied in each cycle, though it is not always explicitly stated.

2. Alienation: By forgetting their God, the people of Israel alienate themselves from him. This estrangement is frequently brought about when Israel turns to the gods of the people groups around them.

3. Consequence(s): As per multiple warnings, the people of Israel suffer great distress upon alienating themselves from their covenant God. The hardship Israel experiences during the period of the judges is normally a result of another people group ruling over them and subjecting them to harsh conditions.

4. Supplication: Israel grieves because of the consequences of their disobedience and cries out to God for salvation.

5. Deliverance: God hears Israel's cry and sends a judge to deliver the people from the consequences of their estrangement from him.

6. Rest: On several occasions, Israel's judge facilitates a period of relief from active oppression by their enemies. During this period of rest, Israel begins forgetting the Lord once again and recommences the downward spiral.

Let us now briefly track this spiral in the stories of the four major judges who precede Samson's narrative. In the process we will highlight a number of the unique characteristics and uncanny situations that contribute to the interpretation of the book as a whole. Then we will reflect on the purpose of the serial repetition of the spiral in the book of Judges.

Ehud

Ehud of the tribe of Benjamin is called on to save the people of Israel after they forget their God, alienate themselves from him, and disobey, doing evil in the eyes of the Lord (Judg. 3:12–15). The nature of Israel's misconduct is not explicitly stated, but the consequence is that God subjects them to Eglon, the Moabite king, for eighteen years. The oppression of the Moabites proves to be too much for Israel, who pleads with God for help. God raises up Ehud to deliver Israel from Eglon by killing him with a sword and, consequently, provides Israel with a period of rest from conflict for eighty years (3:16–23, 30).

What is intriguing about Ehud's narrative is the unnecessarily graphic nature by which the murder of Eglon is recounted. The narrator indicates that Ehud is left-handed, which likely alludes to his deceptive tactics (Judg. 3:15). Readers are also told several times that Eglon is extremely overweight (3:17, 21–22). This last fact is key to illustrating the grotesque image of a roguish judge stealthily puncturing Eglon's belly with an eighteen-inch knife, cramming it deeper and deeper until the handle of the sword was covered with the adipose tissue of the gut of the obese man.

The narrator explicitly mentions one more disgusting detail of the murder scene, stating that Eglon's "bowels discharged" (Judg. 3:22). This fact seems to be a bit of burlesque satire since Eglon's servants think that he is behind closed doors relieving himself. In fact, his bowels *had* discharged, but it was Ehud who had relieved Eglon of his bowels by stabbing him before slyly escaping the residence. The repulsive nature of this story seems needless, and the details could have been avoided. Yet revealing specific vulgarities of stories seems to be one of the features of the book of Judges (4:21; 5:26–27; 9:53–54; 19:27–30) and illustrates the debased situation in which the people of Israel find themselves.

Deborah

Despite being granted a period of respite from conflict, Israel once again forgets the Lord and becomes alienated from God after Ehud's death. This time, the consequence for Israel's disobedience is subjugation to the very people they are commanded to expel from the land: the Canaanites. Jabin, the king of Canaan, and Sisera, the commander of his army, oppress Israel for twenty years. The people of Israel implore the Lord for deliverance, and God responds through the ministry of Deborah, a married prophetess, who judges Israel from under a palm tree in the hill country of Ephraim (Judg. 4:1–5).

Deborah summons Barak, a military leader, and commands him to follow the Lord's injunction to gather troops from Naphtali and Zebulun and fight against Sisera. Barak agrees to obey but only if Deborah will promise to go with him into the battle. Deborah concedes, yet she prophesies that the glory will go to a woman for defeating Sisera, not to Barak (Judg. 4:6–9). This comment misdirects readers a bit because, up to this point, Deborah is the only woman featured in the narrative. Yet the surprise heroine is revealed when the Lord routs Sisera's army, and he runs into the tent of Jael, the wife of Heber the Kenite (4:17). Thinking he has found refuge with an accomplice (see 4:11), Sisera asks for a drink and falls fast asleep. Jael then stealthily approaches him and savagely drives a tent peg through his temple and into the ground. Jael is God's agent to bring rest to Israel for forty years (4:18–22).

The most unique aspect of the section of Judges featuring Deborah and Jael is that the leaders and heroes are women. Some might view the story (and poem) reflecting Deborah's leadership and Jael's bravery as an illustration of the inevitable "downgrade" that comes to pass in disadvantaged societies, destitute of authentic male leadership. This view misses one of the points of the narrative—namely, an emphatic affirmation of the abilities of Deborah and Jael to lead well and act courageously despite unfortunate circumstances around them.

Gideon

In due time, the people of Israel forget their God again and fall into idolatry (Judg. 6:25–35). As a consequence of forsaking the Lord, God permits the Midianites to oppress the people of Israel for seven years. The maltreatment of the Israelites forces them into hiding; their crops are stolen; and their land is destroyed by the Midianites (6:2–5). When the people of Israel are finally humbled, they turn to the Lord to ask for deliverance (6:6).

The angel of the Lord appears to Gideon, who is introduced as he is beating wheat in a winepress for fear that the Midianites will plunder his supplies (Judg. 6:11). Despite a rebuke from the Lord to the people just a couple verses earlier (6:7–10), Gideon seems to be an Israelite who is aware of the works that God has done on behalf of the covenant community. Gideon concludes that God has forsaken the people by contrasting what he has heard about the Lord's former works with Israel's current oppressive situation under the Midianites (7:13). The Lord then speaks directly to Gideon, calling him to save the people from Midianite oppression (7:14, 16).

Several episodes in Gideon's narrative anticipate forthcoming issues in his life. First, Gideon is doubtful: Gideon repeatedly asks God for signs demonstrating that God will *actually* carry out what he *already* said he would do (Judg. 6:17; see the fleece incident in 6:36–40; see also Gideon's son's fear in 8:20). Additionally, Gideon fears his enemy though the Lord has told him that he will be victorious (6:27; 7:10–11). Furthermore, it is striking that Gideon ends up killing his own people—the men of Succoth and Penuel—after he saves Israel from the Midianites (8:1–17).

Eventually, the people of Israel implore Gideon to reign over them. Gideon declines but requests gold from the people, out of which he makes an ephod— a garment that was worn on the upper body by ancient Israelite priests—and sets it on display in Ophrah (Judg. 8:22–27). The narrator then relates how aberrant and abhorrent the scenario actually is: "All Israel prostituted themselves by worshiping it there, and it became a snare to Gideon and his family" (8:27b). It is almost as if the narrator chimes in toward the end of the story to say, "Israel, aren't you glad *this guy* didn't become king?" Nevertheless, because of Gideon's deliverance, the land rested from conflict for forty years.

Jephthah

Gideon's ephod is the predecessor of further apostasy in Israel, since the people shortly turn to full-fledged Baal worship. Toward the end of Gideon's story, the narrator directly states that the people of Israel are already reinitiating the downward spiral: "[The people of Israel] did not remember the LORD their God, who had rescued them from the hands of all their enemies on every side" (Judg. 8:34). Forgetting the Lord leads the people to alienate themselves from him and to worship the gods of Syria, Sidon, Moab, Ammon, and Philistia (10:6). God's consequence for them is to allow the Philistines and the Ammonites to oppress them until they cry out to God and admit the sin of worshiping the Baals (10:7–10). God initially responds by commanding the people to beseech the other gods that they worshiped. However, in keeping with God's compassionate character, he appoints Jephthah to deliver the people of Israel from the hands of their oppressor (10:11–16; 11:1–10).

Jephthah is introduced as bearing three important personal attributes: (1) he is a Gileadite, (2) he is a mighty warrior, and (3) he is the son of a prostitute (Judg. 11:1). Being a prostitute's son causes domestic troubles between Jephthah and his other brothers, who share the same father, Gilead, but who were born to Gilead's wife. They force Jephthah out of their community, refusing to share their inheritance with him. Jephthah's exile in the land of Tob lasts only until the Gileadites need his military prowess to vanquish the Ammonites. Jephthah negotiates with the leaders of Gilead to be their ruler upon delivering Israel from oppression, which is a deal the Gileadites are quick to accept (11:2–11).

Now the story gets really weird.

Jephthah unsurprisingly asks for help from the Lord to defeat the Ammonites. Surprisingly, however, Jephthah vows to offer as a burnt offering the first thing that comes out of the doors of his house upon returning home (Judg. 11:30–31). Jephthah promptly subdues the people of Ammon, and the reader infers that divine assistance was granted to Jephthah and that he must keep his vow (11:32–33). Upon returning home to Mizpah, his only child, an unnamed daughter, merrily comes out to greet him. Jephthah relates his sadness to her, revealing that he has made a vow (lit., "opened his mouth") to the Lord and that it is impossible to rescind on his pledge. Jephthah's daughter is not informed of her father's specific vow, yet oddly she encourages him to keep it, even though she realizes that it concerns her fate. Jephthah's daughter only asks her father's permission to go to the mountains with her companions and weep for her virginity. Jephthah concedes. When she returns to Mizpah, Jephthah realizes his vow and, evidently, sacrifices her as a burnt offering (11:34–39).

There is no period of rest depicted in Israel after this horrific event. On the contrary, Israel engages in even more domestic violence (see Judg. 12:1–6). After Jephthah defeats the Ammonites, the Ephraimites cross the Jordan and quarrel with Jephthah for not summoning them to fight against the Ammonites. This conflict leads to a civil war of sorts between the Ephraimites and the Gileadites in which forty-two thousand Ephraimites are killed. The fact that there is no period of rest after Jephthah's leadership but, rather, a civil conflict, indicates that the situation in Israel is deteriorating instead of improving. Ibzan, Elon, and Abdon judge Israel between Jephthah's leadership and that of the final judge of the book, Samson (12:8–15). None of these judges introduce a period of rest into the land like those that followed the leadership of Ehud, Deborah, and Gideon. This gives the impression that Israel is caught in a rapid downward spiral, facilitated by the bizarre decisions of flawed leaders.

Samson: A Microcosm of Israel

The repetition of the descending spiral functions as a literary impetus that demands interpretation. This is particularly evident since the majority of biblical narrative is not told by repeatedly using such a discernible pattern in close literary proximity as it occurs in Judges. What might the narrator of Judges be doing by retelling several of the stories in such a uniform manner?

The repeated pattern, combined with the peculiarities depicted in scenes featuring the judges, bears a cumulative force that portends the worsening of Israel's spiritual condition. After the pattern is reenacted over and over, the reader comes to terms with Israel's decline, which spirals quicker and descends deeper into self-destruction. This creates an expectation for a strong leader to finally stop the community's decline. Instead, readers are presented with Samson, the ultimate strong man, who, ironically, will serve as the preeminent example of how weakened a society becomes when ensnared in the unremitting downward spiral. Samson's narrative, like that of *Animal Farm*, is more than meets the eye. This narrative depicts Samson as personally mirroring the phases of Israel's downward spiral, which parallels Israel's experience during the period of the judges.

Samson Forgets God

Samson's story begins with the only birth narrative detailed in the book of Judges (see Judg. 13:1–4). Manoah and his unnamed wife are a Danite couple from Zorah. They are unable to have children until an angel of the Lord appears to Manoah's wife and announces that she will conceive. The angel of the Lord specifically reveals two important assignments related to the anticipated baby: (1) the child is to be set apart as a Nazirite from conception, and (2) he will begin delivering Israel from their subjection to Philistine control.

By calling the future baby to be a Nazirite, the angel of the Lord invokes the regulations of the Nazirite vow outlined in Numbers 6:2–8:

> If a man or woman wants to make a special vow, a vow of dedication to the Lord as a Nazirite, they must abstain from wine and other fermented drink. . . . During the entire period of their Nazirite vow, no razor may be used on their head. . . . They must let their hair grow long. Throughout the period of their dedication to the Lord, the Nazirite must not go near a dead body. Even if their own father or mother or brother or sister dies, they must not make themselves ceremonially unclean on account of them, because the symbol of their dedication to God is on their head. Throughout the period of their dedication, they are consecrated to the Lord.

Setting the child apart as a Nazirite is not optional for Manoah and his wife. In fact, the Nazirite vow is immediately operative for Samson's mother, who is commanded to refrain from the fruit of the vine and anything unclean from the moment the angel of the Lord appears to her (Judg. 13:3, 14). Samson's famously long hair, meeting one of the requirements of the Nazirite vow, suggests that Samson's parents had every intention of consecrating their child to serve the Lord and fulfill his mission of inaugurating the deliverance of Israel.

Nevertheless, Samson's parents' commitment to setting him apart is not automatically transferable to their son. Numbers 6 indicates that the Nazirite vow was voluntary, meaning that each person who took the vow had to independently embrace the restrictions outlined therein for a distinct period of separation. Thus Samson's parents ultimately cannot fulfill the Nazirite vow on his behalf. Either Samson has to personally accept being consecrated to deliver the Israelites, or he can forget his calling and neglect to carry out his duty.

Samson deliberately turns from his calling to be a Nazirite. This is evident through his violation of the three major tenets of the vow:

1. Nazirites were forbidden from touching dead corpses, yet Samson touches a dead corpse. Samson is not even forced to undergo a crisis of conscience over touching the corpse of a dead relative, as per the examples given in Numbers 6. Rather, Samson kills an animal in self-defense but is then attracted back to the carcass for a mere mouthful of honey. In this detail, readers can be sure that Samson does not embrace his Nazirite vow (Judg. 14:5–9).

2. Nazirites were forbidden from drinking wine, yet Samson attends a *mishteh* (feast [Judg. 14:10]). This Hebrew word comes from the same root for the word "to drink" (*shatah*) and can mean a gathering in which people consume wine (see Esther 5:6; 7:2, 7–8). The implication of placing Samson at a *mishteh* suggests that he was participating in what the root of the Hebrew word means (i.e., drinking).

3. Nazirites were forbidden from getting a haircut, yet Samson, famously, has his hair cut by the Philistines (Judg. 16:18–22). Toward the end of the narrative, Samson's long hair turns out to be the only remaining sign of the Nazirite vow his parents had made to consecrate him for the work of God. Upon having his head shaved, Samson loses the power to accomplish the mission he was called to perform, demonstrating that his superhuman empowerment for delivering Israel is directly *connected* to his calling of being a Nazirite.

Samson forgetting God is implicit to his story, just like Israel forgetting the Lord is implied in all the other narratives depicting their downward spiral in the book of Judges.

Samson Is Alienated

The narrator is silent concerning Samson's youth, except for mentioning that the Lord was with him as he grew up in the encampment of Dan between Zorah and Eshtaol (Judg. 13:25). The fact that Samson grew up in the area of Israel traditionally allotted to Dan is an important detail of the story, given that the first thing Samson does on his own is leave this area. Samson alienates himself by abandoning the region of Dan, where he was born and raised, to descend to the Philistine city of Timnah.

As expected, once Samson alienates himself from his community, he falls into idolatry. Though equally perilous, Samson's idolatry is more subdued than Israel's sometimes overt worship of icons. Any commitment that Samson had to worshiping the Lord alone evaporates when he sets eyes on Philistine women, who become the objects of his affection (Judg. 14:1; 16:1, 4). Samson leaving the area of Dan to sow his wild oats with Philistine women corresponds to the behavior of the people of Israel, who repeatedly consider what the gods of the land have to offer to be better than the promises of the Lord their God. In this sense, Samson's alienation from his tribe in Israel and his intimate unions with three Philistine women illustrate Israel's apostasy during the period of the judges. Edward L. Greenstein points out that "the Samson story never polemicizes overtly against the Philistine cult. It actually does so covertly, showing how Samson's (= Israel's) liaison with Philistine women (= foreign cults) leads to disastrous consequences."[2]

In Timnah, Samson is left to his own devices to distinguish between right and wrong. During Samson's initial foray into Timnah, he sees a Philistine woman whom he wants to marry and, consequently, insists that his father acquire her for him as a wife. Samson's fetish for Philistine women grows, much to the disdain of his father, who strives to persuade him to remain among and marry within the Israelite people, but to no avail. In a terse retort to his father's objection, Samson demands that his father be complicit in his alienation: "Get her for me, for she is right in my eyes" (Judg. 14:3 ESV).

Samson's phrase "right in my eyes" functions as another clue pointing readers to observe how his narrative corresponds to the story of Israel. Repeatedly throughout the book of Judges, the people of Israel forget the Lord, are alienated from him, and do evil in the "eyes of the Lord" (Judg. 3:7, 12; 4:1; 6:1; 10:6; 13:1). Now Samson forgets the Lord, is alienated from God, and wants what is right in his own eyes. This aspect of Samson's story calls attention to the outlandish trajectory of Israel in which all the people eventually do what

---

2. Greenstein, "Riddle of Samson," 250.

is right in their own eyes (17:6; 18:1; 19:1; 21:25; see further discussion under the heading "Why So Weird?" below).

Samson Suffers Consequences

Samson's willful disregard for God setting him apart and calling him to carry out a special mission ends up bringing about grave consequences and illustrates precisely what came to pass in Israel's story. Two of Samson's unions with Philistine women end in deception, heartbreak, and the death of many people. His first wife coaxes him into telling her the answer to a riddle that he posed to his contemptible companions. This comes to pass, of course, after Samson's Philistine "friends" threaten to scorch his wife alive and incinerate her father's house. In order to pay off his wager for losing the bet related to the riddle, Samson descends to Ashkelon, kills thirty Philistines, and provides the underhanded riddle-responders with the garments of their dead compatriots. Meanwhile, back in his father-in-law's house, Samson's wife is given to another man. Samson is infuriated by losing his wife and enacts retribution by scorching Philistine land. The Philistines, in turn, burn Samson's former wife, who initiated this predicament so that these same Philistines would not set her on fire (Judg. 14:11–15:8). The irony in this story is astonishing.

Philistine women are Samson's kryptonite. After the horrific death of Samson's first Philistine lover, he descends to the Philistine city of Gaza and has relations with a Philistine prostitute. After a failed attempt on his life while he is in Gaza, Samson relocates to the Valley of Sorek with the Philistines still in pursuit. There, Samson falls in love with Delilah, who is bribed by her fellow Philistines into beguiling Samson to reveal the source of his superhuman strength. Samson ultimately falls prey to Delilah's manipulative rhetoric and confesses that the secret of his potency lies in his long hair. The Philistines promptly attack him—draining his strength by shaving off his locks—and gouge out his eyes. Samson's hair is the last tangible sign of him being set apart for God's unique mission. No more hair means no more unique mission; no more unique mission means no more need for unique strength; no more unique strength is an indication that the Lord has left Samson (Judg. 16:20).

Just as Israel yoke themselves over and over again to the gods of the land and suffer horrendous consequences for their apostasy, so Samson repeatedly gives himself over to Philistine women who use him in their egotistic ploys to benefit the people who are oppressing Israel. Samson ends up maimed, blind, and brokenhearted. Nevertheless, toward the end of the story, the narrator provides readers with a bit of commonsensical information with the intent of foreshadowing the continuation of Samson's cycle: "But the hair on his head began to grow again after it had been shaved" (Judg. 16:22).

Samson's Supplication

Just as shaving Samson's hair represented a divergence from his unique mission, so the growth of his hair illustrates a change in his disposition toward the God who set him apart as the one to deliver Israel from Philistine oppression. Like the people of Israel throughout the book of Judges, Samson eventually finds himself in a situation in which he is ruled over by his enemies. With nowhere else to go, Samson turns to the Lord his God and prays for deliverance (Judg. 16:28).

The scene depicting Samson's supplication is utterly pathetic. Samson, the once-promising liberator, is blinded, humbled, imprisoned, and forced into slave labor by Israel's Philistine foes. To the Philistines, Samson is living proof that their god, Dagon, is mightier than the source of Samson's empowerment. Samson is now an object of ridicule for the Philistines and a ludicrously deplorable vestige of who he once was. He is a perfect object of sport for the Philistines to deride when they are drunk and need a good laugh. Likewise, when the people of Israel turn their back on their calling and alienate themselves from their God, they weaken their witness for the Lord to the communities around them and become a caricature of what they are supposed to be as a people group.

Samson's hair continues to grow, and with it his confidence to call on the Lord for the strength to accomplish his original, divinely assigned mission. Samson was empowered by God when his long hair was a tangible sign of a marginal commitment to God (Judg. 13:25; 14:4, 6, 19). Now that his hair is growing back—now that he is completely debased, now that he is entirely dependent on supernatural intervention to relieve him from the consequences of his alienation from God—Samson remembers his God, turns to him, and asks for help. Samson, with the assistance of a hand-holding guide, makes his way to stand between two of the main pillars in the temple of Dagon. He then raises his voice and pleads, "Sovereign LORD, remember me. Please, God, strengthen me just once more" (16:28).

Samson's Deliverance

In keeping with the cyclical pattern evident throughout the book of Judges, readers expect Samson to deliver Israel from the Philistines. Deliverance comes but only in part. In Samson's birth narrative, his parents were told that their baby would "*begin to save* Israel from the hand of the Philistines" (Judg. 13:5 ESV). The dawn of salvation is what is depicted after Samson's final words. Samson petitions God for strength one last time. He lays his right and left hands on different, adjacent pillars. He lifts his voice and expresses his desire to die with the Philistines. His request is granted.

Samson's death is an oddity, since several other biblical heroes petition God to take their lives and are not appeased (e.g., Elijah, Jeremiah, Jonah, Job).[3] However, Samson's death wish is different. In this scene, Samson gives his life and concurrently accomplishes the mission for which he was born. The narrator relates that Samson killed more Philistines in his death than he killed throughout all the conflicts he had with them while he was healthy and strong. Unlike the biblical characters who wish for death out of despondency, Samson wishes for death and, in so doing, fulfills his primary mission of inaugurating Israel's deliverance from the Philistines.

Throughout the stories of the major judges, Israel is delivered from the consequences of alienation from the Lord their God in order that they may remember him and stray from the idolatry of the peoples surrounding them. When Samson dies in the temple of Dagon, he demonstrates that Israel's God is stronger than the gods of the Philistines. Greenstein states that "the Samson story depicts the abandonment of the now abominable alien cult through the image of Samson collapsing the temple of the Philistine god."[4] The fact that Samson began the process of delivering Israel from the Philistines by toppling a rival god's temple would inherently serve as a reminder for all hearers of his story to leave the fragility of idolatry and to return to the strength of the Lord their God.

(Un)Rest in Israel

As the book of Judges progresses, the period of rest from political and military conflict that commonly followed the earlier judges is conspicuously absent at the end of the cycle. The fact that there is no period of rest suggests that Israel lived in a perpetual state of lawlessness leading up to, during, and subsequent to Samson's judgeship. This assessment is confirmed by observing the national free-for-all of chaotic behavior that comes to pass after Samson's death.

Another literary objective is accomplished by not mentioning a period of rest after Samson's narrative. As mentioned above, Samson is a judge depicted as doing what is right in his own eyes. Samson's alienation from the Lord's

3. Greenstein, "Riddle of Samson," 242.
4. Greenstein, "Riddle of Samson," 253.

promises and the covenant community leads to his lamentable judgment while doing what he considered right. The position of Samson's narrative in the book of Judges opens the literary door for all of Israel to do what is right in their own eyes. There are no more judges after Samson. Rather, there are multiple bizarre scenes featuring idolatry, sexual abuse, dismemberment of a human corpse, and a civil war that costs Israel the lives of tens of thousands of its own people (Judg. 17–21). Whatever minor restraint the people had managed to show during the periods of the other judges of Israel has now been removed.

Samson is gifted with everything it would take to singlehandedly deliver the people, yet he ends up ushering in a period of national disarray. What hope does Israel have if a leader like Samson cannot create lasting change? The answer: a king.

Why So Weird? From Disaster to David

In the final portion of the book of Judges, the lack of rest for Israel is directly linked to the fact that there was no king in the land. This is plainly demonstrated through the narrator stating no less than four times in the final five chapters that anarchy reigned when there was no king (Judg. 17:6; 18:1; 19:1; 21:25). This point is particularly accentuated when the narrator explicitly states the condition of Israel in the very last verse of the book: "In those days there was no king in Israel. Everyone did what was right in his own eyes" (21:25 ESV).

The immoral behavior depicted toward the end of Judges combined with the reiteration that there was no king suggests that Israel's spiritual and political fiasco might be subdued if there *were* a king in Israel. Given that the people of Israel were specifically commanded in the Torah to refrain from following the inclinations of their own "eyes" (Deut. 12:8 ESV), perhaps a righteous king would be able to transplant Israel from the path of religious confusion and anarchy back to the trajectory of the Torah (17:18–19). The book of Judges sets readers' expectations for the day in which that type of righteous king would come.

These observations bring us back to the simple question posed earlier in this chapter: Why is the book of Judges so weird? The answer lies in how the book was selectively crafted to depict an appalling situation in ancient Israel just prior to the advent of the kingship. In order to accomplish this, the narrator chose stories that portrayed several of the main characters in quite a negative light. By judiciously retelling some of the most bizarre events of that time period, the author communicates the dire situation of Israel when they are bereft of Torah-oriented leadership.

The selective retelling of the stories in Judges facilitates a contemporary understanding of the (lack of) roles for the "minor judges" in the book (e.g., Othniel, Shamgar, Tola, Jair). Mark Hamilton perceptively states that the minor judges "advance the narrative by allowing the story to skip time without delving deeply into new episodes, thus keeping the focus tightly on other stories, which the book uses to explore the major themes it wishes to address."[5] Whatever role the stories of the minor judges may have played in another narrative, they did not fit the narrator's purposes in the one told in the biblical book of Judges.

Acknowledging that the stories in Judges are told in a selective manner also simplifies reconciling how some of the major characters of Judges can be recognized as people of faith in the New Testament. Despite all the unflattering information given to readers in Judges, the writer of Hebrews perplexingly honors Gideon, Barak, Samson, and Jephthah (Heb. 11:32). When we grasp that Judges paints a picture of chaos leading up to the monarchy, we can come to terms with the fact that the author of Hebrews assesses the Old Testament characters in a broader manner than is presented in the specific stories told about them in Judges.

Judges tells unflattering stories for a purpose. These horrific events uniquely demonstrate how Israel's leadership failed when they alienated themselves from God and how desperately Israel needed a righteous ruler. Oddly enough, this makes Judges a simultaneously weird and holy book to read.

---

5. Hamilton, *Theological Introduction to the Old Testament*, 125.

ELEVEN

Hannah and Ruth

Mothers of the Monarchy

With a few deft strokes the biblical author, together with the imagination of his reader, constructs a picture that is more "real" than if he had drawn it in detail.

—Adele Berlin, *Poetics and Interpretation of Biblical Narrative*

The storyline of the *Lord of the Flies* progresses from bad to worse, from dark to darker. Stranded on a desert island, with no adults to rescue them from themselves, a group of preadolescent boys descends into a state of anarchy. Beginning with an inopportune conflict between the leaders, Ralph and Jack, the story proceeds to vividly portray scenes in which the bloodthirsty, ravenous children participate. Ultimately, lawlessness and savagery reign on the island. Ralph and his socially outcasted friend Piggy are the only boys left who strive for some sort of order. After Piggy is callously murdered, Ralph is forced to run for his life from the relentless pursuit of the sadistic child-savages, who seem intent on decapitating him and displaying his head on a stake as if he were a wild pig. During the chase, Ralph stumbles and falls onto the beach: "Then he was down, rolling over and over in the warm sand, crouching with arm to ward off, trying to cry for mercy."[1] Ralph is in the throes of death without any realistic hope of survival.

1. Golding, *Lord of the Flies*, 258.

Expecting the rampage to continue, Ralph rises to his feet, opens his eyes, and, to his surprise, recognizes a British naval officer standing in front of him on the beach. After the long period of horrific events during which the young boys descend into utter nihilism, the naval officer represents the hope of restored order in their lives. The trajectory toward returning the children to being children again is set in motion by the appearance of a person who represents stability.

Readers of Judges also endure a type of emotional turmoil, having withstood a troubling *Lord of the Flies* type of experience. The overall tenor of the book goes from bad to worse, from dark to darker. One troubling scene after another portrays the people of Israel hastening toward lawlessness and, ultimately, toward their demise. By the end of the book, anarchy reigns, and the people of Israel, like the unruly group of juvenile delinquents on the desert island, are a barely recognizable faction of what they were constituted to be. The Torah has been abandoned. There is no godly leader. Israel simply awaits further self-inflicted violence, chaos, and destruction.

What possible hope is there for Israel?

As readers engage the Scriptures successively, they, like Ralph, slowly rise to their feet, wipe the sand out of their eyes, and behold the hope for restored order. Yet there is a bit of a shock: hope for restoration does not come through the perhaps expected leadership of a strong military leader (e.g., Deborah), a strong man (e.g., Samson), or any other male judge (e.g., Ehud, Gideon, Jephthah). The judges failed to bring about the type of unity and order needed to create a sense of national stability—the type of stability that would correspond to Israel fulfilling their call of being a kingdom of priests and holy nation unto the Lord (Exod. 19:6). As Israel looks up for help with their precarious national predicament, they encounter hope for their future through the lives of two women: Hannah and Ruth—the mothers of the monarchy.

The Royal Trajectories of Hannah and Ruth

The settings of Hannah's and Ruth's narratives, and the content therein, indicate that the same social tenor reflected in Judges should be understood as the backdrop for these stories. The placements of 1 Samuel and Ruth in the Bible seem to put forth Hannah's and Ruth's stories as the trajectory toward the solution to the problem presented in Judges. In the traditional Jewish order of the biblical books, Hannah's narrative immediately follows the final, condemning verse of Judges (21:25). In the traditional Protestant arrangement, the book of Ruth is after Judges and followed by 1 Samuel. Thus Hannah's and Ruth's stories begin, more or less, at the same latitude and, in several ways, take corresponding journeys to the ultimate destination: the Davidic monarchy.

Hannah's and Ruth's stories correspond to each other in a manner akin to how California's famous Pacific Coast Highway and infamous I-5 freeway run somewhat parallel to each other for hundreds of miles, going north–south, and eventually converge at Dana Point, about eighty miles from the Mexican border. The I-5 is California's main north–south freeway and is generally the quickest thoroughfare between major cities. The Pacific Coast Highway, contrarily, facilitates north–south travel in a leisurely manner, following the anatomical vicissitudes of the meandering coast.

Ruth's narrative takes the reader from the period of the judges to David much like the I-5 freeway connects two California cities—quickly and in a straight line (Ruth 1:1; 4:17, 22). In just four chapters, readers observe how King David's paternal lineage develops, with only a couple of main characters and a few changes of scenery. Beginning with the Judahite family of Elimelech, into which Ruth the Moabite is eventually welcomed, Israel is quickly placed on the trajectory toward the Davidic monarchy, signaling an end to the type of chaos depicted in Judges.

Hannah's story can be likened to the Pacific Coast Highway; the route between Hannah and David is more roundabout than straightforward. The narrative spans a larger section of text (1 Sam. 1–16); there are multiple essential characters in addition to Hannah; and several changes of scenery develop before David appears. Nevertheless, the leadership stability that Israel lacked for the hundreds of years represented in Judges is, in a sense, initiated by Hannah's devotion to God. The dedication of Hannah's son, Samuel, to the service of the Lord for the entirety of his life triggers the final stretch of the judges under Samuel, who serves to bring order out of a period of chaos and, ultimately, to anoint King David.

Since Hannah's and Ruth's narratives progress toward the Davidic monarchy, it is not surprising that there are points of similarity relating to how these stories are told: both stories feature women protagonists and record events that came to pass during the time period of the judges. Additionally, though they do not necessarily cohere in the particulars, the narratives of Hannah and Ruth contain several points of general correspondence in the overall presentation of the stories:

- The opening scenes of Hannah's and Ruth's narratives immediately and concisely present extremely distressing predicaments for the women in no uncertain terms.

- The bewildering behavior of Israelite men who function as minor characters in the narratives facilitates the unsettling situations in which these women are depicted.
- Hannah and Ruth eventually become surprise mothers, even though the circumstances at the beginning of their narratives point to the unlikeliness of motherhood.
- The firstborn sons of Hannah and Ruth are crucial in the eventual formation of the Davidic monarchy. Ruth's descendants form the royal monarchic genealogy, and Hannah's son performs David's coronation.

Throughout the rest of this chapter, we will conduct a targeted survey of Ruth's and Hannah's narratives, focusing on these points of general correspondence, in order to observe how the stories reflect Israel's transition out of the period of the judges and into the period of the monarchy. We will consider how Hannah and Ruth are unexpected agents of change who remarkably facilitate this transition and how the despondency of these women turns into the gateway of future hope for Israel. Not only do Ruth and Hannah facilitate a solution to the chaos that came from not having a king, but their stories also provide ancient and contemporary readers hope that the unlikeliest people can be used as key players in the divine plan.

Hannah's Predicament

Hannah's story does not *actually* begin with Hannah; rather, it commences by presenting her husband, Elkanah of the tribe of Ephraim, and immediately foreshadows a problematic domestic issue by communicating that he has two wives, Hannah and Peninnah (1 Sam. 1:1–2). The fact that Elkanah has multiple wives should be disconcerting to readers of the Bible in light of the precedent for marriage embedded in the ancient Israelite creation narrative, which reflects the enduring union of one man and one woman (Gen. 2:24; see further explanation below). There is no divinely authorized stipulation for additional partners within the context of ancient Israel. Both ancient and modern readers immediately recognize Elkanah's introduction as portraying a flawed domestic situation that will likely go awry. This expectation is heightened when we read that Peninnah has children, but Hannah is childless (1 Sam. 1:2).

The narrator characterizes the severity of Hannah's domestic situation by leaving gaps in the narrative. Instead of receiving details about Hannah's complicated home life from the omniscient narrator, the reader is left to imagine the complexities of her unorthodox marriage through the snippets of information provided over a couple of verses (1 Sam. 1:2–8). From this relatively short section, readers apprehend the turmoil that perpetually afflicts Hannah because of her childlessness and develop compassion for Hannah upon conceptualizing how difficult her family situation might be as she shares her husband with another woman—one who can conceive.

The fact that Hannah cannot conceive, however, has nothing to do with Peninnah, Elkanah, or Hannah. It is the Lord who has closed her womb (1 Sam. 1:5). Communicating that the Lord closed Hannah's womb reflects the omniscient narrator's insight into a divine plan behind the infertility, which plays out as the narrative continues. This detail also permits readers to realize how other human beings in the story could misunderstand Hannah's situation. For all intents and purposes, it looks like there is a "problem" with Hannah.

The purposely limited information provided by the narrator permits readers to interpret this truncated version of Hannah's family life in light of other, similar biblical passages. Adele Berlin appropriately captures this idea: "With a few deft strokes the biblical author, together with the imagination of his reader, constructs a picture that is more 'real' than if he had drawn it in detail."[2] Readers are drawn into Hannah's world in the introduction of her story by imagining her perpetual pain, trauma, and domestic drama through the narrator's judicious usage of detail.

Elkanah's and Eli's Bewildering Behavior

Why Does Elkanah Have Two Wives?

Reading 1 Samuel 1:2 and 1:3 in juxtaposition creates a problem for attentive, successive readers of the Bible. Readers are informed in 1 Samuel 1:2 that Elkanah has two wives. The fact that Elkanah is a polygamist could be perceived as an indication that he, like others during his time period, has turned away from the Lord and is doing what is right in his own eyes. However, 1 Samuel 1:3 challenges this impression of Elkanah, since he seems to be respectful of his cultic duties, ascending to Shiloh at least once a year to worship and sacrifice. Why is Elkanah depicted as rejecting God's created order in one verse and then portrayed in the next verse as honoring the Lord?

Maligning Elkanah as another miscreant of the period of the judges can be further called into question considering the narrator's portrayal of

2. Berlin, *Poetics and Interpretation*, 137.

him striving to care for Hannah. Elkanah provides Hannah with a "double portion"[3] of his sacrifice and seems deeply concerned about her emotional well-being (1 Sam. 1:5 and possibly in v. 8). These details of the narrative do not suggest that we diagnose Elkanah with the disorder that infected Israel during the time of the judges. Rather, these particulars in the introduction of Hannah's narrative suggest a possible scenario that could explain her family situation when read in light of other experiences of barrenness in the Bible.

A survey of the Torah shows that producing offspring was a deep-seated value in ancient Israel. This principle is rooted in the creation narrative and the reiterated commands for human beings to be fruitful and multiply (Gen. 1:28; 9:1, 7; 48:4; see also 17:20; 28:3). For example, God meets Israel (a.k.a. Jacob) at Paddan-aram and says to him, "I am God Almighty; be fruitful and increase in number. A nation and a community of nations will come from you, and kings will be among your descendants" (35:11). Thus from their inception, the people of Israel viewed having children as a way to perpetuate their community and fulfill the divine promise that they would develop into a multitude.

This desire to generate progeny transcended the community at large and permeated the lives of individual Israelite families. In a world void of digital images and social media, having an heir was the only way to guarantee that one's name and memory were not blotted out of history upon death. As ancient Israelite tradition progressed, blotting one's name and memory out of history became recognized as a consequence of wickedness: "The name of the righteous is used in blessings, but the name of the wicked will rot" (Prov. 10:7). As a result of this traditional wisdom, not having progeny was at times (mis)understood as a sign of one's wickedness.

This was a legitimate fear in ancient Israel. People who did not have children seemingly perished forever, and their memories were permanently lost. Preserving the name and memory of dead relatives was also one of the reasons that the levirate custom was implemented in Israel (see Deut. 25:5–10; Ruth 4:1–12; see chap. 7). In the Old Testament barrenness was not just a struggle with infertility; it was a struggle with one's family being remembered after death and, in some cases, a struggle between being perceived as righteous and being perceived as wicked.

The Torah presents scenarios in which the matriarchs experience great distress as a result of childlessness and go to extremes in order to relieve

---

3. The literal Hebrew translation of this difficult phrase is "to Hannah he gave one portion, two faces." It appears as if Hannah receives twice the amount that Elkanah gives to the rest of his family (depicted in 1 Sam. 1:4).

themselves of this hardship. In the narratives relating to the infertility of Sarah and Rachel, servants of these matriarchs are given to their husbands for the purpose of bearing children. Adding domestic partners to serve as surrogate mothers to bear children on behalf of the legitimate wives not only is scandalous in light of God's creation order but also causes trouble for those involved in this type of scenario.

Rachel's infertility in particular provides a scenario that lends insight into Hannah's situation. Rachel is Jacob's bride of choice, whom he loves more than his other wife, Leah (Gen. 29:18, 30). God opens Leah's womb and provides a child as a consolation for being unloved by her husband (29:31–35). God does not simply comfort Leah through children but also provides her with future hope. Through Leah, Jacob's name and the legacy promised to him and his family will be perpetuated (28:14).

The fact that Leah has multiple children provokes her barren sister, Rachel, to jealousy and anguish (Gen. 30:1–2). Like her grandmother Sarah (16:1–6), Rachel's childless discontentment leads her to offer her servant, Bilhah, to her husband as a surrogate mother. For Rachel, offering Bilhah serves as a battle tactic that gives her the upper hand in the developing dispute with her sister (30:3, 8). Leah is not to be bested by her more loved sister and follows suit, giving Jacob her servant Zilpah as a surrogate to bear more children on her behalf (30:9–13). It is not until Leah conceives six sons and at least one daughter (Dinah) that God finally remembers Rachel, opening her womb and taking away her "disgrace" (30:22–23).

While the narrator of Hannah's story provides readers with sparse details related to Hannah's predicament, this brief review of infertility elsewhere in the Bible establishes precedent and vivid imagery of the type of problematic situation presented in this narrative. In the two stories featuring the matriarchs, men initially marry but subsequently take other women as surrogate mothers to bear children on behalf of their legitimate, but barren, wives. The descriptive accounts of the negative domestic consequences to these types of unions portray God's displeasure toward the act of taking new partners into the household for the sake of bearing children. These scenarios are accompanied by grief, jealousy, and power plays. In a society in which people feared they might be forgotten or considered wicked if they did not bear progeny, conception meant power. In light of the Torah's narratives, perhaps Elkanah initially married Hannah, yet upon realizing that the wife whom he loved was barren (1 Sam. 1:5), he took another woman into his household, as did Abraham and Jacob. Hannah's predicament is not culturally unusual, but it is still quite problematic.

What's Up with Eli?

Elkanah is not the only Israelite man whose confusing behavior complicates Hannah's predicament. The priest Eli acts in a bewildering manner toward Hannah when she ascends to the tabernacle in Shiloh to pray. As Hannah pours out her heart before the Lord in great distress, Eli observes her lips moving and falsely accuses her of being drunk (1 Sam. 1:13–14). This is quite an absurd misunderstanding of Hannah's predicament, and it portrays Eli the priest as an impetuous character.

There are at least two ironic points to Eli's accusation. First, Eli the priest is depicted as sitting at the doorpost of the tabernacle when Hannah arrives, yet he does not recognize that she is fervently praying (1 Sam. 1:9). Given that the tabernacle was where people would go to worship, one might think that the priest should be familiar with what ardent prayer looks like. Second, Hannah is so terribly vexed that she cannot ingest food (1:7). Yet the priest Eli accuses her of overindulging in alcohol while she is at the house of God to seek the Lord. We can identify the indiscretion of Eli's accusation because the narrator tells us more than Eli knows. Thus we can scoff at the nonsensical nature of Eli's comments[4] and further identify with Hannah's pain of being misunderstood in the narrative (see also 1:8). Hannah crying out before the Lord and subsequently being wrongly accused by Eli the priest compels us to admire Hannah and to be suspicious of Eli.

Eli's ensuing comments are equally as puzzling as his first, yet they humorously bear the opposite tone of his accusation of Hannah. When Hannah implores Eli to recognize that she is deeply troubled and not intoxicated, Eli suddenly changes his tenor and kindly wishes that Hannah's petition come to pass, without ever being informed of the nature of her request (1 Sam. 1:17). Readers smirk at Eli's ignorant and perplexing judgment. Eli's character is portrayed not as wicked per se but rather as simply confusing (see also 2:22–25).

Hannah's Surprise Motherhood: An Answer to Prayer

Elkanah, confusingly, has two wives. Eli the priest speaks to Hannah absurdly in ignorance. Eli's sons, Hophni and Phineas, are depicted as cold-blooded scoundrels (1 Sam. 2:12–17, 22, 27–36; 4:10–18). The narrator contrasts these sons with Samuel, who is the surprise answer to Hannah's prayer and the lone Israelite male who is depicted positively in the opening narratives of 1 Samuel (2:18–21; compare 2:22–25 with v. 26).

---

4. Sternberg, *Poetics of Biblical Narrative*, 164.

Hannah's exemplary character is demonstrated when she takes her case before the Lord, weeping and crying out to God for mercy. Hannah's prayer is simple but ardent: "Lord Almighty, if you will only look on your servant's misery and remember me, and not forget your servant but give her a son, then I will give him to the Lord for all the days of his life, and no razor will ever be used on his head" (1 Sam. 1:11).[5] God answers the prayer by allowing Hannah to conceive, yet the narrator takes pains to supply both the human perspective and the divine perspective of the fulfillment. The fact that Elkanah "made love to his wife Hannah" presents the natural way children are conceived (1:19). However, this is not quite enough information, since readers have been informed that the Lord was initially responsible for closing Hannah's womb, causing her great anguish (1:6). Thus the narrator merges the natural reason with privileged information and communicates what goes on behind the scenes: the Lord remembers Hannah, opens her womb, and permits her to conceive Samuel (1:20; see also Gen. 30:22). God has compassion for Hannah just as he had compassion for Rachel and relieved her of the grief that accompanied her infertility.

Hannah's vow to dedicate the child to the Lord all the days of his life and her promise that no razor will touch (lit. "go up on") the child's head brings to mind the Nazirite vow from Samson's narrative. Samson's parents were also commanded that no razor should "go up on" their son's head (Judg. 13:5). This rhetorical connection links Samson and Samuel and prompts the reader to compare and contrast the two. Both are born as a result of divine intervention after a period of infertility, and both are specially commissioned by God for a specific task. However, Samson ushers a period of unrest into the land of Israel, while "Samuel continued to grow in stature and in favor with the Lord and with people" (1 Sam. 2:26). Samuel eventually introduces one of the most prosperous seasons in Israel by anointing David as king.

Hannah's Highway to King David

After the birth of Samuel, Hannah eventually returns to Shiloh with her young son by her side. There she finally communicates with Eli that her child is what she petitioned the Lord for on the occasion in which Eli accused

---

5. It is not completely certain that Hannah is asking God for a "son" through the phrase that is normally translated as such (lit., "the seed of men"). Additionally, the vow that Hannah makes could have been applied to both men and women (Num. 6:2), especially considering that women served in the tabernacle precincts (cf. 1 Sam. 2:22).

her of being drunk (1 Sam. 1:26–27). At this point, the stage is set for the spotlight to turn toward Samuel as the protagonist as he serves the Lord in the tabernacle at Shiloh. But first the narrator briefly digresses to record one of Hannah's prayers. The final portion of this prayer is key to grasping the trajectory of the following narrative. Hannah concludes by asserting, "The Lord will judge the ends of the earth. He will give strength to his king and exalt the horn of his anointed [*mashiach*]" (2:10). Hannah's mention of a king is curious since there has never been a king in Israel. However, the kingship motif is repeatedly voiced in the book of Judges, foreshadowing a day in which a ruler will be a reality (see also Deut. 17:14–20). Hannah's prayer, which indicates that the Lord will empower an anointed one (*mashiach*) over Israel, continues the kingship theme.

Hannah fades from the narrative at this point, but her impression on the people of Israel is evident through her son, Samuel. Samuel emerges as the main character of the story—the one who has the ear of all of Israel, judges the people, calls them to leave the foreign gods of the land, and leads them to worship the Lord their God (1 Sam. 4:1; 7:3–6; 15–17). Nevertheless, when Samuel's children do not follow in their father's footsteps, Hannah's reference to a king is recalled. Thus "all the elders of Israel gathered together and came to Samuel at Ramah. They said to him, 'You are old, and your sons do not follow your ways; now appoint a king to lead us, such as all the other nations have'" (8:4–5). Despite Samuel's great displeasure with this request, the Lord commands Samuel to obey the voice of the people and appoint a king for them. Israel's desire for a king is not a rejection of Samuel or his children per se. Rather, Israel has shunned the Lord as their king (8:7).

Samuel's obedience leads him to anoint (*mashach*) Saul, the first king of Israel (1 Sam. 9:16; 10:1). Yet Saul's two-time disobedience to the word of the Lord that comes through Samuel leads to the Lord rejecting him as king of Israel (13:8–15; 15:1–35; see chap. 12 below). Samuel communicates with Saul that the "Lord has sought out a man after his own heart" and has "torn the kingdom of Israel from [Saul] . . . and has given it to one of [his] neighbors" (1 Sam. 13:14; 15:28; see also Acts 13:22). God then leads Samuel into Judahite territory, into Bethlehem, to the house of Jesse, to anoint (*mashach*) his youngest son, David, the second king over Israel (1 Sam. 16:3, 13). Through David, Israel experiences some of its greatest national and religious stability. Hannah's faithfulness, which was manifested by her willingness to dedicate Samuel to the service of the Lord, plays a crucial role in the political transition of Israel out of the turmoil of the judges and into a period of relative order.

Ruth's Predicament

As the saying goes, the deck is stacked against Ruth at the beginning of her narrative. Not only is she a foreigner in Israel; she is a Moabite. The Moabites were the ancient relatives of Israel through Lot (Gen. 19:36–38). Yet Israel and Moab have their fair share of problems. During Israel's wilderness wanderings, the king of Moab encumbers Israel's journey by not permitting the people to pass through Moab on their way to Canaan (Judg. 11:17–18). Furthermore, Balak, king of Moab, hires Balaam the prophet to curse Israel (Num. 22–24). This plan seemingly backfires on Balak, since Balaam repeatedly blesses the people of Israel instead of cursing them. However, this situation brings about one of the most infamous scenes in the Torah, in which the men of Israel commit physical and spiritual infidelity with the Moabite women and their god, Baal of Peor. This incident leads to the deaths of twenty-four thousand Israelites in a plague resulting from the Lord's great displeasure with Israel (Num. 25:1–9).

Israel was, therefore, not to permit any Moabite into their community. The Lord commands Israel that "no Ammonite or Moabite or any of their descendants may enter the assembly of the LORD, not even in the tenth generation. For they did not come to meet you with bread and water on your way when you came out of Egypt, and they hired Balaam son of Beor. . . . Do not seek a treaty of friendship with them as long as you live" (Deut. 23:3–4, 6). Israel and Moab are perpetual foes.

Ruth is a Moabite.

The fact that her story appears in the Bible is curious from the very beginning.

Ruth is surely not to blame for her ancestors' misdeeds against Israel. She is, in a sense, experiencing the collateral damage of a conflict that predated her. All the same, as a foreign woman from the land of Baal of Peor, Ruth embodies the perennial downfall of Israel during the time of the judges. However, rather than being depicted as endangering the people of Israel, Ruth is depicted as being the vulnerable one from the outset of the narrative—a poor widow who moves from Moab to Israel with her acrimonious mother-in-law, Naomi. With no husband, financial resources, or children, Ruth is in a particularly troublesome predicament as a foreigner in Israel during the turbulent period of the judges.

How did this Moabite find herself in this situation to begin with?

To answer this question, we must track the perplexing behavior of the Israelite men depicted at the beginning of Ruth's narrative.

Undoing the Exodus: Elimelech's Family's Bewildering Behavior

The book of Ruth presents an antidote for the chaos depicted in Judges through posing a paradox. Readers of Judges recall the anarchy in Israel, and they are reminded that the remedy alluded to in the book is a righteous ruler. Then, readers are paradoxically directed to a story featuring a group of women, of which a widowed Moabite is the protagonist who leads to the enduring Israelite monarchy. This story sounds too incongruous to be true. But truth is stranger than fiction.

Like Hannah's narrative, Ruth's story presents Israelite men whose curious decisions precipitate her difficult situation. In this case, an Israelite man named Elimelech leaves Bethlehem in Judah during a time of famine to reside in the country of Moab with his wife, Naomi, and two sons, Mahlon and Chilion. Mahlon and Chilion marry Moabite women, Ruth and Orpah, while sojourning in Moab. Tragically, Elimelech, Mahlon, and Chilion proceed to die in Moab, leaving three widows: Naomi, Ruth, and Orpah.

Four details mentioned in the introduction to Ruth's narrative are particularly important to understanding how the Israelite men impacted her situation.

1. There is a famine in the land (Ruth 1:1). Famine is presented in the Torah as one of the consequences of Israel not honoring God (Lev. 26:3–4, 18–20; Deut. 11:14; 32:24). Ruth's narrative sets her story in the time of the judges, a time when the Israelites repeatedly turn from the Lord their God, resulting in their once-fertile land becoming as hard as bronze (Lev. 26:19). This leads to the second curious feature in the introduction.

2. Elimelech takes his family to Moab to seek food. Not only were the Moabites Israel's enemies (Num. 22:1–25:9), but their land would have seemingly been just as likely to suffer from famine as Israel's land was—or more so.

3. Elimelech and his family are identified as Ephrathites from Bethlehem of Judah. Bethlehem is geographically in the center of the promised land, which is where the Israelites should be residing during this time period. The decision to move out of the heart of Israel goes against everything the Torah communicates concerning the destiny of the covenant people. God promised the land to Abraham, Isaac, and Jacob hundreds of years before Elimelech's time. The people of Israel sojourned in Egypt for four hundred years; they wandered in the desert for forty years; the Jordan River miraculously divided, and they crossed into Canaan; they endured

numerous military conflicts before finally settling in the land. After all this, the fact that Elimelech leaves the heart of the promised land to cross over the Jordan River and return to Moab is baffling.

4. Elimelech and Naomi's sons, Mahlon and Chilion, both marry Moabite women, Ruth and Orpah. Marrying non-Israelites was not strictly forbidden in ancient Israel as long as the non-Israelites were worshipers of the Lord, the God of Israel. (Even Moses married a non-Israelite; see Num. 12:1). However, there is no indication that either Ruth or Orpah was indeed a worshiper of the Lord when she married an Israelite. In fact, the context seems to suggest otherwise (e.g., Ruth 1:15). Mahlon's and Chilion's marriages to Moabite women are bewildering, given that this type of marriage went against the ancient traditional wisdom of marrying within the community (e.g., Gen. 24:2–4; 28:1–2; see also 26:34–35) and given the recent troubles that Israel has had with the people of Moab.

Naomi is still in Moab when she hears that the Lord, the God of Israel, has broken Judah's famine, and she then decides to return to Israel (Ruth 1:6–7). Upon Naomi's return to Bethlehem, readers are able to perceive the sad consequences of the questionable decisions that the Israelite men made. In Bethlehem the destitute widow Ruth resides as a foreigner with her mother-in-law, Naomi. Naomi blames the Lord for her suffering and would prefer to be alone in her bitterness and have Ruth go back to idolatry, worshiping the gods of Moab (1:11, 13, 15, 19–22).

Elimelech's curious decision to undo the exodus and go back to wandering in a foreign land is puzzling. Mahlon's marriage to a Moabite is confusing. These perplexing decisions that Israelite men made are the primary reasons for Ruth's dilemma.

Ruth's Surprise Motherhood

Be that as it may, the decisions of the Israelite men do not lead to *only* negative outcomes. Even though Naomi urges Ruth to return to her country, her people, and her gods, Ruth sticks by her mother-in-law. This is a decision that Ruth beautifully articulates, stating, "Don't urge me to leave you or to turn back from you. Where you go I will go, and where you stay I will stay. Your people will be my people and your God my God. Where you die I will die, and there will I be buried. May the LORD deal with me, be it ever so severely, if even death separates you and me" (Ruth 1:16–17).

Ruth's determination to go to Bethlehem with Naomi is inextricably linked with her acceptance of Naomi's Israelite people and their God. The rhetoric that Ruth uses to express her commitment to Naomi, her people, and her God is uniquely similar to the type of language God uses in the Torah in reference to his covenant people, Israel: "I will take you as my own people, and I will be your God. Then you will know that I am the Lord your God" (Exod. 6:7; see also Deut. 29:13).

Ruth's commitment to Naomi and to calling Bethlehem her home subjects her to the laws and traditions of her new land and of Israel's God. Ancient Israelite law made provisions for the less fortunate people who lived among them. For example, the Lord commands the Israelites, "When you reap the harvest of your land, do not reap to the very edges of your field. . . . Leave them [i.e., fallen produce] for the poor and the foreigner. I am the Lord your God" (Lev. 19:9–10; see also 23:22; Deut. 24:19). It appears as if Ruth exercises this legal provision upon arriving in Bethlehem, because she does not have enough food. Without anyone to provide for her and her mother-in-law, Ruth takes the initiative to glean in what seems to her to be a random field. The field turns out to be the property of Boaz, a relative of Elimelech's family.

Out of all the episodes that could have been relayed concerning Ruth's and Naomi's lives after they left Moab, the narrator skips to the events of one specific day in the life of Ruth in Bethlehem—the day Ruth meets Boaz. Ruth and Naomi eventually realize that Ruth has stumbled across the field of Boaz, who, because he is a relative of the family of Elimelech, can redeem the women (Ruth 2:19–20). Readers already know of this possibility, since they were tipped off by the narrator before Ruth landed in Boaz's field (2:1). Thus we expectantly wait for this redemption to come to pass throughout the events that follow.

Now that Ruth dwells among the people of Israel, she is eligible for redemption as per the customs of the Israelite community. Naomi works to find an accommodating domestic situation for Ruth and apparently encourages her to propose a marriage of sorts to Boaz (Ruth 3:1–5). The vagueness of Naomi's command to Ruth should be conspicuous to us as readers. We are left questioning whether Naomi encourages Ruth to accost Boaz and perform a suggestive act by uncovering his "feet"—a potential euphemism.[6] Additionally, we wonder why Ruth would petition Boaz to redeem her in the middle of the night. Why would she uncover his feet while he was lying down? Why would Boaz explicitly tell Ruth not to let anyone know that she came to his threshing floor (3:14)? It is difficult to interpret Ruth's actions at the threshing floor. However, through

6. Perhaps, as Adele Berlin states, "Naomi sent [Ruth] on a romantic mission but [Ruth] turned it into a quest for a redeemer." Berlin, *Poetics and Interpretation*, 90.

her conversation with Boaz, Ruth communicates her desire to be redeemed by him, and he expresses his willingness to carry out the redemption.

But what exactly is Boaz to redeem?

Readers are familiar with the concept of redemption from the Torah. For example, land could be redeemed: "If one of your fellow Israelites becomes poor and sells some of their property, their nearest relative is to come and redeem what they have sold" (Lev. 25:25). Israelite law established provisions for family members to redeem property of those who were forced to sell it because of a precarious financial situation. In the book of Ruth, Naomi is selling a plot of land for this reason. However, the situation is a bit more complicated than just the selling of property because of Mahlon's marriage to Ruth. It appears that Israel had developed a custom regarding the redemption of land upon a family member's death. This custom required the person who redeemed land to also care for the wife of the deceased person. This means that the person who redeems Elimelech's property needs to marry Ruth.

In the scene in which Boaz redeems Elimelech's property through Naomi, redemption language is combined with the idea of raising up a name for the dead. This sounds strikingly similar to the custom of levirate marriage, though it is apparently practiced differently in this situation (Ruth 4:10; see also Deut. 25:5–6; see chap. 7 above). At least in the case of Ruth and Boaz, the laws related to property redemption and levirate marriage seem to have been conflated to require the person who redeems the land to also preserve the seller's family. Boaz, consequently, takes Ruth as his wife, the land legitimately becomes his, and he also raises up a name for the dead. Thus Boaz does not simply gain possession of Elimelech's family's land; he also continues Elimelech's family line and frees Ruth from the anxiety of being husbandless, childless, and impoverished.

The redemption proceedings at the city gate lead to the culmination of the narrative, which is matter-of-factly stated: "So Boaz took Ruth and she became his wife. When he made love to her, the LORD enabled her to conceive, and she gave birth to a son" (Ruth 4:13). Upon the birth of Obed, Ruth and Boaz breathe new life into Elimelech's family. This child perpetuates the name and memory of Elimelech's household through the unexpected union of a Judahite and a Moabite (Ruth 4:14, 16).

Ruth's Highway to King David

Ruth's narrative brings to fruition a plan that was set in motion long before her "chance encounter" with Boaz. Upon the joyous occasion of Boaz taking

Ruth to be his wife, the people present at the city gate bless Boaz by stating, "May the LORD make the woman who is coming into your home like Rachel and Leah, who together built up the family of Israel. May you have standing in Ephrathah and be famous in Bethlehem. Through the offspring the LORD gives you by this young woman, may your family be like that of Perez, whom Tamar bore to Judah" (Ruth 4:11–12).

The women mentioned here hark back to a narrative that has been developing from the time of the patriarchs. Jacob had twelve sons with four women, but only the two "legitimate" wives are mentioned in the conclusion of Ruth. This is certainly not because the narrator was unaware of Bilhah and Zilpah. Rather, the mention of Jacob's legitimate wives is necessary to spotlight Judah, Leah's son. Conversely, by mentioning the illicit relationship that Judah had with Tamar, the narrator recalls their offspring, Perez. Perez is the crux of this portion of the book of Ruth, since the narrator begins the final genealogy with Perez, who perpetuates the kingly line of David.

Successive readers of the entire Bible recall the uniquely positive blessings given to Judah by his father, Jacob, as the book of Genesis comes to an end (Gen. 49:8–10). That passage is complex, but for all intents and purposes, it depicts Judah being specially honored by others and bearing unique authority. Ruth marries into the tribe of Judah and perpetuates the genealogical line, which ultimately transitions the people of Israel out of the chaos of the judges and into the stability of the Judean kingship foreshadowed earlier.

Where Hannah and Ruth Meet

Just as the I-5 and the Pacific Coast Highway merge at Dana Point, so Hannah's and Ruth's stories meet at David. Societal order is introduced to Israel by an immigrant Moabite in Judah who marries into the Davidic line and by a "barren" woman who bears the child (Samuel) who anoints David as king of Israel. David, as a descendant of Judah, eventually receives the promise of a perpetual kingship that will transcend his days (2 Sam. 7:16). Hannah and Ruth are the mothers of the monarchical line that brings hope for order and prosperity to the people of Israel by pointing to David.

Hannah and Ruth are genuine examples of faith in the God of Israel in times of vulnerability and grief. They demonstrate what trusting God in difficult circumstances looks like and are relevant examples to all readers. Through these narratives, readers observe how the divine plan uniquely includes women in

great distress to bring about civil order and hope, both for the women personally and among the people of Israel, who had greatly diverged from their call.
We now turn to the monarchy to discuss its development, peak, and eventual
downfall.

TWELVE

King David's True Legacy

> The walls were hung round with tapestry, . . . and, at all events, representing the Scriptural story of David and Bathsheba, and Nathan the Prophet, in colors still unfaded, but which made the fair woman of the scene almost as grimly picturesque as the woe-denouncing seer.
> —Nathaniel Hawthorne, *The Scarlet Letter*

The quote above from *The Scarlet Letter* vividly elaborates on a seemingly minute detail of the home study of one of the book's main characters, Reverend Dimmesdale. How the reader is to visualize the tapestry's imagery reflecting the scenes of 2 Samuel 11–12 (featuring David, Bathsheba, and Nathan the Prophet) is not clarified, except to compare the "grimly picturesque" depiction of Nathan, King David's rebuker, to that of Bathsheba, King David's victim. No further details are provided, since imagining the tapestry's fictitious artwork is not what is significant to the narrator. Rather, what is important is that readers of *The Scarlet Letter* interpret aspects of its scandalous plot in light of their knowledge of the biblical narrative featuring these characters.

King David shares multiple points of affinity with the Reverend Dimmesdale. Both David and Dimmesdale hold positions of authority in their respective communities; both participate in nefarious scandals with married women; both make a concerted effort to conceal their grave misdeeds through deception; both have close encounters with the husbands of the women with whom they participate in extramarital affairs; both use the women to protect their facades of nobility and religious devotion and strive to give the impression of being honorable before their communities.

David's and Dimmesdale's acts of misconduct ultimately constitute self-inflicted wounds that cause drastic consequences, leading to further self-destructive behavior. Dimmesdale is overridden with guilt and shame to the point where his anguish provokes an actual, self-inflicted wound; he bears this wound on his chest, hidden under his clothes, to represent the enduring pangs of his conscience until the day of his death. While David does not inflict a physical wound on himself, his acts of adultery, deception, and murder lead to the breakdown of his public and family lives.

At least one major difference distinguishes David from Dimmesdale. This is also the most notable contrast between David and his royal predecessor, King Saul: David's straightforward manner of repentance. After all King David accomplishes during his reign, he leaves a lasting impression on readers of the Bible by demonstrating confession and brokenness before God. In this chapter, we will set the scene for David's story by first looking at the reign of Saul, Israel's first king. We will then briefly review King David's rise to power and his epic fall from grace, stemming from his ruthless dealings with Bathsheba and her husband, Uriah. During this survey, we will pay close attention to how parts of the narratives featuring Saul, David, Bathsheba, Uriah, and Nathan highlight King David's confession, repentance, and brokenness as key aspects of his enduring legacy.

Saul: The Tapestry of David's Narrative

As alluded to in the previous chapter, David's rise to power is inextricably linked with the judgeship of the prophet Samuel, who anoints Saul and David as the first two kings over Israel. Samuel anoints Saul as the leader of Israel following an ordeal during which they "fortuitously" cross paths as Saul is looking for his father's lost donkeys (1 Sam. 8–10). The private anointing, attended by only Samuel and Saul, is followed by a public coronation at Mizpah. During the public crowning of Saul, an interesting sequence of events comes to pass, shedding light on how readers are to understand subsequent depictions of the characters in the narrative.

As the people of Israel gather at Mizpah prior to Saul's public investiture, Samuel reprimands the community on behalf of the Lord for having spurned their God in favor of an earthly king (1 Sam. 8:7, 19; 12:12). Samuel then obediently proceeds with the coronation protocol during which Saul, the son of

Kish, from the clan of the Matrites, of the tribe of Benjamin, is to be chosen as the first king of Israel. However, as Israel anticipates the installment of their foremost leader, the king-elect is nowhere to be found. The community is forced to ask the Lord where their new supreme commander is. God communicates that Saul, the newly designated king of Israel, is hiding, apparently because he is fearful (cf. Gen. 3:10; Josh. 10:16–17; Judg. 9:5). People from the community are forced to pull Saul from his hiding place and present him before Israel so that he might be crowned as king (1 Sam. 10:20–23).

Knowing that Samuel had already anointed Saul as the leader over the people of Israel (1 Sam. 10:1), readers are in a unique position to inquire about this scene: Why is Saul hiding when he *already knows* that he is the one who will be chosen to lead Israel? This incident also propels us to criticize the prophet Samuel, who at other times of his ministry has harshly denounced foolish actions that challenge God's instructions (e.g., 8:10–18; 12:17–18; 13:13–14; 15:14–23; see also the following section). Yet in this situation, Samuel is conspicuously silent about Saul's hiding, despite knowing that it was the Lord's plan that he be crowned as the leader of Israel (9:15–16). Why doesn't Samuel reprimand Saul for hiding at the most important moment of his life and at such a consequential moment in the community's history? At Mizpah, Samuel disregards the fact that Saul seems completely willing to avoid his call to leadership.

When Saul is eventually brought out before the people of Israel to be crowned as king, the narrator mentions that he stands head and shoulders above the rest of the people. Saul's height and agreeable nature are reiterated throughout his narrative (1 Sam. 9:2; 10:23), and his appearance curiously ends up being the focus of Samuel's introduction of him: "Do you see the man the LORD has chosen? There is no one like him among all the people" (10:24). Deliberate readers are forced to ask, "Why would Samuel ask if the community of Israel 'sees' Saul, when the narrator tells us that he is taller than everyone else?" The answer seems to be in Samuel's emphasis on God choosing someone who had the appearance of a good, strong leader. Samuel is apparently captivated by the moment, focusing on the outward appearance of the king-elect and emphasizing it over Saul's character.

These observations leave readers with the perception that Saul does not want to be king as much as Israel wants to have a king. Additionally, it seems as if Samuel himself facilitates and then becomes absorbed in the hype of the king-elect. These considerations provoke us to wonder how Saul's kingship will unfold. Will the towering king, whom all Israel *must* look up to, be the resolute leader of strong character that everyone will be *able* to look up to? Or does his hiding from his coronation foreshadow his internal weaknesses, insecurity, and lack of leadership ability? Within a few chapters, we have answers to these questions. How these answers play out will directly impact how we perceive David in light of Saul.

The Downfall of Saul

At moments in his life, Saul exhibits shades of the type of leadership needed to unify the people of Israel and liberate them from the hands of those who distressed them during the period of the judges (1 Sam. 14:47–48). Additionally, the Lord's prophet, Samuel, acts favorably toward Saul, supporting him and encouraging him to follow the Lord at the beginning of his reign. Saul's leadership abilities and Samuel's endorsement of his kingship are both evident in Saul's first military campaign. When the Ammonites besiege the Transjordanian town of Jabesh Gilead, Saul, empowered by the Spirit of God, summons troops from Israel and Judah and utterly defeats the oppressors of his people. Saul's military success leads Samuel to call the people of Israel to Gilgal and reaffirm Saul as the leader of their community (11:1–15). Gilgal will become a place of great significance in Saul's narrative. It is here that Saul's kingship is ultimately established. Israel rejoices because they have finally found the leader that will protect them—the leader they have been waiting for who will go out before them and fight their battles (8:20; 12:1–2).

At least, that is what they think.

Saul Sacrifices at Gilgal

Saul's second military campaign is significantly different. Though it is ultimately a successful campaign for Israel, Saul does not carry out the victory (1 Sam. 14:1–23). In fact, the events at Gilgal leading to the battle against the Philistines precipitate the downfall of King Saul. Here is what happens: The perpetual enemy of Israel, the Philistines, gathers thirty thousand chariots[1] and six thousand troops together at Michmash to fight. Saul and his troops are stationed not far away at Gilgal. Panic sets in, and they become frightened to the point that some of Saul's fighters hide from their call to duty in caves and cisterns; others abandon their leader and fellow soldiers and flee to the

---

1. This number reflects the reading of the Masoretic Text. It is quite a large group of chariots relative to the number of soldiers (cf. 1 Sam. 13:5). A recension of the Septuagint and the Syriac version indicates that there were three thousand chariots as opposed to thirty thousand. The smaller number seems to fit better with the quantity of people that accompanied the chariots into battle. Either way, Saul is severely outnumbered.

Transjordanian areas of Gad and Gilead (13:7–8; 14:11). The number of people in Saul's camp dwindles from two thousand men to just six hundred because of the Philistine threat (13:2, 15). Saul fearfully and hopelessly gawks as troops desert him, and he concludes that he must do something to halt Israel's undoing. This leads to big problems.

At an undisclosed point in time, Samuel orders Saul to travel to Gilgal and wait for him there to sacrifice an offering (1 Sam. 13:8). After arriving at Gilgal, waiting seven days, and observing a sizable portion of his troops go AWOL, Saul decides that he has seen enough and carries out the burnt offering without Samuel being present. This action is especially problematic because making sacrifices was reserved for the priests, who were to be from the tribe of Levi (Num. 18:6–7). Saul was from the tribe of Benjamin, meaning that he was not permitted to execute such priestly responsibilities. Samuel, who was a Levite, served in the tabernacle from boyhood and was trained in the cultic activity of ancient Israel (1 Sam. 1:21–28; 1 Chron. 6:33–34). Be that as it may, Saul's fear leads to impatience; impatience leads Saul to spurn the command of the prophet Samuel; spurning Samuel leads Saul to act out of place and violate God's order.

As soon as Saul sacrifices the burnt offering, Samuel returns to the narrative and inquires about Saul's impulsive actions. Saul promptly strives to justify his offense. There are three important components to Saul's misguided rationalization.

1. Saul shifts blame. According to Saul, others are at fault for *forcing* him to sacrifice the burnt offering: the people were scattering; Samuel did not arrive on time; the Philistines gathered (1 Sam. 13:11; cf. Gen. 3:8–13). King Saul is not fighting the battles of the people as Israel desired and expected. Rather, Saul is content to pass along the consequences for his misdeeds to others in the community he was supposed to lead.

2. Saul adds a religious twist to his response. According to Saul, the *real* reason for sacrificing the burnt offering was to seek the favor of the Lord before the impending battle with the Philistines (1 Sam. 13:12).

3. Saul does not repent. Instead of admitting his offense and expressing regret for having disobeyed the word of the Lord that came through Samuel (13:13), Saul is mute. Saul takes no personal responsibility for his actions in his self-justification to Samuel.

Samuel sees through Saul's pretexts and points out that sacrificing the burnt offering out of turn was emblematic of rejecting the Lord's command.

It is extremely problematic for the first king of Israel to deliberately reject God's word, since doing so essentially returns the community to the time of the judges, in which everyone did what was right in their own eyes. Saul's kingdom will, therefore, not be established. Ironically, Saul's kingship was confirmed at Gilgal, and at Gilgal, Samuel confirms that it will end.[2]

Saul Saves Amalek

Though Saul is rejected by the Lord in Gilgal, he is not yet expelled from his office. In fact, Saul is given a second chance of sorts. Samuel reminds Saul of his call to be the leader of Israel and instructs him on behalf of the Lord to carry out another unique military mission: "Now go, attack the Amalekites and totally destroy all that belongs to them. Do not spare them; put to death men and women, children and infants, cattle and sheep, camels and donkeys" (1 Sam. 15:3). Saul must combine his ability to lead with the humility to obey.

The divine instructions for Saul's mission are easily intelligible. The Lord even provides Saul with a reason for the operation: Amalek troubled the people of Israel when they came out of Egypt (Exod. 17:14–16; Num. 14:41–45; Deut. 25:17–19). Additionally, readers know that the Amalekites opposed Israel in the promised land by forming coalitions with the Moabites (Judg. 3:13) and the Midianites (6:3). Given this history, we readers understand that the Amalekites compromise Israel's national security. Thus we might hardly question a military offensive against the Amalekites.

It is safe to say, however, that some of us might ask, "Why does *every* Amalekite person and animal *have* to die?" Those of us with this question might be thinking along the same lines as King Saul. Saul defeats the Amalekites, apparently without questioning the direction to battle that particular people group (1 Sam. 15:7). The issue for Saul is that he does not really believe that "every person" and "every animal" *has* to be put to death. This is particularly evident when he preserves the life of Agag, the king of the Amalekites, as well as the best of their livestock (15:8–9). Saul intentionally shuns God's word a second time, which leads to more explicit consequences than his initial ordeal at Gilgal (15:22–29).

Samuel the prophet is tipped off to Saul's disobedience by the Lord and is deeply grieved when he meets the king on the next day, again at Gilgal. Without Samuel mentioning anything about the Lord's command relating to the Amalekites, Saul promptly establishes a false report concerning his

---

2. Good, *Irony in the Old Testament*, 70.

actions. Again, it is important to notice three aspects of Saul's statement that are strikingly similar to those of his previous words to Samuel at Gilgal.

1. Saul shifts blame: Saul once again shifts the blame of his wrongdoing to his own troops. Saul is sure to note that "they" were the ones who confiscated the cattle from the Amalekites; "they" were the ones who spared the best sheep and oxen to sacrifice to the Lord. Saul then includes himself in the part of his report that reflects obedience to God's command, stating, "But we totally destroyed the rest" (1 Sam. 15:15).
2. Saul begins his response with a religious twist. As soon as Saul sees Samuel coming toward him at Gilgal, he shouts, "The LORD bless you!" Saul then half-truthfully declares, "I have carried out the LORD's instructions" (15:13). Samuel responds by asking Saul a rhetorical question, "What then is this bleating of sheep in my ears? What is this lowing of cattle that I hear?" (15:14). Samuel's question provides Saul an opportunity to repent for disobeying the Lord's command. He does not.
3. Saul "repents." Samuel rejects Saul's excuses and immediately pronounces God's ultimate judgment upon him: God rejects Saul from being king over Israel (15:22–23). Upon hearing the consequences, Saul finally breaks down and admits to Samuel, "I have sinned. I violated the LORD's command and your instructions. I was afraid of the men and so I gave in to them" (15:24). Saul continues to blame the people even in his "repentance"! Saul "repents" because he is interested in protecting his political facade (15:24–25, 30). Edwin Good summarizes, "Saul's apparent motivation does not even rise to the level of piety. He has cared more for his 'public image' than for his royal responsibility."[3]

There is tremendous incongruity between what Saul is called to be and what he becomes. Saul uses his position of privilege and authority as king of Israel to compromise those whom he is supposed to lead and protect. He is a tall leader, giving the appearance of a strong person, yet he does not possess the admirable character that would motivate Israelites (or readers) to look up to him. Instead, Saul spurns the word of the Lord, puts a religious twist on his justifications, shifts blame, and rebuffs authentic repentance. Saul's refusal to accept responsibility for his actions leads to personal instability that is manifest throughout the rest of his life.

Saul's rejection of the word of the Lord seals his fate. Samuel prophesies that God will rip the kingdom away from Saul and give it to someone else more

3. Good, *Irony in the Old Testament*, 72.

fit for the job (1 Sam. 15:28). God will choose a person who is likeminded, after the heart of God (lit., "like his heart" [13:14]).

David's Anointing

Just as the tapestry of David, Bathsheba, and Nathan serves as the backdrop to Reverend Dimmesdale's ordeal, so Saul's narrative serves as the backdrop for important aspects of King David's life. This is particularly the case when we consider Saul's blunders and consequent rejections depicted in 1 Samuel 13 and 15. With Saul's rejection finalized, we anticipate how Israel's king problem will be resolved: Samuel specifically tells Saul that God will give the kingdom to a neighbor (i.e., a fellow citizen) that is better than Saul (1 Sam. 15:28). This comparative language causes us to wonder, What does Samuel mean by "neighbor"? Who is this person, and how will the next leader be better than Saul? Samuel inaugurates the succession of power directly following Saul's second major failure, permitting readers to compare and contrast the newly appointed King David with his predecessor.

Samuel is grieved over Saul's rejection when he receives a command from the Lord to anoint another king. When God orders Samuel to travel to the house of Jesse in Bethlehem of Judah, Samuel grows fearful that Saul will hear of his mission and kill him. This sheds light on why Saul's successor is called a "neighbor." Not only will the king-elect be a fellow Israelite, but Judah and Benjamin are neighboring tribes. Saul's successor is not just any fellow Israelite; he will proceed from a region adjacent to Benjamin, Saul's place of origin and his residence at that time (1 Sam. 15:34).

Samuel obeys the command of God, arrives at the house of Jesse in Bethlehem, and promptly invites Jesse and his sons to a sacrifice. At this point, the narrator shares information that (1) is crucial to understanding the anointing of the king-elect in this scene and (2) helps us fully grasp Samuel's actions in Saul's public coronation (1 Sam. 10:17–27). The narrator tells us that when Samuel sees Jesse's firstborn son, Eliab, Samuel thinks that the Lord's anointed is surely before him (16:6). This information permits us to understand that Samuel judges leadership potential based on appearance. This is precisely what Samuel is depicted as doing at Saul's coronation, when he encourages the people to behold their tall king (10:23–24). Saul's looks give the impression that he will be a strong leader, and so do Eliab's. Yet this time around, God specifically prohibits Samuel from fixating on Eliab's appearance or height and emphasizes that "the Lord does not look at the things people look at. People look at the outward appearance, but the Lord looks at the heart" (16:7). Now Samuel is called to ordain the person that the Lord has specifically chosen, regardless of appearance.

Samuel does not talk back to God; he properly responds to the word of the Lord. Jesse proceeds to march seven of his sons before Samuel, who, now sensitive to the divine command, refrains from judging their leadership abilities based on appearance. Samuel communicates to them one by one that the Lord has not chosen any of them. Attuned to God's leading, Samuel finally suspects that not all of Jesse's sons are present. If it were up to Samuel, he would anoint the oldest, the best looking, and the tallest, as in the situation with Saul. However, since Samuel is sensitive and obedient to God's word, he is able to accept that God might direct him to a better leader, whose appearance may be different from what he expects.

This is precisely what happens. When David is summoned from tending the sheep, Samuel does not reflect on his appearance like he did during Saul's public coronation, but, rather, the narrator tells us of David's comeliness. In contrast to Saul, David is not tall and distinguished but young and handsome (1 Sam. 16:12). In this manner, readers know that David's anointing is not based on his appearance. David is the divinely appointed king over Israel, even though his own family does not consider him worthy to appear before Samuel. No one else's opinions matter in this situation. God's next words to Samuel are all that matter: "Rise and anoint him; this is the one" (16:12).

David: From Flock to Fugitive, from King to Killer

The fact that David is portrayed as handsome is important to how we perceive him as the narrative continues. As Adele Berlin states, "David's outstanding feature is not height but good looks (handsome and ruddy). This creates a different image in the reader's mind—one that is not limited to physical appearance but that extends to a personality with popular appeal (as the narrative confirms)."[4] "Personality" and "popular appeal" end up being David's lifelines throughout his ascension to power after his clandestine anointing by Samuel. Saul eventually develops a crazed jealousy of David that leads him into a deranged state in which he repeatedly tries to murder David (1 Sam. 18:6–16; 19; 23:15–24:22; 26). Beginning around this time, David marries Saul's daughter Michal, who saves his life (18:17–19:24); David's friendship with Saul's son Jonathan becomes crucially important for his survival (1 Sam. 20); David fraternizes with the Philistines with whom he finds asylum (1 Sam. 27); and David gathers hundreds of faithful warriors to protect him (23:13;

4. Berlin, *Poetics and Interpretation*, 137.

25:13; 27:2). David survives these years because he is able to connect with the people. After Saul's death at the hands of the Philistines, the people of Judah—David's own people—formally recognize him as their king (2 Sam. 2:4).

David reigns in Hebron in Judah for a total of seven and a half years (2 Sam. 2:1; 5:5). He is not immediately recognized as king over all of Israel because Ish-Bosheth, Saul's son, has been appointed leader over large parts of the north of the country and of the Transjordanian region (2:8–11). Ish-Bosheth is murdered, facilitating David's recognition as king over all of the tribes (5:1–5). David subsequently conquers Jerusalem, settles in the City of David, and establishes the city as Israel's center of religious and political activity (5:7, 9; 6:1–15).

It is in Jerusalem that God promises David that his house and kingdom will endure forever (2 Sam. 7:16). While living in Jerusalem, David guides Israel into their most successful season as a people group so far, leading military campaigns, defeating Israel's foes, and expanding the kingdom (2 Sam. 8). By staying in Jerusalem when he should be in battle, David embroils himself in another type of battle—one that will result in multiple casualties and jeopardize his family's legacy (2 Sam. 11–12).

What Is David Doing in Jerusalem?

David's battle with the Ammonites begins over foolish misjudgment. When the Ammonite king Nahash dies, David sends his servants to console the king's son, Hanun. Hanun's counselors mistake the servants' intentions and claim that they have arrived to spy out the land. Hanun takes the word of his counselors and embarrasses the Israelites by having their beards half shaved and their garments cut in the middle. The Ammonites realize that shaming the Israelites will result in retaliation, so they take preemptive action, forming a coalition with the Arameans. Joab, the Israelite military commander, consequently leads the Israelite forces into battle against the Arameans, handing them a brutal defeat and causing them to retreat to the Transjordanian town of Helam. King David then travels to Helam and routs the Arameans so badly that they fear ever forming a coalition with the Ammonites against Israel again (2 Sam. 10:1–19). At this point, the conflict between the Israelites and the Ammonites is still not settled and must wait for another day.

The springtime brings about better conditions for battle, which is suggested in 2 Samuel 11:1: "In the spring, at the time when kings go off to war, David sent Joab out with the king's men and the whole Israelite army. They destroyed the Ammonites and besieged Rabbah. But David remained in Jerusalem." With a cursory glance, this verse might merely seem like a drawn-out introduction to a change in scenery. However, the final, terse phrase "But David remained in Jerusalem" suggests that something is not right. David staying in Jerusalem is incongruent with the behavior one might expect, given the information in the first portion of the verse:

- David, the mighty warrior from his youth (e.g., 1 Sam. 17), who previously led multiple successful military campaigns including the conquering of Jebus (Jerusalem), sends Joab to fight his battle while he remains in Jerusalem.
- Other Israelites sacrifice themselves on behalf of the king. "All of Israel" goes to battle against the Ammonites, but David remains in Jerusalem.
- The Israelites ravage the Ammonite city of Rabbah—but David remains in the peaceful city of Jerusalem.

Concerning David lingering in Jerusalem, Meir Sternberg states, "The dynamic norm foregrounds the static exception; the phrase that speaks of kings going to war turns a spotlight on the king who 'is sitting' at home."[5] The incongruity between what readers expect King David to be doing and the fact that he is lying on his bed prompts readers to ask, "What is David doing in Jerusalem?" This is precisely the question that the narrator provokes by contrasting David with others who go out to battle.

King David's Privilege

While Israel is out in battle, the great warrior David is reclining on his bed in the late afternoon (2 Sam. 11:2). It is ironic that David made his name fighting battles, yet his success and prosperity leads to complacency. Now other people fight David's battles for him.[6] This is also ironic since the people of Israel so desired a king who would go out and fight their battles for them (1 Sam. 8:19). Now that Israel needs their warrior king to be in battle, he is at home, reclining on his bed. David leaves the bed to take a midafternoon stroll around the rooftop. From there, he notices an unidentified, beautiful woman bathing.

Exactly what the woman is doing when David observes her "bathing" is never fully explained. Contemporary readers must refrain from importing modern perceptions of "bathing" as "taking a shower" under a showerhead or "taking a bath" in a pool of water, wearing no clothes. It is unlikely that King David is looking at Bathsheba nude or that she is committing any type of provocative act while bathing. Bathsheba is likely partially clothed and

---

5. Sternberg, *Poetics of Biblical Narrative*, 195.
6. Good, *Irony in the Old Testament*, 36.

washing, or even rinsing, a particular part of her body.[7] This image best coincides with the fact that Jerusalem during the time of King David did not boast a contemporary plumbing system. Since David was elevated on his roof, he perhaps could not help but notice her. Yet he does not turn away, affording her privacy. On the contrary, he chooses to use his elevated position of privilege, represented by him standing on the roof of the king's residence, to covet and subsequently prey on this woman.

King David still does not know this woman's name.

Next, he openly probes into the woman's identity. An unnamed respondent answers David's inquiry, seemingly in the form of a rhetorical question: "Is not this Bathsheba, the daughter of Eliam, the wife of Uriah the Hittite?" (2 Sam. 11:3 ESV). The woman's name is Bathsheba, and there are two important components to her identity: (1) She is the daughter of Eliam. Eliam is one of David's thirty special warriors and is the son of Ahithophel, David's counselor (23:34; see also 15:12). (2) Bathsheba is the wife of Uriah the Hittite. He is also one of David's special troops (23:23–24).

Perhaps the identification of Bathsheba comes in the form of a question because David was expected to know the answer to his own inquiry. David *should* have been familiar with the names of the people referred to in the answer. David *should* have considered the potentially devastating implications of further engagement with Bathsheba—the granddaughter of his counselor, Ahithophel, the daughter of one of his special-forces officers, Eliam, and the wife of Uriah the Hittite, his soldier and neighbor. David *should* have been acquainted with and *should* have cared about these people.

David does not care.

David's responds to the rhetorical question by coldly and quickly proceeding toward his desired goal of laying hold of Bathsheba.

King David's Power

King David's abuse of royal power is fully on display when he sends multiple messengers to "get" Bathsheba and bring her to his residence. This is the *only* reason Bathsheba comes to the royal residence. David commits adultery with Bathsheba while she is compelled to be with him. She is forced into this situation by the man with the most power and privilege in all of Israel (2 Sam. 11:4).

Immediately after David's iniquitous act, the narrator provides a concise detail indicating that Bathsheba has been cleansing herself from her impurity (2 Sam. 11:4). This seemingly random note is another example of

---

7. The direct object of the verb "to wash" (*rḥṣ*) is missing in 2 Sam. 11:2, and therefore it is difficult to pinpoint exactly what Bathsheba was doing. See more below.

the omniscient narrator providing specific details in order to communicate information to us that may not have been known to the characters in the narrative. The fact that Bathsheba has been cleansing herself from her impurity refers to purification rituals after the menstrual cycle (Lev. 15:19, 28; 18:19). Evidently, Bathsheba has just undergone the seven-day period of uncleanliness after the menstrual cycle prior to David lying with her. Therefore, when Bathsheba reports that she is indeed pregnant (2 Sam. 11:5), only one conclusion is possible: David is the father of the child. Meir Sternberg states, "This detail, ostensibly so pointless in context, enables the reader to infer and nail down David's paternity."[8]

David uses his privilege and power to seize Bathsheba and abuse her. Bathsheba's pregnancy is unmistakable evidence of David's horrid actions. David promptly concocts a cover-up plan. David begins masquerading, attempting to bury his transgression by committing further transgression.

King David's Masquerade

Committing adultery with a married woman was punishable by the death penalty in ancient Israel (Lev. 20:10; Deut. 22:22). This societal custom predates the Torah and transcends the borders of Israel. For example, Genesis records a situation in which God was on the verge of killing Abimelech, king of Gerar, for unknowingly taking Abraham's wife, Sarah (Gen. 20:1–7). The Laws of Hammurabi suggests that ancient Israel was right at home in the world of the ancient Near East with such strict laws relating to adultery: "If a man's wife should be seized lying with another male, they shall bind them and cast them into the water."[9] Considering this backdrop, David has committed an act that would be considered reprehensible by the people of Israel *and* the nations around them.

David is forced to cover up his tracks to avoid the repercussions of adultery. Though David is guilty of employing terribly unsound reasoning so far in the narrative, his concealment plan is completely logical: if he can only get Uriah the Hittite to have relations with his wife, then everyone, including Uriah, will think that Uriah is the father of Bathsheba's child.

David sends for Uriah from the battlefront. When he arrives, David masquerades as a concerned king. His interactions with Uriah are banal considering the raging battle with the Ammonites: "When Uriah came to him, David asked how Joab was, how the soldiers were and how the war was going" (2 Sam. 11:7). One might appropriately question calling a special-forces soldier off

---

8. Sternberg, *Poetics of Biblical Narrative*, 198.
9. The Laws of Hammurabi 129, quoted from Roth, *Law Collections*, 105.

the battlefield to ask such commonplace questions that any other messenger might be able to communicate (11:19–25). Summoning Uriah makes no sense unless his presence in Jerusalem is necessary to conceal a grave scandal. Only David and the readers know that this is exactly the situation.

After David and Uriah's brief conversation, the king sends Uriah to his house to "wash [his] feet" (2 Sam. 11:8). The narrator judiciously provides this detail to clarify the scene in which David initially observes Bathsheba. The word "to wash" (*rḥṣ*) that the narrator uses to depict Bathsheba bathing in verse 2 is the same word that David uses to command Uriah to wash his feet in verse 8. It appears as if the narrator is letting readers know that Bathsheba was participating in an activity as normal as washing her feet when David began preying on her.

Instead of going home to wash his feet, Uriah spoils David's plan, spending the night alongside the king's servants (2 Sam. 11:8–10). The fact that Uriah is a special-forces soldier who evidently possesses unique physical strength and mental discipline forces the king to masquerade again, this time as a leader who is concerned about his soldier. David asks: "Haven't you just come from a military campaign? Why didn't you go home?" (11:10). Readers now become privy to the only words of Uriah that appear in the Bible: "The ark and Israel and Judah are staying in tents, and my commander Joab and my lord's men are camped in the open country. How could I go to my house to eat and drink and make love to my wife? As surely as you live, I will not do such a thing!" (11:11).

Through Uriah's few words, readers perceive that Uriah is drastically different from David, the king of Israel. In his terse statement, Uriah unknowingly makes several ironic points.

- Uriah demonstrates concern for the people of Israel and Judah, for Joab, and for his fellow soldiers. King David portrays concern only for himself.
- Uriah is out fighting Israel's battle. The people of Israel wanted a king so that he could lead them in battle (1 Sam. 8:19–20). Yet David the king is at home, misusing his power against his own people.
- Uriah does not consider it right to eat, drink, and lie with his wife when his Israelite companions are out in battle. Yet while he was away at war, the warrior-king David was at home, preying on and lying with Uriah's wife.[10]

Uriah's words initiate cover-up plan B, since there is no way for David to conceal his transgression unless Uriah returns home. Therefore, David holds

---

10. See Berlin, *Poetics and Interpretation*, 40, for further points of contrast between David and Uriah.

Uriah back in Jerusalem for another day. David's plan, once again, is wicked, but it is simple and logical: if he can lower Uriah's inhibitions with alcohol so that the discipline exhibited on the previous night might dissipate, then perhaps Uriah will return to his wife. The narrator promptly reports that David "made him drunk" on that night and, just as promptly, states that Uriah slept among the king's servants once again (2 Sam. 11:13). The irony is biting: Uriah restrains his natural yearnings for the sake of Israel's battle, while David, king of Israel, has no restraint over his misplaced desires and should be out fighting.

Uriah has publicly rejected the king's offer of temporary refuge in the comfort of his home. All will know that he is not the father of Bathsheba's child. Furthermore, those close to King David (e.g., those who know of David inquiring of Bathsheba's identity) will suspect that the child is his. Public knowledge of David violating the Torah by committing adultery and fathering a child with the wife of one of his mighty soldiers would be devastating for David's image, popular appeal, and personal relationships (e.g., those with his other wives and his counselor, Ahithophel). Unwittingly, Uriah is unwilling to play along with David's plan A or plan B, leaving only one arrangement that will validate David as the father of Bathsheba's child: David needs to take Bathsheba as a "legitimate" wife. This can only happen if Uriah dies.

David's next facade is that of "incompetent" commander in chief of the Israelite army. Ironically, David is actually a first-rate military commander. Yet this time around, he poses as the leader of the army with instructions that precipitate the demise of his own troops. David concocts a wicked, murderous plan to kill Uriah and to make it appear as a military offensive gone awry. He sends a letter to Joab with these plans by the hand of the man he plans to murder, Uriah the Hittite (2 Sam. 11:14–17).

David implicates Joab in his wrongdoing by providing him military orders that will ensure Uriah's death in battle. Joab implements these orders, and Uriah tragically dies along with other innocent Israelite soldiers in the ensuing combat with the Ammonites. The way David's orders are carried out leads to such terrible results that Joab expects the king to react harshly upon hearing them. Having seemingly deciphered David's goal, Joab strives to strategically disclose in the message that the military defeat accomplished the death of Uriah. Joab instructs the messenger to report the news of the battle, wait for the king to become angry, and then tell David that Uriah is dead. The servant avoids the king's anger by simply cutting to the chase and explicitly stating the most crucial piece of information: "Uriah the Hittite is dead" (2 Sam. 11:24; see also 11:17–23). By the way the messenger communicates Joab's words, we perceive that perhaps even Joab's envoy knows exactly what the king is trying to accomplish.

David is not finished masquerading. His final charade in this narrative is to pose as a benevolent king. Upon the death of Uriah, David once again sends for Bathsheba. This time, however, David takes Bathsheba as a "legitimate" wife (2 Sam. 11:26–27). From the outside looking in, it *appears* as if the compassionate king has consoled the mourning widow of one of his mighty soldiers. To those uninformed of the situation, it *appears* as though David truly loves Bathsheba, and she promptly conceives a child. Bringing Bathsheba into the royal residence *appears* to be an extraordinarily pious move by the king.

But readers know that things aren't always what they *appear* to be.

David Uncovered

The Narrator's Condemnation

The biblical narrator is omniscient but not omni-communicative. At times, the narrator indicates what transpires in characters' minds and hearts. On other occasions, the narrator leaves much of the characters' thoughts and sentiments ambiguous. In the narrative of 2 Samuel 11, the inner lives of the characters are almost entirely hidden from us; the narrator simply communicates one fact after another. Telling the story like this essentially makes the narrator invisible. Therefore, it is shocking and impactful when the narrator interjects with a condemnation of David's actions at the end of the narrative (11:27).

Knowing that the murder of Uriah has been carried out, David commands Joab's messenger to encourage him to not dwell on the setback. "David told the messenger, 'Don't let this upset you [lit., "may the 'thing' not be evil in your eyes"]; the sword devours one as well as another. Press the attack against the city and destroy it.' Say this to encourage Joab" (2 Sam. 11:25). David's words, which eerily portray the calloused heart of a man who has lost all sense of morality, present an opportunity for the narrator to step onto the stage from behind the curtain and assert the divine opinion of the situation. The narrator plays on David's words of encouragement to Joab to not let the "thing" displease him (lit., "may the 'thing' not be evil in your eyes"). As this section of the narrative concludes, the narrator essentially remarks, "Not so fast! David is not going to get away with this!": "The thing David had done displeased [lit., "was evil in the eyes of"] the LORD" (11:27).

While David says to Joab, "Hey, don't worry about that 'thing,'" the narrator tells the reader, "Oh, David better worry about that 'thing'!" Adele Berlin summarizes, "This [is] the narrator's conceptual point of view, the perspective of his attitude toward the story he is telling. He disapproves of David's actions, and by so phrasing his disapproval, he confirms that he is right and foreshadows the fact that they will not go unpunished."[11] This foreshadowing becomes fact when Nathan the prophet confronts David concerning his grave misdeeds.

Nathan's Parable

The scene of David, Bathsheba, and Nathan on the tapestry works for readers of *The Scarlet Letter* because it provokes the memory of a revered leader who bears a destructive secret that could destroy him if it is revealed. Readers know of the secret and continue to read, waiting for the moment in which the main character will be exposed. In the story featuring David and Bathsheba, that moment comes to pass when David is confronted with a parable by Nathan the prophet.

Nathan's story, featuring a rich man with many animals and a poor man with one lamb, is ludicrous. The poor man deeply loves his animal, raising it as if it were his child and even permitting it to drink from his own cup. When a traveler comes to visit the rich man, he unjustly steals the poor man's only animal, kills it, and prepares it as a meal instead of taking from his own multitude. In this outrageous scenario, the rich man behaves contrary to proper social customs in ancient Israel: the rich man is greedy, preys on the poor person, steals, and commits a grave injustice by killing the poor man's beloved companion. David recognizes this and is furious over the rich man's inhumane behavior. He declares that the rich man is worthy of death and commands that he pay back four times what he stole. Nathan then confronts the murderous king, proclaiming a denunciation that will change David's life: "You are the man!" (2 Sam. 12:7).

Nathan's parable is a bit of a riddle—not to David but to contemporary readers. Intuitively, we understand the rich man to be David. He indeed is the wealthy, abusive, covetous predator who stole from a person more vulnerable than himself. Some interpreters then assume that the poor man represents Uriah. However, Bathsheba is the character who survives injustice while her life companion is stolen from her and murdered. Nathan communicates the grave maltreatment that David has carried out against Bathsheba through this parable. In a fit of egocentricity and covetous desire, David has divested her of the object of her affections.

Readers do not know what to expect when Nathan confronts David with his awful sin. Considering this story in the context of recent events and the

11. Berlin, *Poetics and Interpretation*, 47.

reign of Saul, readers are justified in asking, Will David act as the murderous king once again? Will he strive to cover up his misdeeds and protect his image like he and Saul have already done? Will David make excuses and blame others for his actions like his predecessor Saul did when he was challenged for his transgressions? We feel legitimate tension after reading Nathan's parable. Fully aware of David's conduct during the ordeal with Bathsheba and Uriah, we are not sure how far David will go to camouflage his image and masquerade as a pious king.

David in Light of Saul

David's answer to rebuke is different from Saul's in every way. There is no religious twist. There is no blaming anyone else. David immediately confesses his sin. He is truly broken and willing to admit, "I have sinned against the LORD!" (2 Sam. 12:13). After an extended period of deception, living one lie after another, David is ready to establish a crucial part of his legacy. The legacy of repentance.

Through David's brokenness and confession before Nathan, readers are shown how to authentically repent. David's admission of sin, void of any pretexts or blaming, leaves a legacy for readers that arguably transcends his other accomplishments. Many readers of the biblical text throughout history could never have related to David as a king, a warrior, or even a shepherd. However, all readers sense affinity with David when he admits that he has sinned before the Lord.

David's example of repentance is accompanied by his ability to express his contrition through psalms. King David is remembered as a psalmist by the end of his life:

These are the last words of David:

> "The inspired utterance of David son of Jesse,
>   the utterance of the man exalted by the Most High,
> the man anointed by the God of Jacob,
>   the hero of Israel's songs." (2 Sam. 23:1)

As David is in his last stage of life, he is referred to as "anointed" but not as "king." More significant than earthly royalty, his legacy provides us with an example of vulnerability before God.

David's legacy develops, in part, because of his ordeal with Bathsheba. The words of Psalm 51 are traditionally ascribed to David reflecting on this situation. In these words, we can observe the type of repentance he demonstrates after Nathan's rebuke:

> For I know my transgressions,
>   and my sin is always before me.
> Against you, you only, have I sinned
>   and done what is evil in your sight. (Ps. 51:3–4)

Whereas David's repentance is instrumental in his becoming the renowned psalmist of Israel, Saul never truly repents. By the end of the narrative in 1 Samuel 11–12, readers observe the stark contrast between King David, the everlasting king whose songs are used in worship to the present day, and Saul, the temporary king whose epic downfall is his legacy.

King David's Collateral Damage

David's repentance does not eliminate the real-life consequences of his terrible misdeeds. To suggest this would be to ignore the continuation of the narrative and would be an affront to Bathsheba, David's victim. There are serious repercussions for David and for those close to him, just as God communicates through Nathan the prophet: "Out of your own household I am going to bring calamity on you. Before your very eyes I will take your wives and give them to one who is close to you, and he will sleep with your wives in broad daylight" (2 Sam. 12:11). As anticipated, David's personal life becomes quite chaotic in many ways:

- David and Bathsheba's first child dies (12:15–25).
- David's son Amnon rapes David's daughter Tamar (2 Sam. 13). This incident recalls David's own violent passions and unruly and abusive behavior to get what he wants.
- David's son Absalom eventually has Amnon murdered for raping Tamar (13:22, 28–29). Like David, Absalom resorts to murder to resolve a situation.
- Absalom rebels against David, taking his wives. In this act, the Lord's word through the prophet Nathan is fulfilled with precision (16:22).
- Ahithophel, one of David's counselors and a relative of Bathsheba, joins Absalom's rebellion and eventually commits suicide upon realizing that Absalom rejected his advice (15:12; 16:20; 17:1, 14, 23).
- Absalom is eventually put to death because of his rebellion (18:15).

This list shows some of the serious ramifications for David's misconduct. These notorious events happen after David's sins recorded in 2 Samuel 11–12, and the people involved are all somehow connected to David. It appears as if King David is no longer able to manage his household after his misdeeds with Bathsheba. Be that as it may, he admitted to his sin even though Nathan told him that there would be impending consequences upon him and his household. David's ability to admit his sin, knowing that there would be serious repercussions, is a sign that he was truly repentant before the Lord.

Postscript: Bathsheba's Comfort

David and Bathsheba eventually have another child, whom they name Solomon. Solomon is presented as being a comfort to Bathsheba. The Lord loves Solomon. The Lord tells Nathan to call the child Jedidiah, meaning "the beloved of the Lord" (2 Sam. 12:24–25).

Yet Solomon will also bring grave evil to the house of David (2 Sam. 12:11). In fact, Solomon's sin is so egregious that David's sin is not even mentioned in the context of the atrocities that Solomon commits. Solomon's infamous philandering with countless women ultimately leads him to apostasy.

To Solomon's divided allegiances we now turn our attention.

THIRTEEN

Divided Allegiances
to Divided Kingdom
The Tragedy of King Solomon

It is the magician's bargain: give up our soul, get power in return. But once
our souls, that is, ourselves, have been given up, the power thus conferred
will not belong to us. We shall in fact be the slaves and puppets of that
to which we have given our souls.

—C. S. Lewis, *The Abolition of Man*

Toward the beginning of J. R. R. Tolkien's *The Hobbit*, the dwarves fall into
the hands of three trolls—Tom, William, and Bert—as they travel toward
Erebor. These trolls are fed up with eating mutton and are intent on making
a fine meal out of the dwarves. In a characteristically polemic manner, they
argue about whether they should consume the dwarves roasted, boiled, or
jellied. After much discussion, the numbskull trolls decide to roast the dwarves
and eat them later.

Then, out of nowhere, someone contradicts their resolution: "No good
roasting 'em now. It'd take all night."

Not knowing where the voice had come from, William and Bert begin
squabbling over who was being argumentative. After a brief spat, they turn
their attention back to their meal and conclude that it would be best to mince
and boil the dwarves.

Then, for a second time, a voice counters their most recent decision: "No good boiling 'em."

Having just bickered with one another over the previous remark, Bert and William now assume that Tom is the one interjecting commentary. Tom and William get into a fierce argument, which concludes in no definitive judgment about who is dissenting. Rather, the trolls stop arguing when they decide to eat squashed dwarves this time around and boil them on the next occasion.

Then, someone asks, "Who shall we sit on first?"

After they agree to sit first on the last dwarf they caught, another feud breaks out over the color of the last-caught dwarf's socks. Bert claims they are yellow, but a voice sounding like William's says they are gray. William then confirms that the socks are yellow but is reprimanded by Bert for saying they are gray, a claim he fervently denies.

At this moment, the sun begins to rise, and William, Tom, and Bert forthwith turn into stone. Trolls, readers are told, cannot be exposed to the daylight. Once the trolls are immovable rock, Gandalf the wizard emerges from behind a tree for all to recognize that it was he who remarked on the trolls' conversation in order to instigate quarrels among them.[1] Gandalf's antagonistic comments caricature the polemical tendencies of the trolls and give clues to the reader that the dwarves might be rescued.

Interposed comments that appear incongruent with the course of a story cause us to ponder where the narrative is going. In 1 Kings, the narrator begins telling the story of Solomon in a way that paints him in a positive light. Solomon demonstrates the character and strength required to battle adversity to his kingship (1 Kings 1–2); Solomon desires the wisdom of the Lord more than anything else (1 Kings 3:1–15); Solomon has the privilege of dedicating the first temple of the Lord in Jerusalem (1 Kings 8). Yet just like Gandalf, the narrator occasionally interjects brief comments that are incongruent with the apparent trajectory of the narrative. These comments let the reader know of Solomon's divided allegiances, foreshadowing his eventual downward turn and hinting at the day Israel will be fractured. In this chapter, we will discuss how the biblical narrator portends King Solomon's eventual apostasy by providing subtle clues for us in the preceding narrative.

The Destination of a Divided Kingdom

Jesus once said, "If a kingdom is divided against itself, that kingdom cannot stand" (Mark 3:24; cf. Matt. 12:25). Jesus uses a metaphor, arguing that

---

1. Summary and quotations are from Tolkien, *Hobbit*, 36–38.

a group of demons cannot accomplish their collective goals if they destroy one another, any more than a kingdom can thrive if there is internal strife. Jesus, as the master teacher, uses metaphors that his hearers would have understood—things to which they can relate in real life. Solomon's narrative in 1 Kings, when read in conjunction with the other sections of the Old Testament depicting the peoples of Israel and Judah until their respective exiles, plainly demonstrates that Jesus's metaphor is grounded in reality. Once the kingdom of Israel is divided against itself, it becomes destined for downfall. For Israel and Judah, their dissolution ultimately leads to their departure from the land of their inheritance.

The pathway toward the division of the kingdom and, consequently, the exile of the people from the land begins during the reign of King Solomon. This is ironic, since Solomon seems instrumental in unifying Israel. For example, Solomon appears to be, at least in part, responsible for centralizing the cultic activity of ancient Israel in Jerusalem by building and inaugurating the temple (1 Kings 8; see also 2 Sam. 7:12–16). The time during which the temple is dedicated in Jerusalem and the ark is transferred into the house of God is a pinnacle moment in Israel's history. During these events, Solomon blesses the Lord in the presence of all the people. Solomon's prayer, dedication of the temple, and benediction are unmatched in terms of their theology and beauty. Solomon's allegiance to and love for the Lord is seemingly demonstrated through the sacrificing of upward of 142,000 animals on the day of the dedication (1 Kings 8:22–64). On this day, the people of Israel appear united as they worship the Lord together in Jerusalem.

Solomon's Wise Request

Additionally, the account of Solomon's eventual downfall might come as a shock because of the personal care and attention the Lord demonstrates to Solomon by appearing to him twice. The first occasion on which the Lord appears to Solomon is toward the beginning of his reign, at Gibeon (1 Kings 3:5–15). Solomon beholds the Lord in a dream in which God promises to provide Solomon whatever he might ask. The young king reflects on God's goodness to his father David and recognizes his own tremendous responsibility to lead the people. Consequently, Solomon's request consists of one thing: a "listening heart." "So give your servant a discerning heart [lit., "listening heart"] to govern your people and to distinguish between right and wrong. For who is able to govern this great people of yours?" (3:9). Solomon is concerned about remaining teachable, developing understanding, and governing well. This humble answer pleases the Lord, who in turn bestows on Solomon riches and honor for which Solomon did not petition, in addition to the wise and discerning heart he so desired.

At the end of Solomon's dream, the Lord promises to lengthen the days of Solomon's life if he walks in the Lord's ways, which would be evidenced by keeping the Lord's laws and commands just like his father David did (1 Kings 3:14). When Solomon awakens, he praises the Lord. He immediately presents himself before the ark of the covenant, offers various types of offerings, and celebrates the occasion with his servants. At this point, Solomon appears to be a young, teachable leader who reveres the Lord and understands the weightiness of his responsibility to serve the people of Israel well (3:12–15).

Solomon's Prayers Are Received

The second time the Lord appears to Solomon is just after the dedication of the temple in Jerusalem (1 Kings 8:22–66). The Lord hears the prayers Solomon offers during the convocation and assures Solomon that divine favor and attention will perpetually be upon the place he has consecrated (9:3). The Lord then turns his attention from Solomon's building project to Solomon the man and imparts a conditional promise, similar to the one at Gibeon (see 3:14). This time, the Lord emphasizes that Solomon's personal obedience will be instrumental in leading to the establishment of the Davidic throne over all of Israel forever: "As for you, if you walk before me faithfully with integrity of heart and uprightness, as David your father did, and do all I command and observe my decrees and laws, I will establish your royal throne over Israel forever, as I promised David your father when I said, 'You shall never fail to have a successor on the throne of Israel'" (9:4–5).

God's conditional promise has at least two significant implications. First, God expects Solomon to have a heart like his father David had. This heart will produce the type of obedience to God's word necessary to lead the people of Israel for an extended period of time (see more on Solomon versus David below). Second, the Lord assures Solomon that his throne will be established over all Israel forever *only* if Solomon walks with the Lord like David did. By mentioning Israel, God specifies the promise that he made to David and indicates that someone from the Davidic line will reign over all the tribes if Solomon is obedient (1 Kings 6:12).

There is a flipside to the conditional promises that the Lord makes to Solomon. If Solomon turns away from the Lord and leads Israel to other gods, thus failing to provide an example to the people, the Lord guarantees that all of the people will eventually suffer the consequences. The people will be exiled, and the temple will be destroyed: "But if you [plural] or your descendants turn away from me and do not observe the commands and decrees I have given you [plural] and go off to serve other gods and worship them, then I will cut off Israel from the land I have given them and will reject this temple I have consecrated for my Name. Israel will then become a byword and an object of ridicule among all peoples. This temple will become a heap of rubble. All who pass by will be appalled and will scoff and say, 'Why has the LORD done such a thing to this land and to this temple?'" (1 Kings 9:6–8).

Solomon is undoubtedly presented with a unique opportunity to lead the people in a way that will ensure the Lord's tangible presence within Israel. Solomon is to set a precedent of obedience for the people of Israel, who were also implicated in the Lord's conditional promises by God speaking to Solomon in the plural. A lot is on the line for Israel and its king: Will Solomon maintain undivided allegiance to the Lord, providing an example to Israel and facilitating religious and national solidarity? Or will Solomon's allegiances grow divided and drive his people to apostasy, national insecurity, and ultimately exile?

Solomon's immediate response to the Lord's second appearance is silence. Whereas Solomon responds to the Lord in worship after the first encounter with God (1 Kings 3:15), the narrator records no such reaction to the second appearance.

Perhaps this silence is a faint whisper of things yet to come.

Solomon Strays

At some point along the course, Solomon's allegiance to the Lord wanes, and he strays from the pathway set out for him by the Lord. As Solomon's commitment to the Lord weakens, he loses the ability to rule and reign with understanding. Solomon then leads Israel into syncretism and ultimately outright apostasy, which culminates in the division of Israel and the exile of the people from the land. Within a few chapters, Solomon metamorphoses from unifier and worship leader at the dedication of the temple in Jerusalem (1 Kings 8) to apostate and a major cause of Israel's division and ultimate exile (1 Kings 11).

So, what happened?

A perfunctory reading of 1 Kings 1–10 sets us up for shell shock when we arrive at the condemning statements of 1 Kings 11. However, if we pay close attention to the narrator's voice, we will observe subtle clues during the stories of Solomon's "good old days" that foretell his eventual downfall. The narrator whispers information from behind the curtain, pointing to concerning developments in the evolving drama of Solomon's life.

Foreshadowing Solomon's Fall

The narrator discloses Solomon's trajectory toward estrangement from the Lord prior to the fateful denunciation of his collapse by interspersing commentary on his actions throughout the earlier sections of his narrative. These comments tend to be in passing, thrown in as if they were simply additional information for the reader. In reality, the narrator's addition of "incidental" details, understood in light of the Torah's requirements for a king, clearly foreshadow the impending catastrophe.

Toward the end of the Torah, the Lord knows that the people of Israel will soon petition for a king to rule over them like other nations (1 Sam. 8). Therefore, God provides Israel with guidelines that will hold a king accountable for his conduct. The Lord commands through Moses that the king "must not acquire great numbers of horses for himself or make the people return to Egypt to get more of them, for the LORD has told you, 'You are not to go back that way again.' He must not take many wives, or his heart will be led astray. He must not accumulate large amounts of silver and gold" (Deut. 17:16–17). The Torah explicitly forbids the future king of Israel from (1) accumulating horses, (2) having Israelites return to Egypt to acquire horses, (3) collecting excessive silver or gold for himself, and (4) acquiring many wives.

Solomon violates every one of these commands.

This is how the narrator tips readers off from the beginning of the narrative.

Solomon's Love of Horses

Since Solomon humbly petitions for a discerning heart to rule the people instead of requesting worldly possessions, the Lord promises to bless him with great riches. It is, therefore, expected that the narrator will, at some point, detail the tremendous blessings that the Lord provides Solomon. This is precisely what the narrator does in 1 Kings 4:20–34 and 10:14–29. In these sections, the narrator speaks of the abundance of provision there was in Israel, Solomon's bountiful wealth, the expansive kingdom that developed under his reign, and his profound wisdom, among other topics.

These lists of blessings recounted by the narrator mention Solomon's horse collection, as in the following example about the striking quantity of horses owned by the king: "Solomon had four thousand stalls for chariot horses, and twelve thousand horses" (1 Kings 4:26).[2] Read quickly, this might seem like

2. The Masoretic Text of 1 Kings 4:26 clearly indicates that Solomon has forty thousand stalls of horses. This number of horses is reflected in some modern Bible translations (e.g., the ESV and NASB). However, forty thousand stalls of horses seems to be a lot relative to the

just another item in the tabulation of King Solomon's affluence. However, by slowing down and reading with the divinely appointed restrictions from the Torah in mind, readers recall that the king was not supposed to collect horses (Deut. 17:16).

One could suggest that the abundance of horses numbered in 1 Kings 4:26 might simply be another manifestation of the Lord's promised abundance. However, by reading successively, readers observe that the narrator provides a subtle and ingenious commentary on Solomon's actions when horses are mentioned once again. Important data that was previously missing is cleverly inserted by the narrator in 1 Kings 10:28–29: "Solomon's horses were imported from Egypt. . . . They imported a chariot from Egypt for six hundred shekels of silver, and a horse for a hundred and fifty. They also exported them to all the kings of the Hittites and of the Arameans" (see also 2 Chron. 1:16). Not only does the king acquire horses, but he purchases them from Egypt, which is explicitly prohibited by the Torah; not only does Solomon acquire horses from Egypt, but he sends traders to function as middlemen to export horses from Egypt to other kingdoms.

These seemingly minor comments are totally incriminating. The narrator communicates all of these really good things Solomon has, while simultaneously whispering in the reader's ear: "Are all of those horses *really* necessary?" "Hey, Solomon acquired his horses from Egypt. He also sent Israelites down to Egypt." "Hey reader, keep reading. Solomon will be held accountable."

Solomon's Love of Bling

Riches seem to be the last thing on Solomon's mind when the Lord first appears to him. Yet as noted, the Lord provides Solomon with an abundance of wealth. What is unexpected and should alarm readers is how he uses his resources. By relating specific details about how Solomon uses his abundance of riches, the narrator hints at the king becoming enamored with opulence to the point where it distracts him from using his God-given wisdom.

Four hundred and eighty years after the people of Israel came out of Egypt, Solomon finally has the opportunity to build a permanent temple for the Lord. Solomon appears to exert serious effort in constructing this place of worship.

---

twelve thousand horsemen. The parallel passage in 2 Chron. 9:25 indicates that Solomon has four thousand stalls. The difference between four thousand and forty thousand in Hebrew is contingent upon the addition or subtraction of two letters at the end of the Hebrew word for "four." Whether Solomon had four or forty thousand stalls of horses, the point still stands: Solomon accumulates horses, which is something that is forbidden in the Torah. For other, similar passages relating to Solomon's vast collection of horse stalls, chariots, and horsemen, see 1 Kings 10:26; 2 Chron. 1:14, 16; 9:25, 28.

He imports cedar from Lebanon and uses that to build the walls, ceiling, and other parts of the temple. He then overlays the inner sanctuary, where the ark of the Lord dwells, with gold. Solomon is also responsible for crafting the essential components of temple worship such as the golden altar, the golden table for the bread of the presence, the cherubim, the lampstands, and many other elaborate decorations within the complex. After journeying in the wilderness, fighting off their enemies in Canaan, and worshiping for so many years in a movable tent, the people of Israel finally have an enduring temple for the Lord in their promised land. The elaborate temple-building process takes upward of seven years to complete (1 Kings 5:1–12; 6:1–10, 14–38).

Naturally, this magnificent temple needed other furnishings inside and out, as well as vessels so that the cultic activity could be carried out in the complex. The fashioning of these important items is detailed by the narrator in 1 Kings 7:13–51. However, just after mentioning that the temple took seven years to build (6:38), and just before proceeding to detail the crafting of the rest of the items that were fashioned for temple worship (7:13–51), the narrator inserts a subtle comment that gives us insight into where Solomon's priorities really lie: "It took Solomon thirteen years, however, to complete the construction of his palace" (7:1). The narrator could have recounted the building of Solomon's personal residence elsewhere. But it suits the narrator's literary and theological purposes to place the fact that Solomon spends seven years constructing the house of the Lord next to the fact that he spends thirteen years (almost twice as long!) building his own house. This juxtaposition makes us wonder about Solomon's primary concerns as king.

Lest readers conclude that Solomon simply worked more slowly on his own residence, the narrator immediately explains that the royal residence, with all its component parts (i.e., the Palace of the Forest of Lebanon, the Hall of Justice, a palace for Pharaoh's daughter; 1 Kings 7:2–8), is significantly larger than the temple complex (compare 6:2 with 7:2). Solomon is not at all frugal with the materials he uses to build his housing complex, which consists of valuable stones (7:9–12). Perhaps one of the most impressive items that Solomon fashions for himself is a great ivory throne overlaid with gold and accompanied by a dozen decorative lions on six steps leading up to it (10:18–20). Solomon is invested in building the house of the Lord in Jerusalem to a certain extent, but by outlining the ostentatious way he spends his wealth on his own residence, the narrator puts the king's divided heart on display for readers.

The fact that "the king made silver as common in Jerusalem as stones, and cedar as plentiful as sycamore-fig trees in the foothills" (1 Kings 10:27; see also 2 Chron. 1:15, "silver and gold"), demonstrates the fulfillment of the abundant blessings that the Lord bestowed on Solomon and Israel. Yet upon reading of the abundance of precious metals and cedar, readers cannot help but be reminded of how incongruent this is with the Deuteronomic warnings against the king accumulating silver and gold (Deut. 17:17).[3] The issue is not that Israel becomes a wealthy nation; the problem ends up being that King Solomon uses this wealth to serve himself more than the Lord. While he does this, the narrator whispers, "Look at what Solomon constructs with the wealth that God has provided him and Israel. Where do Solomon's priorities *really* lie in his use of the abundance of assets that Israel has been given by the Lord?" Listening to the narrator's whispers permits us to see a huge red flag during a time in which things seem to be going quite well for Solomon and for Israel.

Solomon's Love of Women

Nothing more notably foreshadows Solomon's fall from grace than his infamous love for women. Solomon notoriously "acquires" a myriad of women for himself from the peoples surrounding Israel. Taking women from other nations who did not worship the God of Israel was explicitly forbidden out of a concern that these women would import their foreign religion into Israel (Exod. 34:11–16). This, indeed, turns out to be the main cause of Solomon's tragic downfall (1 Kings 11:1–8).

Early on, the narrator also foreshadows Solomon's love of many women, particularly those who were not from the people of Israel and did not follow the God of Israel. As soon as it is reported that the kingdom of Israel is fully established under Solomon, the narrator interpolates a peculiar comment into the story: "Solomon made an alliance with Pharaoh king of Egypt and married his daughter. He brought her to the City of David until he finished building his palace and the temple of the LORD, and the wall around Jerusalem" (1 Kings 3:1). The fact that Solomon, for political purposes, marries an Egyptian woman who is not identified as a follower of the Lord is problematic (Deut. 7:4). Nevertheless, the narrator's remark is sandwiched between two very good events in Solomon's life—the consolidation of the kingdom under his rule (1 Kings 1–2) and the Lord's first appearance to Solomon at Gibeon (3:14)—making the incongruity even more perceptible. Even though the story relates the events of a fortunate period of Solomon's life, the narrator whispers, "Is this marriage *really* a good idea given that Israel has been repeatedly warned against intermarrying with other people groups that are

---

3. Compare David's handling of the silver and the gold that had been obtained from the nations that he subdued in 2 Sam. 8:8–12.

not worshipers of the Lord? Is Solomon opening up his heart to be led astray this early in his reign?"

Solomon's Egyptian wife makes two more important cameos throughout the narrative. As the narrator retells how much time Solomon spends building his personal residence and the adjacent buildings, the narrator slips in the fact that "Solomon also made a palace like this hall [i.e., the Hall of Justice] for Pharaoh's daughter, whom he had married" (1 Kings 7:8). So one of the reasons Solomon spends more time on buildings connected to his residence than he does on the temple is that he is building his Egyptian wife's house.

How can we be so sure that marrying the Pharaoh's daughter was a bad idea? After all, the first two times she is mentioned, the narrator does not explicitly indicate that she imported the worship of foreign gods. Also, international relations with neighboring kingdoms have always been an important aspect of governing a people group well. Be that as it may, the next appearance of Solomon's Egyptian wife is particularly important to understanding the previous foreshadowing. The narrator conveys the full gravity of the situation in 1 Kings 11:1–2: "King Solomon, however, loved many foreign women besides Pharaoh's daughter—Moabites, Ammonites, Edomites, Sidonians and Hittites. They were from nations about which the LORD had told the Israelites, 'You must not intermarry with them, because they will surely turn your hearts after their gods.' Nevertheless, Solomon held fast to them in love."

At this point, readers comprehend that Solomon's Egyptian wife represents the type of domestic life that Solomon has been living. He has been collecting wives from several different people groups that do not worship the Lord. The Egyptian wife is one of the group of wives who introduces the abominable gods of the neighboring nations into Israel. Solomon is ultimately culpable for his heart being turned away from the Lord, having married seven hundred wives and taken in three hundred concubines (1 Kings 11:3; cf. Neh. 13:26). By specifically stating that Solomon's "wives turned his heart after other gods," (1 Kings 11:4) the narrator demonstrates that the Torah's warnings have been brought to fruition. The Lord previously instructed the people of Israel that their king "must not take many wives, or his heart will be led astray" (Deut. 17:17).

The account of Solomon's tragic downfall recorded in 1 Kings 11 is harsh but not surprising to those who have been tracking the narrator's hints that are ingeniously infused into the story relating his rise. Long before Solomon's heart turns away to the extent outlined in 1 Kings 11:1–8, it had already gradually become divided. The King Solomon we encounter toward the end of his reign is hardly recognizable when compared to the humble leader who petitioned God for wisdom to govern the people or the worshiper-king who dedicated the temple.

Solomon's Divided Heart

The fact that the Lord appears to Solomon twice to reiterate the promises made to David is particularly important to illustrate how far Solomon will stray and to clarify why the Lord becomes angry (1 Kings 11:9). The repeated mention of David in God's communication with Solomon suggests that readers are to understand Solomon's response to God in light of David's dedication to God (3:14; 6:12; 9:4–5). In fact, the narrator expressly compares them for readers throughout 1 Kings 11, which serves as a summary of the grave evil that Solomon eventually commits.

First, in 1 Kings 11:4 the narrator compares Solomon's heart, which is alienated from the Lord, to David's heart, which is wholly devoted to the Lord. Then, in 11:5 and 7 the narrator relates the dreadful account of Solomon worshiping foreign gods. Inserted between these two verses the narrator offers this incriminating denunciation: "So Solomon did evil in the eyes of the LORD; he did not follow the LORD completely, as David his father had done" (11:6).

The fact that Solomon did evil "in the eyes of the LORD" reminds readers of the assessment of David's grave sin with Bathsheba, which was "condemned in the eyes of the LORD" (this is a literal translation of 2 Sam. 11:27, which the NIV translates as "displeased the LORD"). In this manner, Solomon's downfall is presented in light of David's allegiance to the Lord despite David's grave sins—particularly the evil of violating Bathsheba. David's sin against Bathsheba was brought to light and condemned by the prophet Nathan, the narrator, and subsequently God. David repents of his grave misdeeds and subsequently suffers the ominous consequences for them (see chap. 12 above). David's repentance does not alleviate the ramifications for his horrendous behavior, but it does lead him to worship the Lord (2 Sam. 23:1; Ps. 51). Irrespective of how dark David's life grows as a result of the depth of his transgressions, he never resorts to worshiping the gods of the nations around Israel, even though there is no record of the Lord ever personally appearing to him.

Solomon's life, on the contrary, is void of the deceptive, adulterous, and murderous scandal in which David's is mired. Nevertheless, Solomon worships foreign gods even as he concludes his life, and there is no explicit indication in 1 Kings that he ever repents of this apostasy. Solomon ultimately rejects the listening heart and unique wisdom that God gave him (1 Kings 3:14) and inclines his heart toward idols.

The Lord takes special care to encourage Solomon in the direction that will ensure God's presence and blessing in his community. Yet Solomon does not heed the warning that is personally delivered by the Lord (1 Kings 9:6–9). Solomon knowingly and willingly rebuffs God and marries Moabite women whose deity is Chemosh, Ammonite women whose deity is Milcom, and Sidonian women whose deity is Ashtoreth, in addition to Hittite women, Edomite women, and at least one Egyptian woman. Solomon makes a high place for Chemosh and Molech on the mountain east of Jerusalem, which faces the temple that he has built for the Lord (1 Kings 11:7; cf. Exod. 20:3). Molech was traditionally associated with the sacrifice of children (see Lev. 18:21; 20:2–5; 2 Kings 23:10; Jer. 32:35). Readers are therefore justified in asking, "Did Solomon sacrifice the children he had with the wives who worshiped this god?" The simple fact that this question can be responsibly posed demonstrates how far Solomon has departed from the authentic worship of the Lord.

Reading 1 Kings 11:1–8 while considering the narrator's whispers throughout the beginning of Solomon's story shows us that Solomon ultimately endures the consequences of his own decisions. Solomon multiplies horses, amasses wealth, and marries many women. While he is busy getting what he thinks he wants, his divided heart leads to a divided allegiance to the Lord, which in turn leads to Solomon's and Israel's apostasy, resulting in tangible consequences for everyone. The residual effects of Solomon's apostasy impact the people of Israel forever.

Divided Allegiances Lead to a Divided Kingdom

Solomon's divided allegiances lead Israel to a breakdown in societal order and an irreparable rift between the northern tribes (Israel) and the southern tribes (Judah). Indeed, the Lord asserts that this will be one of the consequences of Solomon's grave sin: "I will most certainly tear the kingdom from you and give it to your servant" (1 Kings 11:11). However, since God has already promised David an everlasting house and kingdom (2 Sam. 7:16; 1 Chron. 17:3–15), a son of David will remain reigning over one tribe (1 Kings 11:13). After Solomon's death, these promises set up a scenario in which the people of Israel will necessarily be divided into two separate kingdoms.

The process of division begins with disruption of the peace of Israel from both inside and outside. At one point in his reign, Solomon is surrounded by peaceful neighbors (1 Kings 5:4). As a result of his estrangement from the Lord, that peace is broken, and adversaries arise that oppose him. Three main foes rise against Solomon during this time.

1. Hadad the Edomite: Solomon's father, David, previously stationed troops in Edom, subjecting the Edomites to Israelite control (2 Sam. 8:14). Evidently, David's army commander, Joab, stays in Edom and puts many people to death over the course of about six months (1 Kings 11:15–16). During this period when the Israelites subjugated them, many Edomites, including Hadad, escape to Egypt. Upon hearing that David and Joab have died, Hadad returns from Egypt to Edom and agitates Israel from the southeast (11:14–22, 25).

2. Rezon son of Eliada: The backstory to the rise of this adversary might be related to King David's defeat of Hadadezer of Zobah on his way to reestablish his rule all the way to the Euphrates (2 Sam. 8:3–4). At some point after David's victory and during Hadadezer's reign, Rezon establishes his own gang and relocates to Damascus, where he is recognized as king. In Damascus, he troubles Israel from the northeast of the country (1 Kings 11:23–25).

3. Jeroboam son of Nebat: The greatest threat to Israel's unity eventually comes from within. Jeroboam was once an associate of King Solomon, having been appointed by him to oversee the labor of the house of Jacob (e.g., Ephraim and Manasseh) in Jerusalem. One day as he leaves Jerusalem, he is accosted in a field by a prophet named Ahijah. Ahijah proceeds to rip Jeroboam's garments into twelve pieces (1 Kings 11:11, 30–39; cf. 1 Sam. 15:27–28) and prophesies that the Lord will give him ten tribes of Israel because of Solomon's idolatry. Upon hearing about Ahijah's encounter with Jeroboam, Solomon endeavors to kill Jeroboam because he threatens Solomon's kingship—just like Saul tried to kill David (1 Kings 11:40).

Toward the end of Solomon's life, the kingship is occupied by an unrepentant madman who would rather murder when threatened than admit wrongdoing and ask for forgiveness. The listening heart to rule the people for which he petitioned the Lord has become hardened as it turned to foreign gods. Upon Solomon's death, he has enemies in the northeast, southeast, and southwest. The peace afforded to the people of Israel earlier in his reign is now over. Solomon has positioned Israel to experience internal turmoil and external conflict after his death as they suffer the consequences of his sin.

Rehoboam's Division Decision

After Solomon dies, the people of Israel gather at Shechem to crown Solomon's son, Rehoboam, as their new king (1 Kings 12:1; cf. Josh. 24:1–28; Judg.

9:6). However, the prophet Ahijah already promised Jeroboam a portion of the kingdom. When Jeroboam hears of Solomon's death, he returns to Israel from exile in Egypt. He promptly brings an assembly of Israelites (i.e., northerners) to Rehoboam, petitioning him to lighten the hard work that Solomon imposed during his reign. The proposal is simple: either the king can serve his citizens in the ways his father had failed to serve them, learning from past mistakes and unifying the people, or the king can continue down the pathway leading to division by alienating his people and imposing on them hard work just like his father had (1 Kings 12:2–4).

Rehoboam is counseled by his father's senior advisers to tend to the people with more care so that they will in turn serve him. However, Rehoboam's cronies counsel otherwise, urging him to add to the citizens' burden and demonstrate his authority over their jurisdiction (1 Kings 12:3–10). Unfortunately, Rehoboam heeds the misguided counsel of his friends and decides to harshen his treatment of the northerners, worsening their situation even further than in the days of King Solomon. Jeroboam and those with him renounce any remaining allegiance to the house of David and retreat northward and to the Transjordanian areas of Israel while Rehoboam continues to reign over the southern area, Judah. Rehoboam consequently strives to kill those who threaten his sovereignty as king—just as Solomon did before him, and just as Saul did before him—but is prevented from causing this civil war by a word of the Lord that comes through Shemaiah, a man of God (1 Kings 12:11–24).

Thus the division of the kingdom of Israel is complete, and the word of the Lord that was spoken through Ahijah the prophet is fulfilled (1 Kings 12:15; see also 11:26–39). There are no "winners" in this dissolution. Judah is governed by the foolish king Rehoboam, while Jeroboam immediately leads Israel into apostasy. In doing so, Jeroboam ruins his opportunity for divine endorsement of him and his lineage. The rupture between the north and the south has generational consequences as the resultant kingdoms of Israel and Judah are weakened spiritually and militarily, which ultimately leads to their exiles.

Jeroboam's Apostasy

During their encounter outside of Jerusalem, Ahijah the prophet communicates to Jeroboam a conditional promise from the Lord, saying, "If you do whatever I command you . . . and do what is right in my eyes by obeying my decrees and commands, as David my servant did, I will be with you. I will build you a dynasty as enduring as the one I built for David and will give Israel to you" (1 Kings 11:38). If we take the Lord's promise at face value, it seems like he's giving Jeroboam an opportunity to establish a kingly line over Israel in addition to the Davidic kingdom that is preserved in Judah. Ahijah presents Jeroboam with the opportunity to rescue his people from their oppression and usher them into a kingdom in which the word of the Lord is followed. Jeroboam has a unique chance to build the legacy that Solomon surrendered when he turned his heart away from the Lord.

Sadly, Jeroboam leads Israel into apostasy. In a political maneuver to prevent the people of Israel from returning to the house of David (i.e., Rehoboam, king of Judah), Jeroboam makes two golden calves and sets them in northern sites, at Dan and Bethel. He then discourages the people of Israel from returning to Jerusalem to worship by stating familiar words: "Here are your gods, Israel, who brought you up out of Egypt" (1 Kings 12:28). Notice how eerily similar this phrase is to the alarming proclamation made by Aaron when he fashioned the golden calf: "These are your gods, Israel, who brought you up out of Egypt!" (Exod. 32:4).

Jeroboam creates a new, syncretistic religion in an effort to maintain power in the north by counterfeiting parts of the Lord's religious order. Jeroboam not only sets up altars at Bethel and Dan but also appoints non-Levites to be priests and creates a new feast, similar to the Feast of Tabernacles, that was not outlined in the Torah. Instead of Jeroboam's house being established by his following the Lord's commands like David did, Jeroboam maneuvers in order to protect his kingdom and, thereby, disobeys the word of the Lord and destroys the possibility of an enduring kingship (1 Kings 12:28–33).

Divided Allegiances Lead to Exile

The Lord warns the people of Israel of two major consequences that will come to pass if they turn aside and worship other gods: Israel will be exiled from the land, and the temple will be destroyed (1 Kings 9:7–8). As promised, both of these consequences come to pass in due time.

Israel's exile comes in two stages. First, the northern tribes, weakened by their division from Judah and compromised by their idol worship, fall prey to the Neo-Assyrian Empire in 722 BC. Jeroboam, the king who reigned after Solomon's estrangement from the Lord, sets a trajectory in the north that leads Israel into exile because of their idol worship. Jeroboam's idolatry is repeatedly referred to throughout 1 Kings (15:30; 16:2, 7, 19, 26, 31). Second Kings 17:21–23 summarizes the consequences: "When he [the Lord] tore Israel away from the house of David, they made Jeroboam son of Nebat their king. Jeroboam enticed Israel away from following the LORD and caused them to commit a great sin. The Israelites persisted in all the sins of Jeroboam and did not turn away from them until the Lord removed them from his presence, as he had warned through all his servants the prophets. So the people of Israel were taken from their homeland into exile in Assyria, and they are still there."

As religion in Judah grows increasingly corrupted, the glory of the Lord leaves the temple (Ezek. 10:18–19). This sets the stage for Judah to be exiled and for the temple to be destroyed by the Neo-Babylonian Empire in 586 BC. These events are summarized in 2 Kings 25:8–11: "On the seventh day of the fifth month, . . . Nebuzaradan commander of the imperial guard, an official of the king of Babylon, came to Jerusalem. He set fire to the temple of the Lord, the royal palace and all the houses of Jerusalem. Every important building he burned down. The whole Babylonian army under the commander of the imperial guard broke down the walls around Jerusalem. Nebuzaradan the commander of the guard carried into exile the people who remained in the city."

Solomon's sin clearly has consequences that transcend himself and his lifetime. He establishes a trajectory that forever affects the people of Israel and Judah, both politically and spiritually. While things seem to be going so well for Solomon, the narrator lets us know where the story is really headed by repeatedly whispering throughout 1 Kings 1–10, "Beware. Solomon's allegiances are divided."

FOURTEEN

How Biblical Poets Wrote Poetry

The Importance of Parallelism

> The scene was Mr. Cruncher's private lodging in Hangingsword Alley,
> Whitefriars: the time, half-past seven of the clock on a windy March
> morning, Anno Domini seventeen hundred and eighty. (Mr. Cruncher
> himself always spoke of the year of our Lord as Anna Dominoes: appar-
> ently under the impression that the Christian era dates from the invention
> of a popular game by a lady who had bestowed her name upon it.)
> —Charles Dickens, *A Tale of Two Cities*

This humorous quotation from Charles Dickens's *A Tale of Two Cities* is
a revealing example of how one's distance from words and phrases can facilitate the evolution of gross misunderstandings related to their meanings.
Mr. Cruncher is obviously unschooled in Latin and is centuries removed from
the language being used as the lingua franca in large parts of the world. Thus
he terribly misconstrues the phrase "Anno Domini" (in the year of the Lord)
as the phrase "Anna Dominoes," whose meaning, according to the narrator,
might say more about Mr. Cruncher's own interpretative skills than about the
actual significance of the expression. Mr. Cruncher's grave mishandling of
the phrase "Anno Domini" makes it nearly impossible for him to understand
the real significance of the saying or to even properly use it.

Mr. Cruncher's misusage of the phrase "Anno Domini" is a model illustration of the type of interpretive damage that modern readers can carry out

by misunderstanding the aesthetic devices used in Biblical Hebrew poetry. Biblical poetry is replete with ancient words, phrases, and images that can be easily misunderstood and awfully misapplied if not treated with care. Additionally, biblical poetry is stylistically composed in a unique way that, on the one hand, noticeably conveys poetry to readers, but, on the other hand, is exasperatingly challenging to delineate with precision. Without observing a couple of simple facts concerning figures of speech and how biblical poetry is composed, readers are bound to repeatedly experience the *Anna Dominoes* effect—that is, we will be inclined to superimpose contemporary ideas onto texts that were intended to be understood in an ancient, foreign literary context. If we do this, we may, like Mr. Cruncher, develop amusing construals of ancient language and style, but we will hardly participate in the cultivated poetry of the biblical authors.

In this chapter and the next, we will focus on two prominent features of Old Testament poetry—parallelism and the proliferation of metaphors—and consider how the biblical poets creatively use these devices to contribute to the meaning of their poetry. By engaging with these poems, we can appreciate the art and glean meaning from poetic biblical texts. We should prioritize several basic principles of reading as we engage with biblical poetry. The following two chapters will convey these principles along with practical suggestions concerning how we can read biblical poetry well.

What Is Biblical Poetry?

The artistic expressions of music and poetry may have arisen "in common historical sources of primitive prayer, working chants and the like, and . . . the histories of both have remained in many ways mutually contingent."[1] Coinciding with their assumed shared origin is the fact that music and poetry seem equally challenging for nonspecialists to define precisely. Laypeople ostensibly recognize when they are listening to music in contradistinction to other, cacophonous sounds or when they are engaging with poetry in contrast to an amalgamation of random words. Notwithstanding, these same listeners and readers may find it difficult to properly define what music and poetry *actually* are and the differences between them. Consequently, it is even more challenging to delineate subgenres of poetry and music, even though the common human experience corroborates their indubitable existence. It is, therefore, the task of poetry and music enthusiasts to detail that which is observed in these different expressions of art.

1. *Princeton Encyclopedia of Poetry and Poetics*, s.v. "Music and Poetry," 533.

So, what is "biblical poetry," and how are readers supposed to recognize it? This question might be appropriately answered with an illustration from the related domain of music. The phrase "biblical poetry" is similar in usage to the category of music branded as "salsa music." Salsa music aficionados would be the first to admit that the moniker "salsa music" may not precisely describe the joyful songs played on Spanish-language radio stations around the globe. The phrase "salsa music" is frequently used nowadays as a catch-all to describe several categories of exuberant and danceable music that is often based on a specific Cuban music genre called the "Son." The Son was developed by artists who incorporated elements of other types of music (e.g., Latin Jazz, Afro-Cuban beats) and an array of instruments (e.g., the congas, bongos, cowbell, an assortment of horns). Some of these combinations resulted in "salsa music," whose styles are more accurately labeled as guaracha, guaguancó, and others. There are multiple legends relating to the emergence of the phrase "salsa music," but when all is said and done, "salsa music" broadly refers to several overlapping styles of Latin music that would take a schooled musicologist to rightly delineate.

The classification of "biblical poetry" is similar, in this sense, to the musical category "salsa music." There are multiple types of poems with distinct classifications throughout the Old Testament. For example, in the book of Psalms alone, the following types of pieces are mentioned: *shir, tefilla, mizmor, sheminit, shiggayon, gittit, miktam, maskil,* and several others. All of these compositions are "biblical poetry."

Additional poetic works appear in the Old Testament that are not associated with any specific classification (e.g., Exod. 15:1–15; Judg. 5:2–31; 1 Sam. 2:2–10). Yet these, too, count as "biblical poetry."

Many biblical compositions were evidently intended to be sung in their original settings (e.g., Pss. 4–9). The word *shir* (song) and *mizmor* (psalm) appear together in the titles of Psalms 65–68, 88, 92, and 108, while the phrase *shir hamma'alot* (song of ascent) describes Psalms 120–34. All of these different compositions are included in the term "biblical poetry."

Despite the close connections between biblical poetry and music, only the written words of the biblical text remain for contemporary readers to analyze. As Murray Lichtenstein states, "Biblical poetry, no matter how once closely linked to musical accompaniment, was primarily a medium of words, not melody, and remains all the more so now that only its words have survived."[2] There does not seem to be a single, all-encompassing Biblical Hebrew word that clearly unites all these types of artistic pieces into one category. Despite

2. Lichtenstein, "Biblical Poetry," 107.

the multiple titles associated with poems in the Bible, these highly stylized compositions are broadly identified in English as "biblical poetry." Thus "biblical poetry" is similar to "salsa music" in the sense that different types of artistic pieces are classified under a catch-all title for a considerably diverse genre.

Be this as it may, these texts do have *something* in common. When we engage with this diverse group of songs, prayers, and other expressive compositions, we interact with a group of texts that are fundamentally similar. These works are particularly imaginative, poignant, and considerably distinct from narrative prose. When we engage with them, we recognize their differences from prose similarly to how we understand that salsa music differs from country music. What shared characteristics hold all these pieces of literary art together? The answer to this question, broadly speaking, consists of two parts: rhythm and rhetoric.

Granting that "biblical poetry . . . was primarily a medium of words, not melody," there is still indeed a distinct rhythm to the poetic texts. By referring to "rhythm," I do not intend to communicate "meter" and suggest that it is possible to determine the correspondence of poetic lines through the quantity of syllables and placement of accents. Some lines of biblical poetry may correspond in this manner, but this is hardly the essence of biblical poetry. Rather, rhythm, understood as a repeated pattern in any given composition, is at the heart of biblical poetry through the phenomenon of parallelism.

As we engage with poetic literature in the Old Testament, we observe a systemic arrangement of terse statements that play off each other. Adele Berlin states, "A poem distills and condenses its message, removing 'unnecessary' words and leaving only the nucleus of the thought. At the same time, without losing its terseness, it constructs relationships between its parts such that the final product is unified."[3] These concise, related nuclear statements that ultimately make up a unified final product are generally organized in adjacent lines (e.g., "cola"; see below under the heading "Correspondence in Meaning"), forming parallelism. This arrangement functions as the rhythmic heartbeat of biblical poetry and serves as the unifying force of these artistic texts.

Additionally, biblical poetry seems to revel in the challenging nature of complex words, phrases, and imagery, daring readers to figure out its rhetoric in order to experience the transformative messages therein. Lichtenstein states that "a possible answer to the 'why' of biblical poetry is more likely to proceed from our appreciation of its peculiar genius for effecting the direct, immediate involvement of its audience in a kind of emotional dialogue with both its form

3. Berlin, *Dynamics of Biblical Parallelism*, 6.

and content."[4] A poem's style and rhetoric are both supremely important in terms of the poem's meaning and how it engages its readership.

One of the primary ways the biblical poets captivate their readers is by the proliferation of highly stylized, figurative language—especially metaphors. By repeatedly portraying one object in place of another, the biblical poets ensure that the reader is intellectually engaged in deciphering the poem and communicate an invigorating and divine message to the reader's soul. We will return to metaphors in the next chapter, but it is important to mention their significance at this point since they go hand in hand with parallelism in biblical poetry. The rhythm of biblical poetry is parallelism; the rhetorical technique of using highly stylized, figurative language to engage readers in an emotive discourse is exemplified through the frequent use of metaphors.[5]

Parallelism and metaphors, though fundamental to biblical poetry, are not exclusive to poetry.[6] They also appear in narrative prose (see Lev. 21:8 for parallelism, and Ruth 2:12 for metaphor).[7] For this reason, there are texts in which the idealistic, clear-cut lines between poetry and prose are blurred (e.g., Gen. 1:1–2:3). Typically, biblical poems consist of shared observable characteristics that readers can recognize when deliberately engaging with the texts. As Lichtenstein states, "In the best of any traditional poetry, poetic technique is not some arbitrary set of rules to be followed for their own sake, but a true reflection of shared aesthetic values and a tried resource for effecting their realization."[8] Parallelism and figurative language exemplified through metaphors are the primary shared aesthetic values of biblical poetry, as demonstrated by how often they are used and how essential they are to the meaning of the Bible's poetic compositions.

Biblical poets wrote so that their readership would have ultimately understood their messages and recognized the structure of their texts as poems, since "poets, after all, use the same language and the same linguistic rules as their audience, but it is the way in which they use these that makes them

---

4. Lichtenstein, "Biblical Poetry," 120.

5. Berlin defines biblical poetry as "a type of elevated discourse, composed of terse lines, and employing a high degree of parallelism and imagery." Berlin, "Reading Biblical Poetry," 2185.

6. Berlin states, "Parallelism appears to be the constructive principle on which a poem is built, while a prose passage might have just as much parallelism but not seem to be built on that structure." Berlin, *Dynamics of Biblical Parallelism*, 6.

7. Regarding the parallelism that occurs in the legal sections of the Torah (cf. Exod. 21:11; Lev. 21:8; Deut. 21:3–4), Assnat Bartor concludes that "parallelism is a standard aesthetic vehicle in every genre of biblical discourse. But when parallelism can be understood to serve *a particular purpose*, it is not only a rhetorical ornament but can and should be regarded as a meaningful expression of the lawgiver's intervention." Bartor, *Reading Law as Narrative*, 63.

8. Lichtenstein, "Biblical Poetry," 115.

poets."[9] The issue for modern readers of the Bible is that, for the most part, we no longer speak and write like the authors of biblical poetry did. In order to appreciate the beauty of the compositions and to fully benefit from the spiritual impact of biblical poetry, we should strive to mirror the way that the original readers understood the writing of the biblical poets. This necessitates a study of the structure (i.e., parallelism) and poetic rhetoric (e.g., metaphors) that they employ.

Parallelism: The Heartbeat of Biblical Poetry

Texts can impact readers in a manner that transcends speech since the structuring of written words can uniquely contribute to their meanings. The way a text is arranged facilitates the reader's perception of its significance, particularly if the composition contains internal patterning. Ed Greenstein rightly states, "Our minds perceive in patterns; it is part of our nature. . . . Experience comes organized, and sense reaches us only through form. The meaning that language conveys shifts with any change in linguistic configuration, and the careful writer—not to mention the literary artist—will watch his or her words, sounds, cadences, and syntax."[10]

When we come across a text with a noticeable pattern, we begin reading in a manner that searches for its intentional arrangement, the relevant correlation of the materials, and their meanings.[11] In biblical poetry, the most widespread and rhythmic pattern is parallelism: the juxtaposition of succinct, interrelated lines that markedly correspond with one another. Adjacent lines of biblical poetry might dovetail in terms of their meanings (semantics), how they sound in Hebrew (phonology), shared conjugations (morphology), how words are used in relation to one another (syntax), a number of other correspondences, or a combination of correspondences. This is by no means a comprehensive list of the potential correspondences in the art of parallelism, at which the biblical poets were adept. They controlled the audience's perception of their message and evoked reader engagement through crafting poetic lines to correspond with each other while requiring the reader to reflect deeply to grasp the poem's meaning.

9. Berlin, *Dynamics of Biblical Parallelism*, 80.
10. Greenstein, "How Does Parallelism Mean?," 41.
11. Greenstein, "How Does Parallelism Mean?," 64. This is particularly the case for acrostic poems, whose lines are ordered in agreement with the order of the Hebrew alphabet. See, e.g., Pss. 9–10; 25; 34; 37; 111; 112; 119; 145; Prov. 31:10–31; Lam. 1–4. This explains, in part, the frustration of some contemporary readers upon encountering "incomplete" acrostic poems, in which the letters may be missing from their expected locations (e.g., the "missing" *dalet* between Ps. 9:5 and 9:6).

Rendering the gist of the utterances that biblical poetry is composed of is a fundamental task of Bible translation, and therefore, semantic correspondence persists as a noticeable form of parallelism to those who read translations of the Bible. However, biblical poetry is a complex art form that transcends a simple cognitive knowledge of what words and phrases mean. Poets are artists who intentionally maneuver their compositions' rhythm and rhetoric in order to captivate and, consequently, involve their readers in the process of interpretation. This is manifest in biblical poetry through other types of parallelism in which adjacent lines correspond in a variety of ways that might be lost in translation. Let's look at select examples of semantic parallelism, followed by an example in which phonological, morphological, and syntactical parallelism are evident in Hebrew but are mostly lost in translation. We will then briefly reflect on how parallelism increases a reader's participation in poetry.

Correspondence in Meaning: Semantic Parallelism

Biblical poetry generally consists of short segments of thought frequently referred to by scholars as "cola" (the singular form is "colon"); a bicolon is a set of two thoughts, and a tricolon is a set of three thoughts. These cola customarily appear as two or more alternating indented lines per verse in translations of Old Testament poetry. This arrangement of lines commonly represents distinct phrases in the Hebrew composition and helps us see the correspondences between adjacent lines. This is not a perfect science, nor is it inerrant. Yet, the positioning of the lines in poetic sections of our Bibles helps us compare their meanings which, for the most part, can carry over from language to language.

A technique customary to biblical poetry is the articulation of a grammatically complete clause to start off a group of related phrases, followed by a line (or more) that corresponds with that first statement. In many cases, the following lines correspond by being similar in meaning, being antithetical, or responding to the previous line(s). Psalm 1 provides an example of the first line of a verse making an assertion, followed by two lines that are similar in meaning.

> Blessed is the one who does not walk in step with the wicked,
>   or stand in the way that sinners take
>   or sit in the company of mockers. (Ps. 1:1)[12]

The psalm commences with three parallel statements that correspond semantically in relation to the actions of the "blessed" (i.e., happy) person. The

12. Here, I have slightly altered the line breaks from how they appear in the NIV.

blessed person is mentioned in the first line of verse 1 and is then understood as the subject of the next two lines of the verse. This person is depicted by phrases that present similar imagery to conceptualize a common viewpoint—namely, the blessed person does not associate (i.e., walk, stand, sit) with the behavior (i.e., step [lit. "counsel"], way, company) of the impious (i.e., the wicked, sinners, mockers). Though these lines are similar in meaning, the imagery therein escalates from strolling, to abiding, to dwelling in the way of life of the impious. This escalation in imagery provides a vivid picture of the blessed person distancing him- or herself from anything to do with impiety by not walking, standing, or sitting near impious persons.

The next verse antithetically describes the blessed person by portraying him or her actively taking pleasure in the Word of the Lord. This is communicated through another semantically parallel statement in Psalm 1:2:

> but whose delight is in the law of the LORD,
> and who meditates on his law day and night.

These lines act jointly with the previous verse, but they respond in such a way as to create a favorable parallel. The semantic parallelism within the two lines of Psalm 1:2 enforces the distinction between the manners of living of the blessed, pious people and those of the wicked, who are alluded to in verse 1. These verses contain two distinct instances of semantic correspondence that play off each other in order to creatively portray the conduct of those who are called "blessed."

Semantic correspondence does not necessarily indicate sameness in meaning between multiple lines. In many cases, the semantic play within a poem is a result of the poetic lines being essentially opposite counterparts of one another. Even though the contrasting lines of a poem might make sense when read independently, they end up being dependent on each other for the verse to make full sense. This type of parallelism is frequently exhibited throughout Israel's proverbial literature. For example:

> The words of the wicked lie in wait for blood,
> but the speech [lit. "mouth"] of the upright delivers them. (Prov. 12:6)

The complete impact of these terse, dramatic statements is not fully perceived unless the lines are read in light of each other. The "words" mentioned in the first line are set in parallel with the corresponding substitution (i.e., metonym) "mouth" in the second line. However, the final portion of the two lines depicts contrasting types of speech. The wicked injure other people with their words; the upright, who are set in distinction, use their words to serve fellow human beings. The parallelism between the two lines in this verse creates a contrast that highlights the characterizations of the upright and the wicked alike.

Frequently in biblical poetry, lines participate with one another when the ensuing statements present the results of, elaborate on, or develop thoughts from the preceding lines. A straightforward and concise example of this type of parallelism appears in Psalm 23:1: "The LORD is my shepherd, I lack nothing."

The psalmist presents a declarative statement in the first half of the verse, which is followed in the second half by a concise assertion that presents the outcome of the psalmist's affirmation. Because of who the Lord is to the psalmist, the psalmist will not lack anything.

A similar type of elaboration comes in the form of succeeding lines responding to a question the psalmist posits. For example:

> Who can discern their own errors?
> Forgive my hidden faults. (Ps. 19:12)

And also:

> Who is this King of glory?
> The LORD strong and mighty,
> the LORD mighty in battle. (24:8)

The few examples presented here merely sample the diversity of semantic parallelism. Biblical poets capitalized on the meanings of juxtaposed phrases in order to artistically express that which was impressed on them to impart to their readers. In this manner, the poets adroitly oriented their readers toward the significance of their compositions. Modern students who read the Bible in languages other than Hebrew can be grateful that the art exemplified through semantic correspondence can, for the most part, be observed in translation. Notwithstanding, some other artistic work of the biblical poets is not as easily observed when transferred from one language to another.

Parallelism Lost in Translation: Syntax, Morphology, Phonology

The biblical poets were Hebrew-language wordsmiths and exceedingly skilled at using the linguistic supplies of their mother tongue in their verbal-art projects. Modern readers of biblical poetry, therefore, must consider the fact that elements of the verbal artistry therein are always lost when a composition is translated into another language. This is especially true for poetry, since poems consist of elevated language that is intentionally crafted to be aesthetically pleasing, compelling, and directed toward the emotions of the original-language readers. Accordingly, it has always been, and continues to be, the enduring responsibility of readers of biblical poetry to make an extra effort to decipher how the biblical poets creatively used their Hebrew-language skills to cultivate their artistic pieces and engage their readers.[13]

Hebrew poets frequently arranged parallelisms that reflected the position of words in relation to one another within the line (syntax), the form of words (morphology), and correspondences within adjacent lines relating to the sound of words (phonology). The creative genius of the biblical poets in these realms is frequently lost in translation. Nevertheless, I shall endeavor to demonstrate and explain one example of biblical poetry in which all of these parallel correspondences appear. In the following example, I have provided my own translation in an attempt to imitate the types of parallelisms evident in the Hebrew text.[14]

> Not according to our sins does he deal with us,
>> and not according to our iniquities does he repay us. (Ps. 103:10,
>>> my translation)

Not only do these two lines agree semantically, but correspondences are also evident in other areas of the Hebrew language.

Syntactical correspondence. The words of these two lines are arranged in an analogous manner. Both lines of the verse begin with a negation ("not") followed by a prepositional phrase ("according to our sins/iniquities"). The lines then proceed to a verb ("does deal/does repay") and conclude with an object.

Morphological correspondence. The Hebrew form of the words in both lines of this verse neatly align with one another. The same Hebrew form of the word "not" appears at the beginning of both clauses. The prepositions

13. Those who do not read Biblical Hebrew can still learn to appreciate poetic phenomena. Many English-language Bibles helpfully stagger poetic lines in a way that demonstrates the phenomenon of parallelism well. Exegetical commentaries can also help readers identify lines, phrases, and words that parallel one another. However, there is always an element of interpretation in translation, and that is especially the case in poetic compositions, where figures of speech are plenty, especially metaphors (see chapter 15). Nuancing one's readings of elaborate Old Testament passages is one of the many values of studying Biblical Hebrew and Aramaic.

14. The following example is provided in Berlin, *Dynamics of Biblical Parallelism*, 31–32. My presentation of this verse has been somewhat simplified and differentiated from Berlin's explanation of the verse.

("according to") are both followed by plural objects (sins/iniquities). These objects both have first-person plural suffixes in Hebrew, which indicate possession (i.e., "our"). In Hebrew, the verbs of both lines appear in the third person masculine singular (i.e., "he"). The object, which is the final word in each line ("us"), is a first-person plural suffix in Hebrew.

Phonological correspondence. The relationships between the sounds of the two lines in the Hebrew of this verse are striking. Below, I have included a transliteration of the Hebrew verse underneath my English-language translation, and I have bolded the portions of the lines that sound similar. Readers can easily observe that the phonological similarities appear in the same locations of their respective lines.

Not according to our sins does he deal with us,	*lo' kacheta'enu 'asah lanu*
And not according to our iniquities does he repay us. (Ps. 103:10, my translation)	*velo' ka'avonotenu gamal 'alenu*

In Hebrew, when words have similar forms, they generally sound similar too. Thus the verbs *'asah* ("does he deal") and *gamal* ("does he repay") have phonetically similar vowels, though their consonants are different. The two verbs are in the same tense in Hebrew, which is why they both have two *a*'s in the same locations of the words and in parallel parts of each line.

The terminology in this section may seem a bit complex to those of us who read a translation of the Bible and not the original language, but that is exactly the point. To fully appreciate the brilliance of the biblical poets, we must dig deep into the nuances of their language. The ingenious maneuvers that the Hebrew-language poets carried out in their literary contexts go beyond the limits of what can be reasonably understood and, therefore, appreciated in translation. With these types of parallels, the biblical poets distinctly drew in, engrossed, and influenced their audience—the original readers of the Hebrew compositions.

Parallelism and the Reader's Experience

In concluding this chapter, it is important to reflect on how parallelism uniquely engages the reader of biblical poetry. As mentioned, readers observe parallelism in nonpoetic sections of the Bible (2 Sam. 7:6), yet the constant and distinctive use of parallelism is central to biblical poetry. As Adele Berlin states, "Poetry uses parallelism as its constitutive or constructive device, while nonpoetry, though it contains parallelism, does not structure its message on a systematic use of parallelism."[15] Granting this, how do the biblical poets use parallelism to engage us in biblical poetry? I will briefly mention just a couple of unique ways that the proliferation of parallelism contributes to the reading experience.

In poetry, adjacent lines build on each other and affect the reader by providing a fuller portrayal of the author's thoughts than what could be expressed in just one line or even in prosaic language. The ability to create a powerful effect that is greater than the sum of the text's component parts is one aspect of parallelism that makes it such a valuable tool to biblical poets. When succinct phrases are placed together in parallel, eloquent and compelling imagery can be created to stimulate the reader's imagination and profoundly impact our emotions in a manner that long, prosaic discourses are not equipped to do.

From a reader's perspective, different types of correspondences near to one another facilitate a search for connections between the short, adjacent lines.[16] These parallels might be semantic, morphological, phonological, or syntactic, and these categories can overlap in any given verse or even change throughout the course of a poem. This creates an experience for readers in which we might understand the essence of the poetic phrases but must perpetually search for how the lines interact with other words, expressions, and sounds in the surrounding context in order to grasp their integrated meanings. Thus parallelism keeps us engaged by constraining us to read patiently and attentively if we want to understand the aggregate significance of a word, phrase, or line in the poem. Good readers of poetry frequently analyze and reanalyze texts before fully appreciating the correspondences between parallel lines, fully enjoying the reading experience, and fully recognizing the author's genius.

This short introduction to parallelism in biblical poetry presents how central this literary phenomenon is to our interpretation of biblical poems. Considering how poems are structured goes hand in hand with analyzing the rhetoric used in them. In the next chapter, we will continue to focus on how biblical writers wrote poetry by zeroing in on one of the main rhetorical devices used in biblical poetry: metaphor. We will discuss what metaphors are, how they work, and the importance of tracking them throughout the biblical text.

---

15. Berlin, *Dynamics of Biblical Parallelism*, 16.
16. Berlin, *Dynamics of Biblical Parallelism*, 2.

FIFTEEN

How Biblical Poets
Wrote Poetry

The Proliferation of Metaphors

> Great poets, as master craftsmen, use basically the same tools we use;
> what makes them different is their talent for using these tools, and their
> skill in using them, which they acquire from sustained attention, study,
> and practice. . . . Great poets can speak to us because they use the modes
> of thought we all possess.
>
> —George Lakoff and Mark Turner, *More Than Cool Reason*

Mr. Cruncher's laughable confusion discussed in the previous chapter becomes relevant again when we broach the topic of metaphors in biblical
poetry. "Anno Domini" is a literal saying that represents an attempt to date
events relative to Jesus's birth. Figures of speech, by definition, are not literal.
Thus if Mr. Cruncher's distance from the coining of the literal phrase "Anno
Domini," which has its origins in the contemporary era, could result in such
ridiculous confusion, how much more might we mishandle Hebrew-language
expressions from hundreds of years before the birth of Jesus?

Granted, Mr. Cruncher's confusion is fictional, but the illustration aptly
demonstrates how reading ancient expressions without serious consideration
of their intended meaning can lead to misunderstandings and chaotic reap-
propriations of idioms. This issue is especially problematic in poetry because

its elevated language is replete with figurative expressions. Modern Christian readers of ancient Hebrew-language poetry will have difficulty applying the principles communicated through the poetic compositions if we do not understand (or if we misunderstand) their essence. Ancient figurative speech must be discerned with care. We should consider the ancient context and refrain from imposing private guesses, so as to avoid running the risk of repeating the "Anna Dominoes" blunder.

The biblical poets pointedly used creative language to prod readers' imaginations and affect their sensibilities. In this chapter, we will discuss how to read poetry well by considering the metaphor, a frequently used rhetorical device. This is a continuation from the previous chapter, in which we discussed the use of parallelism as biblical poetry's driving rhythm. After briefly exploring how metaphors work, we will discuss how tracking them helps us trace motifs across the biblical texts. The chapter concludes with practical reminders about how to engage with biblical poetry well based on its prevalent features.

Metaphors: The "Heart" of Biblical Poetry

Metaphor is the figure of speech most conspicuously used in biblical poetry. This means that it is of primary importance for the interpreter to locate and decipher metaphors within individual poetic compositions and to trace their use throughout the biblical text. Concerning the importance and proliferation of metaphor in poetry, I have previously remarked that "metaphor is ubiquitous in poetry. . . . The establishment of metaphor and its coherent iterations throughout a poem is a work of art in and of itself. On many occasions, the usage of connected metaphors within a literary work presents the reader with a puzzle; its component parts must be found, ordered, and connected in order for the reader to appreciate the significance of the composition. In this sense, discerning metaphors is part of the joy of reading poetry."[1]

Metaphorical language is the rhetoric that largely composes the rhythm of parallelism; both phenomena are at the "heart" of biblical poetry, to use a metaphor.[2] Parallelism provides the necessary steady "pulsations" that invigorate the compositions by supplying predictable and regular movements throughout the text. Metaphors are the "life force" running through the vessels, providing liveliness to the composition. In order to draw near to the

1. Hernández, "Metaphor and the Study of Job," 391–92.
2. Berlin, *Dynamics of Biblical Parallelism*, xii; also see p. 4.

"heart" of biblical poetry, readers must work to understand these ancient figures of speech.

How Metaphors Are Recognized

Adele Berlin rightly states that "much of the difficulty in understanding poetry arises from the difficulty in recognizing what is metaphorical (and what is not) and in perceiving the meaning of the metaphor."[3] Readers of biblical poetry frequently encounter nonliteral (figurative) language, in which words and phrases are not used in their most basic senses. One of the most common figures of speech, the metaphor, at its essence promotes "understanding and experiencing one kind of thing in terms of another."[4] In many cases, we intuitively process these metaphors. Without consciously analyzing the figure of speech, we recognize that one concept is—at least to a certain degree—being presented in terms of another concept. For example, when speaking of the Lord's protection of his followers, the psalmist comments:

> He will cover you with his feathers,
> and under his wings you will find refuge. (Ps. 91:4)

We do not need to be experts in zoology to recognize that "feathers" and "wings" belong to birds. Yet the pronoun "he" in the first line of the verse refers to the Lord (see Ps. 91:2). So readers of the poem are presented with two options for interpreting these lines: (1) either the Lord assumes the body of a bird, spreads his wings, and encourages followers to gather under them for protection, or (2) the poet creatively uses nonliteral language to illustrate a concept that is difficult to make concrete, by using a tangible image adopted from the realm of animals. Since readers would hardly believe that the Lord assumes the body of a bird in order to protect human beings, we instinctively use our previous knowledge of God and birds to discern the expression.

Yet how do we grasp the significance of the metaphor? How do we decipher the metaphor, and how can we use this process to comprehend metaphors that are not as intuitive as this one? Knowing the basics of how metaphors work permits us to approach them with a reading strategy that facilitates understanding their originally intended meanings and comparable present-day applications. In this manner, we can remain faithful to the meaning of the figure of speech and avoid outlandish interpretations of nonliteral language.

3. Berlin, "Reading Biblical Poetry," 2189.
4. Lakoff and Johnson, *Metaphors We Live By*, 139.

How Metaphors Work

Not all scholars agree on how the human mind processes metaphors. Therefore, in this section, I intend to provide a cursory introduction to how some scholars who subscribe to Conceptual Metaphor Theory (CMT) postulate that humans decipher these figures of speech. There is a good deal of diversity among those who study CMT, but, generally speaking, these scholars suggest that humans tend to think in terms of metaphor—that is, many metaphors that we use and understand reflect ways humans naturally conceptualize their experiences.

Common metaphors that are adopted and discerned by intuition are referred to as "conventional metaphors" or "general conceptual metaphors." These metaphors "structure the ordinary conceptual system of our culture, which is reflected in our everyday language."[5] Lakoff and Turner comment on the use of general conceptual metaphors in poetry, stating: "General conceptual metaphors are not the unique creation of individual poets but are rather part of the way members of a culture have of conceptualizing their experience. Poets, as members of their cultures, naturally make use of these basic conceptual metaphors to communicate with other members, their audience."[6]

Common metaphors are not the unique invention of poets, but they are aesthetically pleasing rhetorical devices that poets can use for their purposes. In the case of biblical poetry, the poets used a lot of metaphors to express word pictures concisely, portraying concepts that might require extensive elaboration in ordinary prose. Since humans conceptualize their experiences in similar ways and express their conceptualizations through metaphors, comparable metaphors could conceivably materialize in diverse cultures, across multiple languages, and in an assortment of composition types. Accordingly, contemporary students of the Bible are able to recognize some figures of speech and process basic metaphors in biblical poetry. The foundation of conceptualized experiences that modern readers share with the biblical poets emerges through many conventional metaphors in Old Testament poetry.

An oft-used and quintessential example of how conventional metaphor is structured into the human conceptual system is how intuitively people liken arguments to war. Consider how the concept WAR is alluded to by the italicized words in the following typical sayings related to an ARGUMENT:

- Your claims are *indefensible*.
- He *attacked every weak point* in my argument.

5. Lakoff and Johnson, *Metaphors We Live By*, 139.
6. Lakoff and Turner, *More Than Cool Reason*, 9.

- His criticisms were *right on target.*
- He *shot down* all of my arguments.[7]

These types of sayings are, time and again, alluded to in different languages and in distinct geographical locations when referencing people engaging in an argument—a "verbal conflict" that a "combatant" either "wins" or "loses." In the metaphor ARGUMENT IS WAR, the less structured concept ARGUMENT is partially understood in terms of the concept that is more delineated by shared human experience WAR. The more concrete concept WAR is the SOURCE DO-MAIN for the metaphor, which serves as the pattern used to illustrate the more abstract concept. The abstract concept that is (at least partially) understood in terms of the SOURCE DOMAIN is called the TARGET DOMAIN. "Mapping" the metaphor consists of tracing the set of correspondences by which we understand one domain in terms of another. Generally speaking, the image provided through the SOURCE DOMAIN mapped onto the TARGET DOMAIN facilitates a nuanced understanding of the abstract concept in terms of the concrete concept based on common human experience.

At this point, let us briefly return to our example in Psalm 91 and outline how we might process the metaphor therein:

> He will cover you with his feathers,
> and under his wings you will find refuge. (Ps. 91:4)

GOD (i.e., the Lord) is the TARGET DOMAIN of the metaphor, which clarifies an abstract aspect of the divine character. The exact manner in which the Lord protects his followers is seldom tangibly visualized, and thus this feature of the divine character is portrayed in commonly observable terms that are easier to delineate (i.e., the SOURCE DOMAIN)—namely, a bird caring for its offspring with its wings. The resulting metaphor GOD IS A BIRD uniquely expresses the Lord's loving care for his followers by mapping the clear image of what a bird does for its offspring onto the vague notion of how the Lord preserves and defends his people. Just as a bird cares enough for its brood to spread its wings over them in protection, so the Lord safeguards those who follow him.

Biblical poets frequently employ metaphors as a rhetorical tactic in order to portray illustrative and compact word pictures that critically engage their readers. This frequent use of terse, illustrative language generally contrasts with narrative prose. When modern readers read biblical poetry, it is

7. The examples are from Lakoff and Johnson, *Metaphors We Live By*, 4. All the italics are original.

consequential for us to strive to decipher its metaphors in order to appreciate what the poetic text may have meant to the original audience, and in turn to grasp its meaning for contemporary readers.

Additionally, it is important to recognize metaphors and to know how they work so as to avoid inventing peculiar interpretations that were never intended by the poets. Readers who carefully discern figurative language will escape the common blunder of developing bizarre readings of passages under the auspices of having a high view of Scripture. Taking the Bible seriously without recognizing the conceptual metaphor in Psalm 91:4 might result in thinking that the Lord assumes the body of a bird, feathered wings and all.

Why Is Tracking Metaphors Important?

In many cases, deciphering metaphors in biblical poetry lends insight into how certain concepts may have been perceived by the biblical authors and understood by their audiences. Yet examining individual metaphors is only the beginning when it comes to observing how impactful a metaphor might be across the whole biblical text. Sometimes, the biblical authors use the same metaphor in different locations in the Bible to broach similar topics and make agreeing or contrasting points. Tracking metaphors throughout Scripture permits us to observe how motifs develop and to follow themes throughout the biblical text. Related metaphors give modern readers a more comprehensive view concerning how the biblical authors spoke to an issue on the whole or how they participated in conversation about a particular topic in the world around them.

Tracking the course of a metaphor and how it is used admittedly presents some challenges. For example, metaphors are not always equal in their per-ceptibility. Also, sometimes readers simply do not have enough information relating to a metaphor's SOURCE DOMAIN in order to grasp how it is supposed to facilitate an understanding of the TARGET DOMAIN. In other cases, the bibli-cal poets created unconventional (and also new) metaphors that may present ways of thinking about concepts that were not a part of the natural conceptual system of the original audience. These types of metaphors are challenging for contemporary readers to decipher because the set of correspondences between the SOURCE DOMAIN and the TARGET DOMAIN might not be easily noticeable. Yet there is great payoff to discerning unconventional metaphors because they permit us to uniquely delve into the world of the author—into the realm of the source of the metaphor. The rarer or more creative the metaphor, the more difficult it is to discern but the more potential it has to uniquely communicate on behalf of the author.

Whether metaphorical language is conventional or unconventional, its prevalence means that tracking it in biblical poetry can be a key to following what is happening in different parts of the Bible. Repeated metaphors sometimes function as the dots that are connected throughout the text, permitting readers to see the genius of biblical authors and the unity of compositions across the entirety of the Bible. For example, tracking the GOD IS A BIRD metaphor facilitates understanding a claim that Jesus makes in the New Testament. Let's briefly look at how this happens.

Apparently, the SOURCE DOMAIN of the GOD IS A BIRD metaphor was commonly understood in ancient Israel. Since ancient Israelites would have been able to observe birds and their behavior, they generally understood that birds protected their broods with their wings. This can be reasonably concluded by observing how frequently this metaphor is used just in the book of Psalms. For example:

- "Guard me as the apple of the eye; hide me in the shadow of your wings" (Ps. 17:8).
- "All people may take refuge in the shadow of your wings" (36:7).
- "In the shadow of your wings I will take refuge, until the destroying storms pass by" (57:1).
- "For you have been my help, and in the shadow of your wings I sing for joy" (63:7; see also, "the shelter of your wings" in 61:4).

The frequency of this metaphorical expression suggests that it was not simply an illustrative saying that Israelite poets invented. Rather, its repeated use implies that the Israelite experience made it relatively natural for them to map out how the SOURCE DOMAIN (i.e., BIRD) illustrates how the Lord protects people. By observing the correspondences between how the image of a bird is used and how that represented God in ancient Israelite poetry—that is, the transfer of information between the SOURCE and TARGET DOMAINS—contemporary readers acquire knowledge about the ancient Israelite understanding of birds (SOURCE DOMAIN), as well as their perception of God (TARGET DOMAIN).

The importance of deciphering metaphors becomes increasingly obvious when similar language appears in different types of biblical literature. For example, in the book of Ruth, Boaz alludes to the GOD IS A BIRD metaphor, stating, "May the LORD reward you for your deeds, and may you have a full reward from the LORD, the God of Israel, under whose wings you have come for refuge!" (Ruth 2:12). Boaz, an Israelite, is depicted as using this metaphor in his commendation of Ruth for leaving her homeland of Moab and settling in Israel with her destitute mother-in-law, Naomi. Boaz's statement portrays not only that ancient Israelites would have used and understood this allusion to God as a bird but also that it may have been understood by those who lived in the surrounding area and spoke related languages (i.e., the Moabites).

The fact that the metaphor is recorded in the narrative prose of Ruth provides an example of how similar metaphors can be a valuable tool in different kinds of discourse, depending on the rhetorical purposes of the speaker or author. This is an important point since similar metaphors reappear or are alluded to in various biblical compositions to make points specific to each context. This is precisely the case for the GOD IS A BIRD metaphor in the Gospels. Understanding the metaphor in the Old Testament is key to comprehending the imagery alluded to by Jesus. By recognizing, deciphering, and tracking this metaphor, readers observe the poetic genius displayed in the psalms, view the extent of its use through the narrative prose of Ruth, and also discern how Jesus references the GOD IS A BIRD metaphor and expands on previous conceptions of God (the TARGET DOMAIN).

Matthew and Luke record Jesus's allusion to the metaphor in question (Matt. 23:37; Luke 13:34). In both Gospel accounts, Jesus is depicted as speaking near Jerusalem in the presence of the Pharisees (Matt. 23:2–24:1; Luke 13:22, 31). Jesus's religious, Torah-observant, Jerusalemite listeners would likely have been familiar with the imagery that was repeatedly used by the Old Testament writers (cf. Deut. 32:10–11). Within the context of this discourse Jesus states, "Jerusalem, Jerusalem, the city that kills the prophets and stones those who are sent to it! How often have I desired to gather your children together as a hen gathers her brood under her wings, and you were not willing!" (Luke 13:34).

Jesus, the master teacher, capitalizes on his audience's familiarity with the GOD IS A BIRD metaphor to encourage his listeners to realize the consequential nature of his teaching. In doing this, Jesus has slightly modified the imagery to illustrate facets of his own character and ministry by switching out the original TARGET DOMAIN (God) for himself. The metaphor GOD IS A BIRD is frequently used in the Old Testament to emphasize the Lord's loving and protective character. By stating, "How often have I desired to gather your children," Jesus changes the metaphor to JESUS IS A BIRD. Jesus, then, stands in where all his listeners would have expected the metaphor to refer to GOD (i.e., the Lord, the God of Israel). Jesus alludes to this metaphor in a situation in which his listeners would have understood that it reflected an aspect of the Lord's character. He then applies this feature of the Lord's character to himself, implicitly suggesting his oneness with God. Through the allusion to the GOD IS A BIRD metaphor, Jesus asserts that he could have cared for the inhabitants of Jerusalem just like the Lord, their covenant God, protects his followers.

Reminders for Reading Biblical Poetry

The theological implications of Jesus's use of the GOD IS A BIRD metaphor illustrate the importance of recognizing, analyzing, and tracking metaphors throughout the biblical text. The manner in which Jesus alludes to this particular metaphor to imply his oneness with the Lord affords an occasion for us to pause and consider our attentiveness to details in biblical poetry and how they might be bases for understanding other biblical literature. This provides a timely opportunity to hark back to our core reading commitments, nuancing them specifically for biblical poetry, so that we can appreciate the text and personally glean from the principles therein.

As mentioned in chapter 2, Christians who engage with the Old Testament humbly, successively, and entirely progress in the right direction in terms of holistically engaging the Bible as Scripture. This book has also emphasized reading the biblical text deliberately; we have been consciously striving to pay special attention to how, what, and why biblical writers communicated in order to provoke a response from their readers. The discussion of biblical poetry in this chapter and in chapter 14 returns us to the conversation but this time with an eye on how to engage with biblical poetry deliberately. Multiple reading tips could be mentioned at this point, but the review of biblical parallelism and metaphor provokes two suggestions: (1) We *really* need to refrain from rushing while reading biblical poetry. (2) We must be intentional about reading "for the affect."

Really Refrain from Rushing While Reading

The idea of slowing down while reading is not new to us. In chapter 2 we briefly discussed reading slowly when deliberately engaging the biblical text. However, reading slowly is particularly important with poetry. Rushing is highly unadvisable to begin with, but the consequences become even greater when we encounter poetry. This is based on the simple fact that it is sometimes difficult to recognize poetry while speeding through a text. Reading quickly can pose difficulty if we do not discern that we are engaging with poetry because of the rare words, flowery expressions, and ingenious imagery that frequently appear on the pages of the poetic sections of Scripture. Other aesthetic devices that are characteristic to poetry are sometimes lost in translation, and other times, they are simply not noticed. Not recognizing that an author is waxing poetic can bear tremendous consequences on interpretations. Really slowing down in reading helps contemporary, distanced interpreters make fewer mistakes in understanding the actual words of biblical poetry and in interpreting the meaning of these texts for their communities. Some misguided readings can be traced, at least to a certain extent, to reading too quickly and missing cues indicating poetry. The unfortunate consequences of this hastiness can include misapplications of biblical texts among the community of faith. We have already mentioned the absurdity of suggesting that the Lord assumes the body of a bird, as might be the interpretation of Psalm 91:4 if readers hurriedly ran their eyes over this verse without recognizing the metaphor. Yet perhaps a more prevalent and applicable example of the consequences of rushing through poetry is the well-known reading of Proverbs 31:10–31 as solely a checklist of everything a woman must do if she is to be considered a woman of valor.[8] This type of interpretation is misguided. One reason this passage is frequently misread can be directly linked to readers zipping through the first verse of the poem:

> A warrior woman, who can find?
> Her price is worth far more than precious jewels. (Prov. 31:10, my
> translation)

There are a few indicators in the very first verse of this poem that help us recognize that the section does not exclusively consist of a checklist of things women have to do in order to be considered virtuous. These cues can hardly be noticed when we are rushing through the process of reading.

- First, the verse uses parallelism. As mentioned in the previous chapter, sometimes lines of verses correspond with one another by posing a rhetorical question and then answering it. Slow, deliberate readers observe that this is precisely what the author does in Proverbs 31:10.
- Second, figurative language appears in the second line of the verse, in which the woman is likened to highly priced jewels. The metaphor here might be understood as A WARRIOR WOMAN IS AN EXPENSIVE COMMODITY, through which readers are able to understand the characteristics of the warrior woman based on the value of another costly object (jewels). Readers may process this intuitively, because it is relatively common to speak of someone's value or worth in certain contexts without

---

8. The following example is adapted from Hernández, *Proverbs: Pathways to Wisdom*, 105–30.

considering that person to be literally procurable by exchanging currency. Nevertheless, careful readers recognize that they are dealing with nonliteral language without needing to delineate exactly how the metaphor gets its message across.

- Third, the first line of Proverbs 31:10 begins with the first letter of the Hebrew alphabet (*aleph*). As we continue to read, we realize that the second verse begins with the second letter of the Hebrew alphabet (*bet*). This acrostic pattern continues for the twenty-two verses of the poem, with each verse beginning with the next letter of the Hebrew alphabet until the sequence is complete. An acrostic is an unmistakable indicator that the poet is purposely employing an aesthetic device to provide a design and increase the enjoyment of the reading experience. Thus as per the author's request, the reader of this poem *should* be concerned with its beauty. The contents of the poem cannot be considered apart from its aesthetic devices, meaning that it is not the right of the reader to switch the beauty of an acrostic into an idealized checklist that is only applicable to women readers.

Granted, the Hebrew-language acrostic is lost in translation, but the point remains: readers cannot appreciate the level of intentional artistry present in the poem if they run past the parallelism and metaphor evident in the translation of its very first verse. Within a few verses, measured readers are able to recognize that they are engaging with a highly stylized poem. When we notice this, our interpretations of the passage can reflect the author communicating through his poetic style, rather than reflecting an imposition of our own paradigms upon information extracted from the words of the text.

The "checklist" interpretation is symptomatic of a broader issue. It actually evidences reading through the entire book of Proverbs too quickly to be attentive to the rhetoric and motifs of Proverbs 31:10–31 that are broached in other areas of the book. For example, Proverbs 31:10 speaks of the warrior woman, whose "price is worth far more than precious jewels." There is a connection between how this warrior woman is presented in Proverbs 31:10 and how wisdom is presented in other areas of the book. For example, the same word for "jewels" that appears in Proverbs 31:10 also appears in the following verses to speak of wisdom:

- "She [wisdom] is more precious than jewels, and nothing you desire can compare with her" (3:15 NRSV).
- "For wisdom is better than jewels, and all that you may desire cannot compare with her" (8:11 NRSV).

What becomes discernible through these connections in language is that the concept of wisdom is thoughtfully associated with what the poet was trying to communicate in Proverbs 31:10–31. More specifically, the woman of this poem is the embodiment of wisdom, and the principles of the passage apply to all people who desire to be wise. This understanding is corroborated when we compare some of the major motifs related to wisdom throughout the book of Proverbs to how the warrior woman is depicted throughout the poem.

- She is depicted as speaking with wisdom: "She speaks with wisdom, and faithful instruction is on her tongue" (31:26). Proverbs repeatedly emphasizes that the use of language to build others up is wise, while quarreling indicates foolishness (see, e.g., speech being referred to as a "rare jewel" [like wisdom] in 20:15; see also 10:21, 31; 12:17–19; 15:2, 4, 7; 16:24).
- She is depicted as working hard: "She selects wool and flax and works with eager hands" (31:13; see also vv. 15, 18–19). Proverbs repeatedly promotes working hard as wise living and ridicules the lazy (see, e.g., rhetorical connection with "hand" in 21:25–26a; see also 10:4; 12:15, 27; 13:4; 19:15; 20:13; 26:16; 28:19).
- She is depicted as being committed to the family unit: "She gets up while it is still night; she provides food for family and portions for female servants" (31:15; see also vv. 18, 21, 27a). Proverbs repeatedly emphasizes that wise people holistically care for their family unit (4:3–4; 13:24; 19:18, 26; 20:7; 22:15; 23:13–14; 30:11).

Further examples could be presented (e.g., humility, caring for the vulnerable, etc.), but these three motifs of wise speech, working hard, and relationships to family sufficiently illustrate the point: By reading the book of Proverbs slowly, attentively, and entirely, readers are able to pick up on the imagery in the warrior woman poem that is repeatedly mentioned throughout the rest of the book. Rushing through Proverbs transforms the composition into simply a book of short adages that provide bits of advice. This type of reading inevitably disregards much of the book's important rhetoric and imagery, and thereby misunderstands the climax of the book as a glorified to-do list that is exclusively relevant for women.

Slowing down in reading has a quieting effect; it reduces the noise of our own interpretive contrivances. It draws our ears to listen to biblical poetry's heartbeat and thereby perceive the lifeblood of the compositions. We permit the ancient poets to impact our minds and hearts by taking the time to not only receive what they had to say but also to appreciate how they went about doing so.

Reading "for the Affect"

Encouraging readers to slow down and read is admittedly a bit of a double-edged sword. We just discussed the benefits of refraining from rushing in our reading, yet reading too slowly might be symptomatic of overanalysis. On the one hand, it takes time to make keen observations; on the other hand, enthusiastic students of the Bible run the risk of endlessly floundering in discourses concerning morphology, phonology, syntax, the SOURCE DOMAIN, the TARGET DOMAIN, and metaphorical mapping. Wallowing in the mire of poetic scrutiny is not necessarily synonymous with developing reasonable interpretations and applications of the text's principles. On the contrary, overexamination of this kind can lead to discounting the poet's ability to communicate to the heart of the reader. Whereas some of us might fall short of analyzing the beauty of compositions, others who are skilled in analysis might forget that the beauty was crafted by the poet for specific reasons—one of which was to impact us by appealing to our affect.[9]

Oftentimes, biblical poetry lets the reader into an intimate meeting between the writer and God—either by relaying an actual conversation between the two or by inviting the reader into the private spaces of prayer, praise, and lament, revealing the writer's theological reflection on God. Thus when reading poetry, we are compelled to permit it to influence our affect and to respond with proper emotions, desires, and behavior. Let's begin elaborating on this point by quoting our exemplary verse one last time:

> He will cover you with his feathers,
> and under his wings you will find refuge. (Ps. 91:4)

At the core of this verse is the idea that the Lord is a protector of his people. This is evidenced by the second line indicating that God's wings provide refuge. If the author wanted to plainly communicate that God safeguards his followers, he could have stated that with a simple, indicative statement void of figurative language. However, the psalmist did not do this. The psalmist used bird imagery so that it would be possible for readers to understand God's protection through the way birds instinctively and attentively care for their broods. This image does more than communicate with our heads; it provokes us to consider how God might care for and protect us when we need refuge

9. For the sake of clarity, I am referring to the noun form of the word "affect," which essentially refers to human emotions.

in life. The image allows the poet to influence our emotions in a way that simple, nonfigurative statements do not.

Another well-known example might be helpful in portraying how biblical poets used aesthetic devices to nudge the feelings of their readers. Psalm 23:1 states, "The LORD is my shepherd, I lack nothing."

We mentioned this verse in the previous chapter as an example of the type of parallelism in which ensuing statements present the results of, elaborate on, or develop thoughts from the preceding lines or from earlier in the line. What we did not point out then is the distinctly metaphorical language that likens the Lord to a shepherd. Since the Lord is not literally a shepherd who rears sheep, readers naturally consider how a shepherd caring for his sheep reflects God's care for the author and, by extension, for the reader. Thus two metaphors are implied in the first line of Psalm 23:1: GOD IS A SHEPHERD, and GOD'S FOLLOWER IS A SHEEP. The psalmist then alludes to the relationship that God has with his followers by amplifying the shepherd-sheep relationship over the next several verses:

> He makes me lie down in green pastures,
> he leads me beside quiet waters,
>   he refreshes my soul.
> He guides me along the right paths
>   for his name's sake.
> Even though I walk
>   through the darkest valley,
> I will fear no evil,
>   for you are with me;
> your rod and your staff,
>   they comfort me. (23:2–4)

By providing vivid imagery of a shepherd bringing about rest for his sheep in the pasture, accompanying his sheep by the still waters, and using his rod and staff to comfort, the author illustrates the tender relationship that a shepherd has with his sheep. Implied in the verses is the fact that the sheep depend on the shepherd for guidance, protection, and safekeeping. This depiction of the shepherd's care combined with the sheep's trust in the shepherd, reflects intense affection between the two. That feeling of affection is precisely one of the things the author was intent on portraying in order to have a holistic impact on the readers. For the author, it was not enough for the readers to simply know that the Lord cares for the author and even for them. The psalmist used metaphorical language in the first line of the verse followed by an indicative statement (i.e., "I lack nothing") that presents the result of the metaphor so that readers will *feel* that the Lord cares for his followers like a shepherd cares for his sheep.

In biblical poetry, the focus customarily shifts from communicating facts in discourse to affecting the readers' sentiments through rhetoric. Evidence for this lies in the way some prose narratives are retold in a concise, poetic manner. For example, Psalm 136 recounts parts of the Exodus story in a concise, memorable way that explicitly calls for the reader to perceive these past events as evidence of the Lord's steadfast love:

> To him who struck down the firstborn of Egypt
> *His love endures forever.*
> and brought Israel out from among them
> *His love endures forever.*
> with a mighty hand and outstretched arm;
> *His love endures forever.*
>
> to him who divided the Red Sea asunder
> *His love endures forever.*
> and brought Israel through the midst of it,
> *His love endures forever.*
> but swept Pharaoh and his army into the Red Sea;
> *His love endures forever.*
>
> to him who led his people through the wilderness;
> *His love endures forever.* (136:10–16; see also Exod. 15:1–18)

Readers are quickly drawn into and inundated with compact statements through which the author strives to influence the reader's emotions by repeatedly presenting the reason for what the Lord did for Israel. The prose of the Exodus narrative includes details relating to the events, while the poetic account in Psalm 136 uses concise word pictures to illustrate the purpose of the Lord's exploits for Israel. The biblical poets could have simply restated the facts: God supernaturally protected Israel and delivered them from Egypt. Instead, this author does what poets do: he jabs at the reader's emotion and expects that they will openly engage their affect. After reading—or, maybe, audibly repeating—that the Exodus from Egypt came to pass because of the Lord's steadfast love for his people, the original readers were supposed to *feel* what their covenant God had done for them and respond accordingly.

As we refrain from rushing in our reading, we enable our emotions to be influenced by the biblical poet's style and rhetoric. Readers who recognize metaphorical language, track metaphors through biblical texts, slow down, and engage their affect permit the ancient poets to continue to speak to their readers and prevent "Anna Dominoes" moments from replacing ancient art. We will continue to look at biblical poetry in the next chapter, but our focus will shift to what poetic texts say about a theme that is prevalent in many of them—the issue of just retribution.

SIXTEEN

Metaphors and Retributive Justice in the Poetry of Job

As for Job, no one is ever finished with it.
—Edwin M. Good, *Irony in the Old Testament*

Danny's body sagged as the tension went out of him. He glanced at me, his face a mixture of surprise and relief, and I realized with astonishment that I, too, had just passed some kind of test.
—Reuven Malter, in Chaim Potok, *The Chosen*

A Saturday afternoon, crowded service in a Brooklyn synagogue is the scene in which Reuven Malter not only passes an evaluation of his knowledge of gematria (i.e., the numeric value of Hebrew words) but also experiences a formative educational episode alongside his friend, Danny Saunders. Danny and Reuven meet through a neighborhood softball league, and the two become improbable friends—improbable because Danny is a member of a strict, ultra-orthodox community led by his father, the tzaddik Reb Saunders. That day in the synagogue, Reuven is nervous about meeting the well-known Rabbi Saunders for the first time because, despite being a practicing Jew, he is not part of the Hasidic community. Tension builds in the synagogue when Reb Saunders—a prophet-like figure to this community—directs his attention to his son after bestowing his customary, sagacious teaching upon his admiring congregants, and asks Danny if he has anything to say. The reader of the novel wonders, Why would this tzaddik (Hebrew for "righteous man") ask his adolescent son if he has any comments about his lesson? As readers come to find out, Reb Saunders intentionally embeds intermittent blunders into his teachings. His astute son and assumed successor, Danny, is responsible for calling attention to the incongruities while the rest of the community observes and learns from their lively exchange. Reb Saunders's discourses are so broad, and the rhetoric so cogent and convincing, that it takes knowledge of countless rabbinic texts and of Jewish history spanning hundreds of years to discern and redress the problems with the rabbi's speech. On that day in the Brooklyn synagogue, Danny brilliantly discerns everything except for an error related to gematria—a test that the Rabbi embedded into his discourse to be solved by Danny's newfound friend, Reuven Malter.

An engaging and contentious dialogue between learned interlocutors in the presence of spectators is an ingenious method of instruction, constructive for all involved. Ideally, the participants are drawn closer to truth by discovering and critically engaging with faults in their interlocutors' arguments or through refining their points of view based on the soundness of their friends' points. The spectators in the crowd vicariously engage by not only receiving information from the speakers but also learning how the verbal participants use rhetoric to propose convincing arguments. Reb Saunders teaches everyone in the synagogue during that evening Shabbat service by testing the knowledge of his primary interlocutors, Danny and Reuven. The verbal exchange between the three speakers accomplishes the task of engaging and informing the whole community.

Likewise, the book of Job captivates and enlightens contemporary readers by presenting the characters' dispute over the theological explanation for Job's suffering. In the first round of speeches, Job's companions—Eliphaz, Bildad, and Zophar—initially encourage him to return to God from some sort of misdeed in order to be restored. Job, in turn, argues that he has not done anything to receive the type of hardship that has come upon him and that, consequently, God does not have a system of consistent just retribution. In fact, Job claims that the reality of his situation and his observations of the conduct of those around him demonstrate the previously unthinkable: God actually favors the wicked (Job 10:3). By the end of the second round of speeches, upon hearing Job's unorthodox comments about God's injustice and inconsistency in retribution, Job's friends count Job among the wicked. This conclusion leads to a breakdown in communication and a resolute impasse in the conversation in the third round of speeches. The third round of speeches (chaps. 22–27) appears to be disordered, but it is in fact arranged in a way that demonstrates the disintegration of effective communication.

In this, readers learn how *not* to be effective conversation partners. We recognize that all of the characters' speeches are based, at least in part, on ignorance, since they lack knowledge of the heavenly scene, outlined in Job 1–2, during which the reason for Job's suffering is narrated (see below). Readers who are aware of the prologue must pay close attention to the content of the discussion in order to detect the characters' disagreements with one another, as well as the erroneous claims they make concerning the reasons for Job's suffering.

Rhetorical content is never separated from its stylistic packaging. Thus readers not only take note of Job's and his friends' propositional statements but also pick up on the presentation of their arguments. Readers learn from *what* Job and his friends say as well as *how* they say it. In the exchange between Job and his friends, the characters employ the finest biblical poetry, saturated with both common metaphors and novel ones. In the debate, Job and his friends use language and imagery that transcends the immediate context of the book of Job. This brings to mind other sections of the Bible that reflect on just retribution and even language reminiscent of extrabiblical compositions that describe how others in the ancient world evaluated similar issues. When we engage with Job in its literary context, we observe an exquisite example of rhetorical argument from the world of the Bible in its ancient Near Eastern environment.

Tracking metaphors in the poetic dialogues of Job is crucial to following the arguments between the participants and, ultimately, tracking their conversation to their eventual impasse. When we pay attention to the metaphors used in Job and his friends' communications, we can understand the content of their disagreements and appreciate the genius in the presentation of the overall composition. We are like the crowd in the crowded Brooklyn synagogue when reading the dialogues of Job: we are sometimes amused and other times disquieted. Yet as observant spectators, we are always enthralled by the content and presentation of the characters' arguments in the debate about just retribution. This chapter will focus on one specific thread of metaphorical imagery (the light/darkness dichotomy) employed by Job and his friends as the theme of retributive justice develops throughout the dialogues.

The Backdrop of the Retribution Debate

The issue of just retribution is arguably the most prevalent theme that appears in the dialogues between Job and his companions. This is especially the case in the first two rounds of speeches, in which Job, Eliphaz, Bildad, and Zophar take turns speaking about the tragic circumstances that have come upon Job. Throughout the discourse, the characters wax poetic, using particularly vivid imagery in an endeavor to get through to one another.

Yet the book of Job is not all written in poetry. The composition begins with a section of prose through which the reader obtains information that the characters never possess. This is significant for reading Job since the narrative context of the book frames the story and helps us understand the poetic dialogues. In other words, the information we are privy to allows us to perceive the reality behind the story and, in turn, make judgments about the characters' assessments of the situation. This is a key point to reading the book of Job well and permitting the dialogues to have their full impact on us as readers. We are like captivated spectators watching a drama play out as the characters argue with one another, from a position of partial ignorance, over the significant issue of divine retribution. Not only is it important to be familiar with the gist of the content of Job (which can be attained in part by reading the narrative prologue and epilogue); but to be good stewards of our privileged information and to come to reasonable conclusions about the book, we must also be familiar with how the content is presented.

The narrative that leads into the dialogues is found in Job 1–2. The protagonist, Job, is depicted as an upright and blameless man who is particularly concerned for his family and the things of the Lord (1:5–6). Straightaway, we are brought into a celestial meeting in which the Lord, other members of the divine council, and the Satan[1] are present. The Lord addresses the Satan and curiously points out the unmistakable devotion of his servant Job. The Satan retorts that the obvious reason for Job's devotion is that the Lord supernaturally protects him, causing him to prosper and prohibiting him from experiencing adversity in life. The Satan's comments suggest that if Job experiences calamity, then his disposition toward the Lord will change, and he will become just like a person who interprets personal tragedy as punishment. Job, in turn, will act like one who does not fear God, and he will curse God to his face (1:6–10).

God accepts the challenge and begins by permitting the Satan to sabotage the world around Job, without touching his body. Job's moral uprightness is immediately put to the test as he is promptly depleted of his financial

1. "The Satan" is a literal translation from the Hebrew text, in which the definite article "the" is before the word *satan*. The Hebrew word *satan* means "adversary," coinciding with the fact that the personage depicted in Job 1 challenges God and thus appears to be an adversary-type figure. The inclusion of the definite article "the" before the word *satan* leaves open the possibility of this being the adversary that eventually became known as "Satan" (1 Chron. 21:1) or some other celestial challenger.

prosperity (i.e., his cattle), his servants, and, in one fell swoop, all ten of his children. Yet Job's response is not quite what the Satan expects: Job falls on the ground in worship and refrains from uttering anything offensive against the Lord, even after all of these tragedies have come upon him (Job 1:11–22).

But the Satan will not concede defeat.

In a second celestial scene nearly identical to the first, the Satan appears before the divine council once again. On this occasion, the Satan insinuates that the proverbial deck was stacked against him, which is why the first venture did not have its expected conclusion. The Satan reasons that Job did not curse God because Job himself remained unscathed. All of the calamity fell on others around him. If Job is touched, if Job personally experiences the effects of the devastation, if Job can feel the pain, misery, and distress of *personal* torment, then, according to the Satan, Job will indeed curse God to his face (Job 2:1–5; see also 1:5).

On the grounds of this appeal, the Satan is given permission to physically afflict Job, with the limitation that Job must not die from the assault. Upon leaving the Lord's presence, the Satan immediately inflicts physical agony on Job, other unknown skin conditions, and bad breath, among other physical issues (Job 2:7; see also 7:5; 19:17, 20; 30:30). By way of his undeserved suffering, Job becomes the lead in a drama that plays out over the subsequent chapters relating to whether God's servant will hold to his integrity, irrespective of his lot in life. Readers follow along, wondering how upright people can maintain their integrity despite being victims of undeserved tragic circumstances.

Job Changes His Tune

Job's temperament shifts once his body is touched by the Satan. Job is no longer depicted as silent; he speaks up and out in a progressively shocking manner throughout the rest of the composition. During a brief and baffling interaction with his unnamed wife, Job appears intent on accepting his lot from God, whether good or bad. But then Job's friends, Eliphaz, Bildad, and Zophar, arrive on the scene, initially to empathize with and comfort him (Job 2:6–13). The combination of Job's personal affliction, his wife's confrontation, and the presence of his friends provokes a poetic monologue in which Job changes his tune, cursing the day of his birth and wishing he had never been born. At the beginning of Job's monologue, he indignantly proclaims,

May the day in which I was born be damned,
and the night that said, "A man has been conceived." (3:3)[2]

In this verse, Job vividly expresses his desire to eradicate the day he was born in order to extirpate his presence from the world. Job's usage of imagery related to light and darkness is particularly significant in communicating his desire to eliminate the day of his birth:

[4]May that day be **darkness**.
May God not seek it from above
and may **light** not shine upon it.

[5]May **darkness** and **deep gloom** desecrate it.
May a cloud dwell on it.
May **deep darkness** of the day terrify it.

[6]That night—may **darkness** take it.
May it not rejoice among the days of the year.
Into the number of the months, may it not come. (Job 3:4–6; see also
3:9)

The bolded words above illustrate the light/darkness dichotomy that Job uses to express his desire for the elimination of the day of his birth. The various expressions related to darkness do not come from the same words in Hebrew, which can be attributed to the stylistic variation that biblical poetry frequently displays (e.g., the five words for "lion" in Job 4:10–11). Even though this passage uses an assortment of words for darkness, the concepts of light and absence of light depict the existence/nonexistence dichotomy that Job is intent on illustrating. This dichotomy is particularly evident in 3:4: Job hopes that the day of his birth will be considered darkness, and then in a parallel line, Job wishes that light may not shine upon it. Reading verses 3–4 successively, we observe the development of the following metaphors: if NONEXISTENCE IS DARKNESS, then, by inference, EXISTENCE IS LIGHT.

There is a subtle development in this imagery as Job continues to speak in Job 3:5–6. Darkness is embodied, and Job hopes that it will "desecrate," "terrify," and "take" the day of his birth. This image is consistent with the idea that being driven out of existence is intimately linked with the concept of darkness. Recognizing personification is key in tracking the progression of Job's usage of this light/darkness imagery, since it reveals an additional aspect

---

2. All of the translations in this chapter from the book of Job are my own and are adapted from Hernández, *Illustrated Job*. I have bolded the text for emphasis here.

of the imagery of darkness: if darkness were incarnate, it could wreak havoc on Job's birthday by extinguishing its light (i.e., existence). As Job continues his monologue, the imagery further develops as he uses the domains of LIGHT and DARKNESS to patently relate to life and death, respectively. Later in his speech, Job disconcertingly questions:

> Or why was I not as a buried stillborn?
> Why was I not as babies who never saw light? (3:16)[3]

In this verse, Job alludes to the light/darkness dichotomy to refer specifically to human life and death. Quite literally, stillborn babies do not see light because they do not live outside the womb. Instead, the dead perpetually remain in darkness, never having seen light. Job proceeds to use this imagery metaphorically to complain that he was forced to live by being given light when he would have preferred death (i.e., darkness). Job poetically expresses this toward the end of his monologue.

> [20]Why does he give light to the sufferer,
> and life to the bitter of soul,
> [21]those who wait for death, but it is nonexistent;
> and those who dig for it more than hidden treasures? (Job 3:20–21)

Job does not want the LIGHT that God gave him, because it represents LIFE. The concept LIGHT overtly corresponds to LIFE in the two parallel lines of Job 3:20 and thus alludes to the image of the stillborn baby that Job mentions in 3:16. Job wishes he had not seen literal light, because it means that he was born alive and that the life he is forced to live is quickly leading him toward death. Job's monologue, in part, is intended to simply communicate his belief that he would be much better off in the realm of the dead (3:17–22). Job prefers DARKNESS because it represents not only NONEXISTENCE but now also DEATH. DEATH is desirable, according to Job, because it is the way he could find respite from his difficult life. These more specific metaphors develop by the end of Job 3: DEATH IS DARKNESS and LIFE IS LIGHT.[4]

---

3. The questioning in v. 16 is picked up from v. 12, despite the absence in Hebrew of the interrogative word "why" and the phrase "why was I not" in both lines of the verse, respectively. The interrogative phrase "why was I not" in the second half of v. 16 is understood in light of the parallelism with the previous line.

4. The light/darkness dichotomy is not exclusively used to represent life and death in the Bible. In other sections of the book of Job, and in other biblical literature, the imagery of light and darkness is used to represent related concepts. For example, light is used to convey a pleasant physical life (Job 18:18; 33:28, 30; 38:15, 19) as well as wisdom and spiritual enlightenment (22:28; 24:13, 16; 28:11; 29:3). The image of darkness is also used to symbolize the netherworld

Job's friends can easily identify this light/darkness trope, since it is common in biblical and extrabiblical literature. Job's friends take issue with how he uses the light/darkness dichotomy to represent life as terrible and death as bringing about rest for his afflicted self. Thinking that they can fix Job's fallacious reasoning, Job's companions respond to his monologue, encouraging him to admit some fault and thereby concede to traditional wisdom concerning divinely oriented retributive justice, which asserts that one gets what one deserves.

Eliphaz, the oldest of the group, accuses Job of not practicing what he has preached. Eliphaz finds it unsettling that Job has helped others in the past, but now that he has suffered tragic circumstances, he prefers to have not been born (Job 4:2–5). Bildad and Zophar also chime in, encouraging Job to turn back to God from some hidden sin so that he can be restored to his former glory (8:5–7, 20–21; 11:14–19). Job repudiates his friends' suggestions that he has committed some sort of misdeed and summons God to appear for a trial (9:32).

What starts as a difference of opinion among friends in the first round of speeches disintegrates into quite an unpleasant altercation by the second round of the dialogue. Job's friends move away from encouragement to turn back to God toward warnings of the impending disaster that awaits Job because of his impiety. Of course, Job and his friends have only partial knowledge of his circumstances, while readers have access to extremely vital information relating to Job's suffering. We follow the dialogues in light of the narrative and Job's monologue. This creates tension for us as the characters begin to argue about what they consider to be the main cause for Job's suffering—namely, Job's friends believe that he endures affliction because of misdeeds carried out in his personal life, while Job complains about God's injustice. We know that the actual reason for Job's suffering is the divine contest between God and the Satan. This strained relationship between the knowledge of the informed reader and the propositions of the comparatively ignorant characters is part of the drama of reading Job. Discerning the nature of the characters' disputes requires paying close attention to the vivid imagery they use throughout the dialogues, since their arguments are mostly couched in metaphor, as is the argument of Job's monologue. Let's continue to track how the imagery of light and darkness is used by Job and his friends in their second round of speeches (Job 15–21) as they continue arguing about retributive justice.[5]

(10:21; 15:22–23, 30; 17:13; 18:18; 20:26) as well as folly and a lack of guidance (5:14; 12:25; 19:8; 22:11; 29:3; 38:2).

5. Some of the conclusions below concerning the discussion in the second round of speeches in Job are detailed in chapters 3–6 of my book *Prosperity of the Wicked*.

The Poetic Dialogues: A Battle of Images

Instead of prosaically communicating with Job that his arguments are illegitimate, Job's friends inform him of his dire fate in poetic form—in exactly the same way he communicated with them in his monologue that he desired to die. By the second round of speeches, Job's companions suggest that the darkness metaphor he broached in his monologue most appropriately applies to the retributive death of the wicked. Since, for all intents and purposes, Job appears to be dying the death of the impious—and DEATH IS DARKNESS—it seems justifiable to Job's friends to warn him of the impending darkness and to let him know that he is a bit confused in his use of the light/darkness dichotomy.

Job's companions' use of the light/darkness symbolism to reveal to Job that his own imagery ironically relates the consequences of wickedness that he has brought upon himself. Their use of metaphors, especially related to darkness, seems to be the proverbial "nail in the coffin" in terms of proving their point that Job must quickly return to God. In Job 21, Job responds in turn to their use of the light/darkness dichotomy.

Eliphaz: "He Will Not Depart from Darkness"

Even though Eliphaz initially responds to Job in the role of a learned and concerned senior adviser (Job 4–5), his second speech is replete with severe warnings targeted at Job. Eliphaz claims that the eventual penalty for wickedness is death in God's consistent system of just retribution. He explicitly invokes the imagery of darkness to which Job alludes in his monologue to make Job aware that he is on his way to suffering the traditional consequences of being wicked. According to Eliphaz,

> [22]He [i.e., the wicked person] does not believe in his return from
> darkness,
> and he is spied out for a sword.
> [23]He wanders for bread—"Where is it?"
> He knows that the day of darkness is established in his hand.
>
> [30]He will not depart from darkness.
> A flame will dry up his branch.
> He will depart by the breath of his [i.e., God's] mouth. (15:22–23, 30)

The first line in Job 15:22 alludes to the demise of the wicked person by using the imagery of darkness. This becomes particularly evident after reading the second line of the verse, in which the sword is referenced as a lucid metonym (i.e., word substitute) relating a horrid death. Thus in Eliphaz's reference to darkness in verse 22, he implicitly notifies Job of his potential fate if Job does not take quick, corrective action in his situation. Another reference to death comes in the second line of verse 23 in the phrase the "day of darkness."[6]

Eliphaz subsequently parallels the concept of darkness with the image of a branch dwindling under the heat of a flame (Job 15:30). According to Eliphaz, death is as sure for the wicked as being scorched is for a branch over a fire. In the final line of this verse, Eliphaz reveals why he is confident that this judgment will come to pass: God takes personal retribution on the wicked. The wicked departs from the land of the living because they have been blown away by the breath of God's mouth. Eliphaz similarly stated in 4:8–9:

> As I have seen, those who plow iniquity,
> and those who sow mischief, will reap it.
> From the breath of God they will perish
> and from the breath of his nose they will be consumed.

Job's judgment is certain, according to Eliphaz, because God implements the retribution. Since he is confident that God carries out justice in this manner, and thus God is on his side, Eliphaz believes his doctrine to be impregnable. Job, then, had better turn back to God quickly before God gives Job the darkness that he claims he wants—but not the darkness he expects. Job will receive retribution and not rest, pain and not peace.

Job: "I Spread Out My Bed in Darkness"

Just as in any good debate, the interlocutors respond to their adversaries' points in due time. Job is paying keen attention to Eliphaz and responds to his use of the concept of darkness in his next speech. Job counters Eliphaz's alarmist use of darkness imagery and suggests that ending up in darkness is not such a bad fate for those who are suffering like he is. In fact, Job resorts to again using darkness imagery, as he did in Job 3:17–22, to reiterate his

---

6. The parallel line in Job 15:23 "He wanders for bread—'Where is it?'" must be understood considering Eliphaz's statement in 4:10–11, where he subtly reminds Job of the fate of the wicked by using lion imagery. Eliphaz likens an iniquitous person to a lion whose consequence for its misdeeds is starvation as a result of a "lack of prey." "Bread" is used by Eliphaz as a metonym for sustenance in 15:23, comparable to how "prey" is used in 4:11 to express similar points in both contexts: wicked people are deprived of food and, thereby, progressively meet their demise through starvation.

desire to die so that he might finally be at rest from his turmoil. In 17:13–16, Job responds to Eliphaz's comments by saying:

> If I hope for Sheol, my home,
> in the **darkness** I spread out my bed.
> I have called to the pit, "You are my father"
> and to the worm, "My mother" and "My sister."
> And where, where is my hope?
> And my hope, who will see it?
> It will go down to the bars of Sheol;
> together on the dust of rest.

By stating that he wishes to spread out his bed in darkness (i.e., the place of the dead), Job once again uses darkness imagery to relate to death in terms of respite from his calamitous, and therefore hopeless, life. Job wants to die so that he might rest from the grave distress that he has experienced in the land of the living, where there is light (i.e., life). Thus darkness is not to be feared as a consequence of some sort of hidden sin in his situation. There is no poetic justice in darkness; according to Job, there is only rest.

Eliphaz and Job both use darkness to allude to the netherworld and, thereby, to refer to the state of being dead. The abode of the dead being referred to as a place of darkness seems to have been an understandable image in the world of the Bible. This is evident since the underworld is also depicted as bereft of light in other ancient Near Eastern literature. For example, the Akkadian-language composition known as the *Descent of Ishtar to the Netherworld* similarly uses the light/darkness dichotomy to depict the realm of the dead. As the title of the composition suggests, the account tells of an occasion in which the goddess Ishtar resolves to enter the netherworld. The following lines provide a brief depiction of the realm of the dead in this composition:

> To the **netherworld**, the land of no return,
> Ishtar, daughter of Sin, set her mind.
> Indeed, the daughter of Sin did set her mind
> To the gloomy house, the seat of the **netherworld**,
> To the house that none leaves who enters,
> To the road whose journey had no return,
> To the house whose entrants are **bereft of light**,
> Where dust is their sustenance and clay their food.
> They see **no light** but dwell in **darkness**.[7]

---

7. Foster, *Before the Muses*, 499 (bold added). Another ancient Near Eastern composition named *Nergal and Ereshkigal* uses imagery corresponding to the *Descent of Ishtar to the*

This composition likens the place of the dead to a house, the residents of which are cut off from light and thus dwell in darkness. These images are similarly used in Job to represent the place of the dead and the inhabitants therein. Considering these observations, we note that light and darkness were well-known concepts in the ancient Near East, used to refer to life and death. This is why the characters in Job are depicted as intuitively understanding each other. Additionally, it is important to note that the narrator does not emerge to explain these concepts to the reader. This signifies that the imagery used in Job would have likely been understood by readers and that readers were able to track the argument between Job and his friends concerning how the source domains of LIGHT and DARKNESS were being used. If we, as contemporary readers, can position ourselves closer to the text of Job by similarly grasping how these images may have been used in the Bible and its world, we set ourselves up to best track the thread of conversation in which these images are used.

Job and his friends use common tropes from their world relating to light and darkness for their own rhetorical and theological purposes. More specifically, Eliphaz uses the concept of darkness to depict the horrid end of the wicked; Job uses this concept to depict what he perceives to be the ideal place for rest. Job's friends are not finished arguing over which use is correct—and neither is Job.

Bildad: "The Lamp of the Wicked Will Wane"

As might be expected, Bildad disagrees with Job and is compelled to condemn him for his impiety. Bildad takes a slightly different approach to using the light/darkness imagery in order to reiterate the traditional wisdom that the wicked eventually suffer an excruciating death. Bildad, like Eliphaz, eventually grows impatient with Job's claims of blamelessness (Job 18:2–4) and communicates to Job that Job really does not want to experience the darkness he so adamantly claims to desire. Darkness, according to Bildad, should be understood as the tragic fate of the godless, which is how Job is acting since he refuses to turn back to God. In 18:5–6, Bildad states,

> Yes, the light of the wicked will wane.
> The flame of his fire will not gleam.
> Light will darken in his tent,
> and his lamp will wane on him.

Netherworld in telling of the travel of the plague god, Nergal, to the realm of the dead. See Foster, *Before the Muses*, 516.

Instead of focusing on darkness like Eliphaz, Bildad switches to focusing on light. Light-giving sources are depicted by the words "light," "flame," and "lamp," which appear in all four lines of these two verses. The lamp imagery is particularly interesting in this context since it refers not to light in and of itself but, rather, to a light-emitting device. This is a unique image that Bildad introduces into the conversation. According to Bildad, the wicked have the light of their lamp snuffed out, and, by implication, the righteous possess lamps that consistently provide light. The introduction of this type of creative imagery is a move that an attentive conversation partner would observe and use to respond.

This is precisely what happens.

However, Bildad is not quite finished using the light/darkness dichotomy to preach traditional wisdom. As anticipated, Bildad asserts that the wicked are destined for death. Even if they are permitted to live for a while in their tent, the light in their abode will eventually fade. Before death, the wicked's impending doom is made manifest in the waning of their lamp—their lives become progressively worse (e.g., Zophar's comments in Job 20:11, 22–26). As Bildad continues in his second speech, he explicitly mentions the domains of LIGHT and DARKNESS in order to intensify the distinction between those who remain in the land of the living and those who die. There is no question about Bildad's belief in the grim end of the unrepentant sinner after he emphatically uses the light/darkness dichotomy in the following manner:

> He [i.e., the wicked person] will be driven from light into darkness,
> and from the world he will be banished. (18:18)

Though Bildad can take credit for introducing the lamp imagery into the conversation in Job, he cannot take credit for creating it. In fact, the concepts of light and darkness are joined with the lamp elsewhere in the Old Testament. The image of the lamp is an ancient trope that transcends the conversation in Job and relates to a broader discussion concerning retribution. For example, the language of Proverbs 13:9 corresponds to Bildad's comments:

> The light of the righteous shines brightly,
> but the lamp of the wicked is snuffed out.

Considering how the light/darkness dichotomy is used to describe the fate of the wicked in Job, this verse speaks to the retribution issue by suggesting that the lives of the righteous are cheerful while the lives of the wicked disintegrate as they progress toward their demise. The imagery of the fading lamp is used to communicate similar messages in Proverbs 20:20 and 24:20.

If someone curses their father or mother,
   their **lamp** will be snuffed out in pitch darkness. (See also Exod.
   21:17; Lev. 20:9; Deut. 27:16)

For the evildoer has no future hope,
   and the **lamp** of the wicked will be snuffed out.

These verses from Proverbs apparently offer the typical view of retribution that Bildad expresses by using the same lamp imagery in his second speech. Bildad reuses and intensifies Job's light/darkness dichotomy by bringing up the lamp in order to point out that Job has not only misunderstood his own fate but also misused the well-known light/darkness imagery as it relates to his situation. Wicked people are dispossessed of their lives by being pushed out of the domain of light (e.g., the world in which they live) and into the darkness. According to Bildad (and Eliphaz), Job is mistaken: darkness is not restful; it is retributive. Job must understand and accept this quickly.

Job: "How Often Does the Lamp of the Wicked Wane?"

The idea of consistent, divinely appointed retributive justice is a farce to Job. This is not simply because he is suffering; even greater evidence supporting the absurdity of just retribution is the fact that the wicked actually prosper, according to Job. The success of the wicked is emblematic of divine injustice and undermines the principle of consistent, just retribution. Job again challenges his companions' traditional wisdom by using the metaphorical light/darkness dichotomy. By using this imagery once again, Job demonstrates that he is paying close attention to their argumentation and informs them that they are sorely misguided.

Job also now has a new image at his disposal in his rhetorical repertoire: the lamp.

Job shrewdly adopts the lamp imagery that Bildad introduced into the conversation. Job uses this imagery to refute what Bildad tried to assert. Bildad says that the light from a lamp of the wicked diminishes and eventually dies out in order to assure Job that the wicked are afflicted during life, which leads to their eventual ignominious death. Job sardonically wields Bildad's image and poses several confrontational, rhetorical questions:

How often does the **lamp** of the wicked wane,
   and their calamity comes on them?
How often does God distribute pains in his anger? (Job 21:17)

By questioning whether the wicked are *really* deprived of light/life, Job parodies Bildad's use of the lamp imagery and rebuts his claim that the light of their lamp wanes until it eventually goes out. According to Job, this rarely happens, meaning that there is no such thing as consistent just retribution.

Job spends the lion's share of his speech in Job 21 striving to back up his claim that the lamp of the wicked does not incontrovertibly wane by pointing out that the wicked actually prosper. Job claims to have observed the impious living lives of good fortune, with no decrease in quality at all, thereby suggesting that the lamp that gleams with light is the one that belongs to the wicked. In order to prove this point to his friends, Job gives specific examples of how he has actually seen the wicked prospering. For example,

- Job's friends argue that the wicked fail to have descendants carry on their name and memory into successive generations (15:32b–33, 34a; 18:16–17, 19). Job considers this claim to be utter nonsense, given that the wicked are surrounded by plenty of joyous children (21:8–9, 11–12).
- Job's friends argue that the wicked are deprived of their financial prosperity (15:27–29; 20:10, 15–18). This claim is ridiculous to Job, who notes that the cattle of the wicked are particularly fertile (21:10). Zoological plenty is one of the ways in which ancient people were able to maintain abundance throughout generations (1:3).
- As we have observed in part, Job's friends repeatedly state that the wicked die horrible, ignominious deaths (see Zophar's comments in 20:6–8, 16, 23, 26, 28 in addition to the citations above). Job deems this erroneous and asserts that the wicked live long, productive lives and are even honored in their deaths (21:7, 13a, 32–33).

At this point, the characters' dispute comes full circle. Their fundamental disagreement concerning whether there is consistent, divinely appointed retribution has gone nowhere in terms of them convincing one another of their opinions. Readers do see, however, that the theological battle quickly turns into a battle of imagery throughout the dialogues, with LIGHT and DARKNESS being among the domains the characters use to illustrate their positions. We have been examining one thread of the dispute over just retribution in which the interlocutors debate specifically about the proper theological understanding and use of the light/darkness dichotomy. This thread can be lightheartedly summarized in the following manner:

- Job: "I wish I had never seen light. I want darkness because I want to rest in the place of the dead" (Job 3).

- Eliphaz: "Aah, no you don't, Job. Darkness represents death—but insofar as it is a punishment for the wicked" (chap. 15).
- Job: "I want darkness because I want rest!" (chap. 17).
- Bildad: "Aah, no, you really don't, Job. Darkness is reserved for the wicked, who are pushed out of the land of the living. The light of the lamp of the wicked wanes until it is eventually extinguished" (chap. 18).
- Job: "Yeah right! How frequently have you seen this happen? Not frequently. . . . Yeah, that's what I thought! By the way, have you observed how prosperous the wicked *actually* are? This means that there is no consistent system of just retribution" (chap. 21).

After Job's comments concerning the prosperity of the wicked in Job 21, the conversation breaks down in the truncated third round of speeches (chaps. 22–27). God eventually appears to Job in a storm and quiets him and his friends by, ironically, never replying to any of Job's questions concerning his suffering or retributive justice (chaps. 38–41). Job and his companions presumably finish their ordeal not having received a definitive answer related to why Job suffered, and therefore, they never settle their argument concerning the proper use of the domains of LIGHT and DARKNESS.

This void in the divine speech might be disheartening if the reader expects the composition to answer the questions that Job so passionately advances. Yet what if the composition was written for readers in the way that Reb Saunders and Danny's dialogue was conducted in front of the crowd in the synagogue? What if at least one of the purposes is to engage the reader in the argument by encouraging us to think critically about the issues broached in the dialogues while observing the blundering characters striving to set each other straight?

How Job Teaches

In this chapter, we have discussed only one group of related images used in the poetic dialogues of Job. This has permitted us to track just one theme in this multifaceted composition. Understanding and tracking how the DEATH IS DARKNESS and LIFE IS LIGHT metaphors are adopted, reused, and revised by the characters permits us to follow one aspect of the argument concerning retributive justice. We readers of Job are privileged with knowledge that enables us to track problems in the characters' arguments as they dispute the issue of just retribution in the dialogues.

As we have seen through glancing at Proverbs and other ancient Near Eastern examples, neither the light/darkness dichotomy nor the lamp imagery was novel in its literary environment. Therefore, it comes as no surprise to us that Job and his companions understand how their dialogue partners use and rework the common imagery for their purposes. The ways they nuance this imagery make for engaging reading, given that the dispute is lively, logical, and highly cultivated. This type of learned conversation in which we must follow threads in order to grasp the essence of the drama can be a challenge, but it also comes with a significant payoff: as we catch on to the figures of speech being used to make significant points, the conversation between Job and his friends becomes increasingly captivating and prompts us to consider issues of just retribution, the sovereignty of God, and suffering, among other significant themes.

The author of Job is quite a sagacious teacher here.

The author of Job could have flatly recounted the conversations between Job and his friends in a way that provided readers the theological gist, using narratival comments in order to straightforwardly answer the most pressing issues in the ancient Israelite context. Yet instead of blandly spewing acceptable standards of thought about God and behavior toward God, the author leaves the theological mistakes of the characters in the highly stylized poetic dialogues, while providing readers with privileged information in straightforward prose. This ingenious pedagogical method forces readers to pay close attention to figures of speech in dialogues in order to track the important motifs and message of the composition. We stand back and watch as the characters of Job blunder in their disagreements, knowing that their misjudgments and quarreling are for our good.

From Poetry to Prophecy

In the preceding two chapters, we have discussed how biblical poets write and how to engage with their compositions well by focusing on how the poets used parallelism and metaphors. In this chapter, the subject matter has shifted to how portions of Job and other select poetic biblical and ancient Near Eastern texts similarly use the source domains of LIGHT and DARKNESS and how this common imagery is used by the characters in Job to communicate their views on just retribution. Many metaphors could have been followed in Job and other biblical poetry to demonstrate a conversation thread relating to a number of predominant biblical motifs. Nevertheless, in this chapter we have been able to see how crucial reading poetry well is to following themes in a biblical book and beyond.

Poetry pervades all areas of biblical literature. As we see in the book of Job, the Bible contains long poetic compositions in which narrative comments appear (e.g., Job 1–2; Prov. 25:1). Additionally, there are extended sections of biblical narrative in which poems of varying lengths strategically appear (e.g., Gen. 49; Num. 23:7–10, 18–24; 24:3–9, 15–24; Deut. 32–33; 1 Sam. 2; 1 Chron. 16:8–36). There is one more use of poetry alongside narrative that cannot be overlooked: biblical prophecy. The biblical prophets are commonly recognized as fire-blowing, future-telling characters. Yet the prophets, as we read them in our Bibles, are not just preachers but also poets. In the next section, we will observe how reading narrative and poetry well helps us understand some of the most dynamic characters and powerful poetry in the Bible.

SEVENTEEN

How Prophets Prophesy

> So much has been done, exclaimed the soul of Frankenstein—more, far
> more, will I achieve; treading in the steps already marked, I will pioneer
> a new way, explore unknown powers, and unfold to the world the deepest
> mysteries of creation.
>
> —Mary Shelley, *Frankenstein*

The name "Frankenstein" is often understood in contemporary English to
allude to a colossal and sinister monster who embodies morbidity. "Frankenstein" might invoke unsettling imagery of a patchworked mythological
creature who epitomizes the hair-raising consequences of trifling with the
synthetic vivification of dead tissues and materials. This understanding of
Frankenstein has developed in popular folklore to refer to any type of oversized
and scary being. Yet those who use the term this way may not be particularly
familiar with the details of Mary Shelley's classic 1818 novel by this name. In
Frankenstein, Mary Shelley tells the account of a scientist, Victor Frankenstein, who strives to make an indelible mark on his discipline by compiling and
animating dead matter. Upon assembling miscellaneous parts, Frankenstein
animates them, bringing unity and mobility to a formerly lifeless composite
creature.

The scientist responsible for enlivening the human collage, Victor Frankenstein, is the real Frankenstein—not the creature. The essence of the creature, however, is of critical importance to capturing the reader's attention,
which is likely a primary factor facilitating the contemporary use of the

title "Frankenstein" to refer to the composite brute. The inextricable link between the scientist, Victor Frankenstein, and the intriguing creature he creates explains why the monster is sometimes inappropriately conflated with the designer.

The aesthetic features of biblical prophecy result in the compositions sometimes being conflated with their main characters in a manner similar to how Frankenstein's creation is called by his name. When contemporary readers engage with the prophetic sections of the Scriptures, we commonly refer to them by the name of the protagonist in the compositions or by the name of the professed prophet (e.g., "the Elijah/Elisha narratives" or Nahum, Habakkuk, and Zephaniah). Yet just as Victor Frankenstein imaginatively arranged and fused his work, so the biblical authors planned, outlined, and fashioned artistic expressions of divine communication. The prophetic, inspired, and artistic hand responsible for compiling and composing the biblical work (i.e., the scribe) is the real "Frankenstein." In this chapter, we consider how the biblical prophets prophesy, noting that the compositions that traditionally bear their names are the creations of literary, inspired Victor Frankensteins— gifted artists who worked behind the scenes to shape the biblical prophetic literature and bring it alive in its current form.

The Prophets Functioning like Frankenstein

Traditional opinion suggests some overlap in authorship between the historical prophets and those who wrote the biblical prophetic compositions. Surely some of the authors and the prophetic characters depicted in the compositions could be the same people—particularly in instances in which prophets are depicted as writing and as providing first-person accounts (Ezek. 1:1; 43:10–11). Yet it is curious that these texts rarely provide clear and detailed information about who the actual authors are. This lack of information concerning the historical figures behind the compositions suggests that the author wants the reader to consider these compositions as the divine word; the composition itself is the prophetic voice to the reader.

Irrespective of whether we know exactly who wrote the prophetic materials, we have a systematically and ingeniously organized amalgamation of stories relating prophetic activity and divine words communicated through the prophets. Just as the monster did in Mary Shelley's novel *Frankenstein*, the Old Testament prophetic literature demonstrates that a science has been applied to carefully selecting and putting together these texts. This matter has been brought to life by the literary scientist in a way that makes the compound more powerful than its individual parts. The real and inspired author (the Victor Frankenstein, if you will) selectively and artistically composed the prophecy and the life events (if they are included) of the characters who utter words from God.

We do not have exhaustive accounts of the prophets' lives or all their prophecies. For example, in 1 Kings 22, Micaiah is represented as a true prophet of the Lord who delivered other divine, yet unfavorable, messages to King Ahab of Israel. The narrator records King Ahab's interaction with King Jehoshaphat of Judah: "The king of Israel [Ahab] answered Jehoshaphat, 'There is still one prophet through whom we can inquire of the LORD, but I hate him because he never prophesies anything good about me, but always bad. He is Micaiah son of Imlah.' 'The king should not say such a thing,' Jehoshaphat replied" (22:8).

Recording all of Micaiah's prophecies was not particularly important to the writer of 1 Kings. Rather, this specific interaction with the kings of Israel and Judah was chosen because the author thought it was important to the narrative (22:13–28). Selectively compiling and arranging the prophetic materials like this has a calculated effect on the reader. The final composition now affects readers in a way that far surpasses the effect of the individual component parts. When we refer to the prophetic books by the prophets' names, we are calling the product "Frankenstein" often without remembering that the complex creation of each composition relating the life and ministry of an Old Testament prophet had its own mad scientist behind the scenes.

So Then, What Is a Prophet?

Simply stated, the English word "prophet" in the Old Testament generally refers to someone who claims to speak on behalf of the divine.[1] The content of the word from the divine is largely irrelevant in terms of categorizing the intermediary as a "prophet." Rather, the message of the prophet is important in determining whether the prophet is a "true prophet." Authentic prophets exclusively deliver the word of the one true God of Israel, the Lord. The

---

1. The Torah suggests that a prophet speaks in the name of the divine but can also serve as a spokesperson for someone else (Exod. 7:1). It is important to note that the title of the person who communicates the divine message changes throughout the Bible. For example, Samuel and Gad are called "seers" in the same context in which Nathan is called a "prophet" (1 Chron. 29:29). Additionally, the type of divine message received by the prophet is classified differently in various texts (e.g., oracle, prophecy, vision, word of the Lord). The distinctions between these terms are not particularly relevant for the goals of this chapter. Here, a "prophet" is anyone who received a divine message and communicated that with other people.

fact that other prophets claimed to have heard from the divine (Jer. 14:14; 21:21–23; Ezek. 13:1–7; Mic. 3:11) and that certain magicians were able to produce remarkable signs (Exod. 7:8–8:7) made determining who the true prophets were of particular importance to the people of Israel—especially early in their formation as a community.

The Torah depicts God verbally communicating through the divine, audible voice as well as through his messenger, Moses, prior to the divine word being written down (see Exod. 3–4). Specific instructions were embedded in this early communication to help the Israelites determine which prophets were false and which were true. These directives for assessing authentic prophecy were necessary during the formation of the people of Israel as the Lord's community, since anyone could conceivably claim to be a prophet and thereby lead the community astray. Consequently, the people of Israel were not to heed anyone speaking in the name of another god, since there was to be no other god before the Lord, who was exceedingly jealous for the covenant people (Exod. 20:3–5; 34:14; Deut. 4:24; 5:7; 6:15; Josh. 24:19; Nah. 1:2).

The Torah outlines the grave consequences for the prophets of alien gods among the people of Israel:

If a prophet, or one who foretells by dreams, appears among you and announces to you a sign or wonder, and if the sign or wonder spoken of takes place, and the prophet says, "Let us follow other gods" (gods you have not known) "and let us worship them," you must not listen to the words of that prophet or dreamer. . . . That prophet or dreamer must be put to death for inciting rebellion against the Lord your God, who brought you out of Egypt and redeemed you from the land of slavery. That prophet or dreamer tried to turn you from the way the Lord your God commanded you to follow. You must purge the evil from among you. (Deut. 13:1–3a, 5)

According to this text, a sign or wonder from a supposed prophet is not necessarily indicative of *true* prophecy. This is particularly evident given the fact that Israel is warned in this passage not to be duped by a sign or wonder if it is coupled with an encouragement to follow any god other than the Lord, the God of Israel. Signs and wonders must be accompanied by proper theology, which necessarily consists of directing the people to the Lord. If this is not the case, the people are commanded to actively expel this wickedness from among them. Striving to persuade the people of Israel to follow a god other than their covenant God is a capital offense. That "prophet" is to be executed; their message is a rebellion against the Lord, and their sleight of hand intentionally subverts the Lord's ways.

Deuteronomy 18:20–22 similarly calls for the community to be circumspect regarding the claims of those who purport to communicate a prophetic word from the Lord:

> But a prophet who presumes to speak in my name anything I have not commanded, or a prophet who speaks in the name of other gods, is to be put to death.
>
> You may say to yourselves, "How can we know when a message has not been spoken by the LORD?" If what a prophet proclaims in the name of the LORD does not take place or come true, that is a message the LORD has not spoken. That prophet has spoken presumptuously, so do not be alarmed.

The passage describes two kinds of prophetic impersonators—one who attributes a word to the Lord that God has not spoken and a second who is under the delusion of speaking in the name of a false god. When a person claims to speak on behalf of the Lord, the community is to test the veracity of that word by waiting to see if the message rings true and if all accompanying indications associated with the message come to pass. If this does not happen, Moses reiterates that such a prophet is to suffer the death penalty.

As we see in these two texts from Deuteronomy, the title "prophet" is used to refer to (1) those who claim to be intermediaries for the Lord and who speak a true word from him, (2) those who claim to represent the Lord and who speak a false word that is not from him, and (3) those who claim to speak on behalf of another divine being.

Biblical prophetic literature is commonly understood to be the passages that focus on authentic prophets of the God of Israel. Yet various accounts of "false prophets" appear throughout the Old Testament (e.g., Zedekiah in 1 Kings 10–12; the prophets of Baal in 1 Kings 18:19–40; a group of prophets in 1 Kings 22:6 and 2 Chron. 18:5; Hananiah, the false prophet in Jer. 28).

Several accounts of the false and true prophets are relayed in narratives, suggesting that such sections could also be considered "prophetic literature" since they feature accounts of the prophets and/or the divine word communicated through them. Biblical prophecy is not inextricably linked to a specific style of writing, since the accounts of the prophets and the divine messages they received are recorded in a variety of compositions.[2]

---

2. The traditional naming of the prophets might also imply that the role was exclusive to men. However, on several occasions women are depicted as prophetesses in the Old Testament. Miriam (Exod. 15:20), Deborah (Judg. 4:4), Isaiah's wife (Isa. 8:3), and Huldah (2 Kings 22:14; 2 Chron. 34:22) are all prophetesses. Compare against the false prophetess Noadiah, who Nehemiah claims was among those who tried to scare him (Neh. 6:14).

Unity in Diversity: The Prophets and Prophetic Texts

Biblical prophetic literature, by our definition, is twofold: (1) It consists of the Scriptures that feature accounts of the authentic prophets, and/or (2) it is composed of the divine word communicated through them. This broad definition leads to understanding a range of biblical material as "prophetic" that might push the boundaries of what Christians have traditionally thought of as prophetic literature. The Old Testament is generally divided between the historical books (Joshua through Esther) and the prophetic books (Isaiah through Malachi). Therefore, some Christians understand the prophetic literature as including only the texts that bear the names of the prophets (e.g., Jeremiah, Ezekiel, Micah). Notwithstanding, well-known prophetic accounts can be found in largely narratival historical books that do not traditionally bear the names of the prophets featured in them (e.g., the narratives of Elijah and Elisha in 1–2 Kings). In the biblical prophetic books that are traditionally named after a prophet, the prophetic word tends to be expressed in eloquent poetry, while in historical books, the prophetic biblical material is normally related in prose. In some instances, a combination of narrative and poetry appears in prophetic literature (e.g., Jonah). Irrespective of how the prophetic literature is presented, these diverse compositions are united in that they feature a character who receives a divine word, speaks on behalf of the Lord, and becomes the focus of attention of (at least a section of) a biblical book.

Christians further tend to divide the prophetic compositions into the "major" and "minor" prophetic books, whose names reveal the major prophetic character featured in the book. The major and minor prophets are mostly written in poetry, with sections of narrative that vary from brief explanatory remarks (e.g., Amos 7:12–14) to longer scenes written mostly in narrative prose (e.g., Isa. 36, 39; Jer. 27–29, 32–45; Hosea 1; Jon. 1; 3–4; Haggai; Zech. 1–8). As a result of this similarity in style, we might tend to understand prophetic biblical literature in light of the predominant overriding *genre* of the major and minor prophets. Yet the designation of "minor" and "major" prophets covers only a portion of the biblical prophetic literature that falls within our definition since it does not include all the accounts of authentic prophets communicating the divine word that was disclosed to them.

Looking to the traditional divisions of the Hebrew Bible is helpful in terms of engaging with all the prophetic literature. In the Hebrew Bible, prophetic literature is divided into the former and the latter prophets, with the former prophets essentially consisting of what many Christians call historical books (i.e., Joshua, Judges, 1–2 Samuel, and 1–2 Kings). Setting the traditional Christian designations aside for a moment, let us briefly consider how these mostly prose narrative books communicate prophetically—that is, instances in which the focus of the composition turns to a character who communicates on behalf of God.

- *Joshua*: Joshua the son of Nun, who is the protagonist throughout much of the book, is uniquely consecrated as Moses's replacement to lead the people of Israel. In the Torah, Moses is called a prophet and depicted as the mouthpiece of God (Deut. 34:10). The people are to listen to Joshua just as they listened to Moses, and God promises to be with Joshua just as he was with Moses (Josh. 1:5, 17; see also Exod. 33:11; Num. 14:14; Deut. 31:1–8; 34:9–10). Joshua is not only to lead the people of Israel in their conquest of the land but also to serve as a prophetic voice to the people, encouraging them to follow the revealed Word of God (Josh. 1:1–11).

- *Judges*: Several of the leading characters in Judges have prophetic voices. For example, Deborah is explicitly called a judge as well as a prophetess (Judg. 4:4). Through a rhetorical question, Deborah discloses the Lord's will to Barak and prophesies future events (4:6–9). In another situation, when the people fall under the oppression of the Midianites, the Lord sends an anonymous prophet to rebuke the people for not having obeyed the word of the Lord (6:7–10). This event occurs just prior to Gideon's ascent to be a judge of Israel while also apparently doubling as a prophet (see 7:2–18).

- *1–2 Samuel*: The namesake of the book of Samuel (according to the Hebrew Bible designation) is depicted as repeatedly hearing from and speaking for God (e.g., 1 Sam. 3:1–4:1; 9:9; 10; 15:10). The prophetic activity at the beginning of Samuel paves the way for the narrative that begins after the death of the prophet (25:1). Additional prophetic activity by the prophet Gad is recorded in Samuel (1 Sam. 22:5; 2 Sam. 24:11, 18–19). Last, Samuel records the well-known instances in which Nathan the prophet appears to David with a word from the Lord—famously, to provide him with a divine promise, and then, infamously, to rebuke him (2 Sam. 7:4–17; 12:1–25).

- *1–2 Kings*: The prophetic activity of the renowned prophets Elijah and Elisha is spread throughout the book of Kings according to the Hebrew Bible (see esp. 1 Kings 17–19; 2 Kings 1–13). Additionally, several other prophets are mentioned within the composition, substantiating the notion that prophecy makes up a considerable portion of the book (1 Kings 1; 11:29; 13; 14:2, 18; 16:7, 12; 18:4, 13).

These observations suggest that the ordering and naming of the Hebrew Bible continue to be helpful when considering prophetic literature. The compositions that some readers regard as merely historical books in actuality contain a significant amount of biblical prophecy. The narrative and poetic content in the former and latter prophets (i.e., the historical books and the major and minor prophets) can be understood as prophetic literature, insofar as it relates the words and activities of the prophets—those who receive an authentic message from the Lord and whose activities and message coincide with the regulations and theology set out in the Torah.

Back from the Future

A broad definition of prophetic literature helps us best engage with this diverse material on the text's own terms as opposed to imposing on the text our own presuppositions about what prophecy should be. Recognizing that prophetic literature consists of a wide range of material helps us interpret prophetic books and prophecies by calling into question a common practice of interpreting them as primarily a compilation of futuristic utterances. Surely, the prophets do claim to anticipate the future (e.g., Zech. 14). However, much of the prophetic material turns out to be quite mundane and applicable to contemporary readers (of both that day and today) as opposed to being utterances about the future that lie dormant, waiting to be decrypted. Peter Gentry asserts, "The biggest part of the message of the biblical prophets has nothing to do with predicting the future. . . . The majority of what they had to say constitutes proclaiming a message that explains how the word of God, already revealed and received in the past, applies to present circumstances and situations."[3]

Misperceptions of prophecy as mostly telling the future can lead to misreading these texts. Readers' expectations that prophets consistently talk about the future will inevitably push the meaning and application of some currently relevant principles these texts contain into the future. Therefore, we as contemporary readers have to pull our perceptions back from the future, away from the assumption that prophecy necessarily means foretelling the future. We do this first by engaging with the prophets as literary material that was developed to instruct the community of God that received these texts. The moment the prophets' words were inscribed by their Dr. Frankenstein, the written, prophetic Word of God was set to endure so that all subsequent readers could know the character of God. Thus when the author records the

3. Gentry, *How to Read and Understand the Biblical Prophets*, 30.

life events and words of the prophets through narratives, we should recall how narrators narrate (see chap. 6). Similarly, when the author records the divine word in poetry, we should bear in mind how biblical poets use poetry to communicate with their readers (see chaps. 14–16). Certainly, engaging with biblical prophecy can be further nuanced, but broadly classifying prophetic literature into these two categories and implementing the interpretive principles for narrative and poetry serves as a starting point for us to read prophecy well in its literary context and to hear the Word of God through the prophets.

Two realities help us read these texts in their contexts and apply their messages in our communities. First, remember that behind the revelatory words uttered (some of which are recorded in the Scriptures) stand the prophets as people. These people became literary characters when an author fashioned them as the protagonist of a composition and made their words the driving theme of at least a portion of a prophetic text. Everything the prophets did and said came to pass in a variety of contexts. Studying as much as we can about the prophets as people permits us to grasp as much of that context as possible and to incorporate that information into our reading of the prophet's words.

Second, a responsible engagement with the prophetic books acknowledges that select accounts of the prophets' lives and words were recounted and crafted into compositions by the biblical authors for the purpose of illustrating their theological purposes. These narratives and this poetry feature the same type of ingenuity we previously discussed relating to these types of writing. Normally, the prophets' lives are chronicled through selective narratives, whereas their prophecies are often related as poetry. This point is crucial for contemporary readers, because we must continuously bear in mind that all accounts of words and deeds that were written down were necessarily stylized. Thus through reading deliberately we can observe both the genius of the biblical writer and the enduring application of the bygone prophets of ancient Israel.

In the rest of this chapter, we will expound on how the prophets are presented as people, focusing on how and when the prophetic compositions lend insight into the contexts of the prophetic personages. The next chapter will focus on aesthetic devices used in poetry by the prophets to encourage readers to turn to the God of Israel. The final chapter in this section will provide an example of deliberately engaging with a specific poetic prophetic text (Isa. 52:13–53:12). This particular prophetic word provided hope to the community that received it, foretold a time of restoration, and remains applicable to contemporary readers of the Bible.

The Prophets as People

The Contexts of the Prophets

The prophets were people whose words and actions came to pass in a number of contexts (e.g., historical, social, political, religious). When the prophets appear in prose, the narrator often crafts the backdrop of the prophet's word from the Lord by recounting some of the circumstances relevant to the advent of the prophet. For example, just prior to the renowned prophet Elijah's appearance onto the biblical scene, the narrator makes the following comments that are crucial to understanding Elijah's ministry:

> In the thirty-eighth year of Asa king of Judah, Ahab son of Omri became king of Israel, and he reigned in Samaria over Israel twenty-two years. Ahab son of Omri did more evil in the eyes of the LORD than any of those before him. He not only considered it trivial to commit the sins of Jeroboam son of Nebat, but he also married Jezebel daughter of Ethbaal king of the Sidonians, and began to serve Baal and worship him. He set up an altar for Baal in the temple of Baal that he built in Samaria. Ahab also made an Asherah pole and did more to arouse the anger of the LORD, the God of Israel, than did all the kings of Israel before him.
>
> In Ahab's time, Hiel of Bethel rebuilt Jericho. He laid its foundations at the cost of his firstborn son Abiram, and he set up its gates at the cost of his youngest son Segub, in accordance with the word of the LORD spoken by Joshua son of Nun. (1 Kings 16:29–34)

This section of the narrative might appear to be mundane to contemporary Bible readers because it seems to just provide the facts related to yet another transition of Israel's kingship. Additionally, we might tend to be more interested in the thrill of Elijah's prophetic narrative, which contains scenes relating harsh confrontations, fire falling from heaven, and a hot pursuit, among other excitement. Thus texts like the six transitional verses from 1 Kings 16:29–34 are especially prone to being skimmed, skipped, or quickly forgotten because we are more interested in the thrill of the texts that portray the action. However, these verses prove to be exceedingly consequential to the "action" sections of Elijah's narrative, since they provide the historical, geopolitical, and religious contexts of the Northern Kingdom of Israel just prior to the emergence of the prophet.

The religious situation of Israel during Elijah's time that is depicted by the narrator is particularly relevant at the beginning of the prophet's ministry. Elijah bursts onto the scene by asserting a polemical promise: "As the LORD, the God of Israel, lives, whom I serve, there will be neither dew nor rain in the next few years except at my word" (1 Kings 17:1). Whereas, on the one hand, a lack of water is universally understood to be a threat to human life, on the other hand, the reader wonders, "Why does Elijah threaten drought instead of another plague?" "What is specifically significant about a lack of water in Elijah's context, and why would he address these comments to King Ahab?"

These types of interpretive questions facilitate an appreciation of the contexts that present Elijah as a person who was deeply entrenched in the historical, religious, and social contexts of his time. The details outlined just before Elijah's introduction, which might hardly appear to be part of the prophetic narrative, are essential to understanding the full significance of Elijah's confrontation with King Ahab. Elijah is not randomly threatening a retributive drought because Israel is unfaithful. Rather, Elijah addresses the specific type of apostasy that King Ahab has permitted to enter into the land through his intermarriage with his Sidonian wife, Jezebel.

The narrator notes that King Ahab "married Jezebel daughter of Ethbaal king of the Sidonians, and began to serve Baal and worship him. He set up an altar for Baal in the temple of Baal that he built in Samaria" (1 Kings 16:31–32). It appears as though the deity mentioned in this passage is more specifically Baal Hadad, the Canaanite storm god who was believed to govern rainfall and, thereby, the fertility of the land.[4] John Day comments relating to the ancient Israelites' being drawn to worship this deity: "Reading the OT, it becomes clear that it was the Baal cult that provided the greatest and most enduring threat to the development of exclusive Yahweh worship within ancient Israel. The fact that the Israelites were settled among the Canaanites, for whom the worship of Baal was so important, and that Palestine is a land utterly dependent for its fertility upon the rain, which was held to be Baal's special realm of influence, accounts for the tempting nature of this cult as well as the strength of the OT polemic against it."[5]

Considering this information, we can develop a picture based in the religious context of Elijah's day. Withholding rainfall was a spectacular attestation that the God of Elijah (Elijah's name means "my God is Yahweh") was actually the true storm God. Immediately after announcing this word of judgment to Ahab, Elijah is commanded by the Lord to go east of the Jordan River and hide himself in the Kerith Ravine. There, God supernaturally provides for

---

4. "With the discovery of the Ug[aritic] texts it became clear that there was one great Canaanite storm-and-fertility deity Baal-Hadad of cosmic stature, so that we must assume that these OT allusions refer to particular local manifestations of this one god" (Day, "Baal," 547). The word "Baal" simply means "lord" or "master." Admittedly, Elijah seems to counter all forms of Baal worship, which is evident by the fact that the word is plural in 1 Kings 18:18.

5. Day, "Baal," 547.

him by sending ravens to bring him bread and meat in the mornings and the evenings (1 Kings 17:3–6). Interestingly, the same God who holds back rain in Israel sends the prophet where there is water and commands the prophet to trust in the Lord for his provision.

By paying close attention to the contexts in which the prophets live (when these details are provided), we are more likely to perceive the impact of the prophetic words. In the case of Elijah, the contexts of his narrative noted prior to his arrival show us that his first words to King Ahab communicate an implicit judgment of Baal worship and allude to the fact that the God of Israel is Lord over the rainfall in and fertility of the land. Elijah's initial proclamation is a polemical assurance that all who meddle with Baal, the false deity who supposedly controls rain and fertility, will see that the God of Israel is the true Sovereign, and because of this, they will suffer the consequences of their apostasy (see 1 Kings 18).

The Ordination of the Prophets

When the prophets are called to their ministries, the narrator supplies important details that portray the biblical prophets as God's spokespeople. We learn about their "ordination" and sometimes other significant aspects of their lives. Some prophets have a formal call story, while others are confronted with a word, oracle, or vision from the Lord. Each of these introductions confers the prophet with the very voice of God, communicating to readers that we are engaging with the divine word in written form.

Not all prophets are called with great drama or grandeur. In many prophetic compositions, the prophets are introduced abruptly; in other compositions, so little information is provided that we barely know who the prophets are. For example, the prophetic books Nahum, Habakkuk, and Zephaniah present different amounts of personal information during their respective prophet's introduction:

- Nahum provides some but not many details for readers. Nahum is not explicitly called a prophet at the beginning of the composition. Rather, he is depicted as having received a vision that was (at least in part) subsequently written in a book (Nah. 1:1). The book communicates an oracle (i.e., burden) concerning Nineveh on behalf of the Lord through Nahum, making Nahum both a prophet and ultimately responsible for the messages in the book that bears his name. Additionally, Nahum is identified as an Elkoshite. Scholars are uncertain about the location of "Elkosh," but this detail also depicts the prophet as a person who speaks into the geopolitical circumstances of his day.

- Habakkuk bears the least amount of introductory information among these three prophets. Almost nothing is stated about him as a historical figure, except that he saw an oracle and was appointed as a prophet (Hab. 1:1). Later in the composition, we encounter a cursory remark that likely depicts him as a musician (3:1). This detail helps us engage with Habakkuk's psalm (in chap. 3) accordingly. Nevertheless, Habakkuk's oracle (chaps. 1–2) is uniquely recorded in the form of a dialogue between the Lord and the prophet. The lack of information relating to the prophet shifts emphasis away from the prophetic person and to the prophetic word. Because of the relative lack of introductory information, we are immediately ushered into a lively discussion between the prophet and God, and we are left to draw on internal clues to discern the historical context in which the prophetic word originally applied. For example, the fact that God proclaims that the Chaldeans are being raised up in 1:6 suggests that the prophetic word was likely delivered shortly before the Babylonian invasion of Judah.

- Zephaniah provides the most detailed information of these three compositions and sketches the prophet as a person. The book begins by stating that it is "the word of the LORD that came to Zephaniah son of Cushi, the son of Gedaliah, the son of Amariah, the son of Hezekiah, during the reign of Josiah son of Amon king of Judah" (Zeph. 1:1). Through this one verse, readers are informed of Zephaniah's family line and observe that he may have been a descendant of Hezekiah, king of Judah. Additionally, readers are provided an idea of the general vicinity and approximate time period in which the prophet received and delivered this word from the Lord.

The books of Nahum, Habakkuk, and Zephaniah serve as examples of how the prophets are briefly presented as conducting their ministries in space and time. Some prophetic compositions give specific information about the prophets (Amos 1:1; 7:14; Hag. 1:1–3; Zech. 1:1), while others present the prophets based on their place of origin (1 Kings 17:1; Mic. 1:1). Some provide a bit of the family line of the prophets (Joel 1:1; Jon. 1:1), while others provide hardly any information other than referring to the prophets as people (Obad. 1; Mal. 1:1). Irrespective of the quantity of information provided, these pithy comments encourage us to remember that the biblical prophetic compositions are stylized, selective representations of the divine word that began with real people in diverse contexts.

Any bit of information we can glean about the prophets as people helps us understand the prophetic word delivered to that prophet and recorded by the author of the composition. The better we are able to locate the prophetic word in its context(s) by paying close attention to the information provided in the prophet's introduction, the better we are able to discern what the oracles meant to the community that received them and then to apply the prophetic message to our day and age.

The Calls of the Prophets

Several of the prophetic books reveal a good deal of personal information about the prophets, primarily by describing their prophetic calls to ministry but also through details included throughout the compositions. Extended scenes depicting the prophets' calls to ministry are instrumental in communicating how, what, and why God is communicating to the prophets' communities at their respective times. Some of the more well-known call stories that depict the prophets as people make up significant portions of the books of Isaiah (6:1–13), Ezekiel (1–3:15), and Jeremiah (Jer. 1). Yet no other call story may be as (in)famous and disturbing as that of Hosea.

Hosea begins like other prophetic compositions that provide personal details relating to the prophet's life: "The word of the LORD that came to Hosea son of Beeri during the reigns of Uzziah, Jotham, Ahaz and Hezekiah, kings of Judah, and during the reign of Jeroboam son of Jehoash king of Israel" (Hosea 1:1). Through this introduction, readers learn that Hosea speaks a word from the Lord (i.e., he is a prophet), become aware of Hosea's lineage, and discover that he likely served as a prophetic figure in the north. Nevertheless, instead of the book heading directly into the word that the prophet receives from the Lord, an extended narrative section follows, detailing Hosea's call into public ministry. This call consists of a counterintuitive directive: Hosea is commanded to join himself to a promiscuous wife—to a person whose lifestyle repudiates the Torah's teaching (Exod. 20:14; Lev. 20:10; Deut. 22:22).

Hosea obeys and marries Gomer, and she bears three children. At this point of the introductory narrative, the reader observes that the divine call of the prophet does not just repeat historical circumstances leading to Hosea's public ministry but also serves as an object lesson through which God will teach the people. The three names of Gomer's children represent the spiritual condition of Israel and the consequences for their waywardness: "Jezreel" represents the fact that the house of King Jehu of Israel is going to suffer divine chastising in the Jezreel Valley; "Lo-Ruhamah" (Hebrew for "not having received mercy" [NIV: "not my loved one"]) represents that God will not have mercy on the house of Israel; and "Lo-Ammi" (Hebrew for "not my people") represents that the once covenant community of the Lord is no longer God's people. Be that as it may, God subsequently plays on these same names to provide hope of restoration to the community of Israel:

> "In that day I will respond,"
>   declares the LORD—
> "I will respond to the skies,
>   and they will respond to the earth;
> and the earth will respond to the grain,
>   the new wine and the olive oil,
>   and they will respond to Jezreel.
> I will plant her for myself in the land;
>   I will show my love to the one I called 'Not my loved one
>   [Lo-Ruhamah].'
>   I will say to those called 'Not my people [Lo-Ammi],' 'You are my
>   people';
>   and they will say, 'You are my God.'" (Hosea 2:21–23; see also
>   1:10–2:1)

The descriptive introduction to the book of Hosea, including the intimate details of the prophet's call to ministry, sets the stage for the words of the prophet in chapters 4–12, in which the Lord, through Hosea, levels harsh criticism at the people of Israel for their covenant unfaithfulness (e.g., 4:10–19), while intermittently providing hope for restoration of their exclusive relationship (1:10–11; 2:14–23; 11:8–11; 13:14; 14:4–7).[6]

Conclusion

Reading prophetic literature well involves a sustained integration of multiple aspects of reading narrative and poetry deliberately. In this chapter, we have focused on the words spoken *about* the prophets and their contexts. Nevertheless, the prophets' actual words are hardly recounted in stale presentations of facts. Rather, the prophets' words tend to be expressed in poetic compositions that demonstrate a literary artistry that impresses attentive readers and calls them to action even today.

6. Other eccentric personal experiences are recorded in the prophetic books to serve illustrative purposes. For example, Isaiah the prophet is commanded to wander around Jerusalem naked for three years as a demonstration of how the king of Assyria will lead away Egyptian and Cushite captives (Isa. 20:1–4). Ezekiel is commanded to sleep on his left side for 390 days, which represents the 390 years of punishment that the house of Israel will bear. He then switches to his right side for forty days, with each day again representing a year (Ezek. 4:4–6). Also, Ezekiel's wife dies, which turns out to be a divinely orchestrated event so that he might have the opportunity to further his prophetic message (24:15–25).

The poetic sections of the prophetic books bear the markings of their authors—their literary Dr. Frankensteins; that is, they are tied together by coordinated statements that introduce the prophetic word, bridge different prophecies, or conclude sections. Additionally, poetic sections of prophecy bear the markings of Biblical Hebrew poetry. We have already discussed the fundamental aspects of poetry in biblical literature in chapters 14–15, and yet focusing on prophecy provides an opportunity to explore other characteristics of poetry that appear specifically in prophetic compositions. The prophetic books' respective authors strove to faithfully communicate the messages of the Lord that came through the prophet and, in doing so, fostered aesthetically pleasing and theologically impactful poetry. In the next chapter, we will focus on the prophets as poets, observing the expressiveness of the prophetic words in their written forms.

EIGHTEEN

How to Engage Poetic Prophecy

> The prophets' messages were communicated not only by what they said,
> but—more importantly—how they said it. . . . For all their eccentricity,
> the prophets were artistic geniuses, crafting their words to maximize the
> effectiveness of their message.
>
> —Al Fuhr and Gary Yates, *Message of the Twelve*

Contemporary poet Billy Collins's heartrending yet humorous poem "On Turning Ten" relates the disconsolate musings of a nine-year-old child who is on the verge of turning double digits. The youngster draws the reader in by hyperbolically and metaphorically likening the very thought of aging to physical discomfort: it is comparable to a stomachache or a headache that one gets when reading without enough light, or like "measles," "mumps," and "chicken pox" to the "spirit," "psyche," and "soul," respectively. In the second stanza the child addresses a conversation partner and accuses him of not understanding:

> You tell me it is too early to be looking back,
> But that is because you have forgotten
> the perfect simplicity of being one.[1]

According to the downcast youngster, the older interlocutor cannot understand the child's plight. He is too old to remember every single digit: the

---

1. Collins, "On Turning Ten," 63.

242

complicated winsomeness of turning two, the fantasies of Arabian wizardry that accompanied the child upon turning four, the military aspirations of turning seven, the royal prowess of turning nine. The inauguration of ten is the commencement of sadness, the young child realizes while "traversing" the universe in sneakers. As one approaches the age of ten, life imminently becomes more serious, presenting an irreversible turning point in which the guilelessness of the past is undone and interchanged with the daunting realities of maturation.

"On Turning Ten" represents Billy Collins's uncanny prowess in using expressive language to engage the affect and imaginations of his readers. The poem discloses the select thoughts and experiences of the speaker to provoke readers to *discern* the child's perceived unrest, *feel* the child's emotional turbulence, and to *move* readers to recall their own aversion to adulthood and empathize with the child. Readers enter the child's world through the poet's colorful remarks, consisting of hyperbole, metaphors, and vivid imagery to which readers can relate.

This is *how* the poem works. This is *why* the poem works.

The realistic information in the poem (e.g., the child's age, aspirations, property, and even imaginary friends) is not *just* an account of connected thoughts, events, or facts. Rather, the poet stylistically includes these true-to-life details to urge the reader to action as they engage with the poem.

The reader becomes the child's interlocutor.

Approached in this manner, the protagonist's words can be read, on the one hand, to address a particular audience that the child had in mind and, on the other hand, to transcend the composition and abruptly impose on the readers' unexpected vulnerability: "'You tell me it is too early to be looking back.'"[2] The "you" suddenly becomes "us" as we are captivated by the emotions of turning ten through the charm of the poem.

Billy Collins's contemporary poetry exhibits characteristics and outcomes similar to poetry that appeared thousands of years prior in prophetic biblical compositions. Careful readers of biblical prophecy recognize that factual information appears in the poetry but that it is stylistically arranged to maximize the impact that the prophetic compositions have on readers. If information *can* be stylized in prophetic biblical literature, it *is* stylized with the purpose of urging readers to discern the meaning of the text, to feel the sentiments provoked by the author, and to be moved to action. Inasmuch as the prophetic compositions were written and then preserved as the divine word delivered through the prophets, successive generations of

2. Collins, "On Turning Ten," 63.

readers have become contemporary interlocutors of the prophets. The new audience becomes those of us who are captivated by the aesthetic devices of the poetic prophets and driven to internalize the main points of their compositions.

There are manifold styles of prophetic compositions written in poetry that originally extended to a multitude of contexts. Likewise, the functions of poetic compositions in modern readers' lives are varied and doubtless influenced by the reader's circumstances. Nevertheless, poets inspire us by crafting their words in a way that not only is authentic in their contexts but also aspires to move all those who engage with their compositions in subsequent generations. In the rest of this chapter, we will evaluate the contemporary applications of prophetic biblical compositions that were written in poetry. We will observe how these writings were aesthetically crafted so that all readers might discern the principles eloquently communicated therein, feel the sentiments evoked by the composition, and be moved to action in their respective contexts.

Poetic Prophecy to Israel, the Nations, and the Reader

This call to discern, feel, and take action begins with *actually* engaging with the poetic prophets on their terms. Readers of the prophetic books cannot help but notice similarities in the compositional makeup and content of their poetic sections. On the one hand, in Biblical Hebrew poetry the prophets communicate messages from the Lord that came to them in comparable ways: a burden/oracle (Isa. 14:28; Zech. 9:1), a vision (Isa. 1:1; Obad. 1), a parable (Ezek. 17:2; Mic. 2:4), a simple "word" (Jer. 1:4), or a combination of modes of communication (Nah. 1:1; Hab. 1:1; 2:2–3). Notwithstanding the technical distinctions that exist between these types of messages, it follows that the themes and deliveries of the prophets' messages bear resemblances since the prophets wrote for a Hebrew-speaking and Hebrew-reading constituency who bore a common history and lived in the same general region of the world. It simply makes sense that prophets broached related topics and crafted their messages similarly in poetry.

On the other hand, it is unreasonable to curtail the meaning and/or purpose of *all* of the prophetic compositions that are written in poetry to a single main idea. Despite general similarities, the poetic prophecies represent varied communication from God for different types of people, in different locations, and at different times. All of the prophecies were contextualized messages that the Lord communicated through the prophet. This diversity suggests that it simply does not make sense to posit narrow and simplistic objectives for all of the prophets who wrote in poetry based on their resemblances to one another.

Ironically, the contextualization of the individual prophetic compositions is what brings a bit of harmony to the distinctiveness of the poetic prophets and facilitates reading them as applicable to this very day. The common threads that emerge from the poetic prophets, which were originally contextualized for different settings, can be further contextualized by modern readers. Readers seeking a present-day application will observe that at least two broad themes materialize while reading the poetic prophets: (1) the call for the covenant community (e.g., Israel, then Israel and Judah) to respond to God with all their heart and (2) the call to the nations to heed the word of the Lord, the God of Israel. These motifs are directly relevant to how we read this sometimes esoteric feeling poetic literature.

A Heart Response

The prophets urge their readers through poetry to genuinely respond from the "heart" to their messages. Heart language is patently metaphorical, but it is also clearly biblical, first arising in the Torah. Moses commands the people of Israel to respond properly to God's revealed word through a changed heart: "Circumcise your hearts, therefore, and do not be stiff-necked any longer" (Deut. 10:16; see also 30:6). The language relating to circumcision recalls the Lord's covenant with Abraham and his descendants in which circumcision served as a sign of them being set apart for the purposes of God (Gen. 17:1–14; Lev. 12:3). Circumcision of the heart, therefore, relates a similar concept: it was meant to function as an indication that the community internalized God's call upon them and responded with devotion.

Moses's command to circumcise the foreskin of the heart was written in narrative prose in a section of the Torah that contextually provides an idea as to what a heart response is to look like for the covenant people. Shortly before the command for Israel to circumcise their hearts, Moses reminds the people of Israel of practical steps they need to take in order to stay in proper communion with the Lord: "And now, Israel, what does the LORD your God ask of you but to fear the LORD your God, to walk in obedience to him, to love him, to serve the LORD your God with all your heart and with all your soul, and to observe the LORD's commands and decrees that I am giving you today for your own good? To the LORD your God belong the heavens, even the highest heavens, the earth and everything in it" (Deut. 10:12–14).

The demands set out for Israel hinge on "observ[ing] the LORD's commands and decrees." In other words, the circumcision of the heart will be manifest when the Lord's community embraces the previously revealed, divine word in obedience. The required heart response of Israel consists of permitting God's word to influence their essence to the point where they will love God and their actions will demonstrate this fact. This idea of Israel internalizing the word of God and acting out of devotion to the Lord goes all the way back to Israel's days of wandering in the wilderness.

Yet Israel disobeys. They are not completely devoted to the Lord. Ultimately, they suffer the consequences of their rebellion by losing sovereignty over their own people group and over their land. Nevertheless, the poetic prophets pick up the call to a heart response, and they use poetic devices to point the community to the Torah and urge them to return to their God. For example, Jeremiah reiterates the call for the readers to respond to God in obedience in language similar to that of the Torah:

> Circumcise yourselves to the LORD,
>   circumcise your hearts,
>   you people of Judah and inhabitants of Jerusalem,
>   or my wrath will flare up and burn like fire
>   because of the evil you have done—
>   burn with no one to quench it. (Jer. 4:4)[3]

In the context of Jeremiah 4, the prophet suggests that circumcising the heart is akin to properly responding to God through obedience and reciprocating the fellowship of their creator. Jeremiah asserts that the people's disobedience and apostasy is a result of not heeding the voice of the Lord (3:24–4:1). This implies that a proper heart response includes attending to God's revealed communication. The prophet proclaims serious impending consequences if the people of Judah and Jerusalem continue to repudiate the voice of the Lord and, thereby, ignore the call to circumcise their hearts (4:4b). A call to genuine communion with the Lord through internal change is a topic that is belabored by the prophets (9:25–26; Ezek. 44:7).

Poetry is a particularly effective way of calling people to a change of heart since poetic compositions give an important place to the expression of emotion, thereby prompting readers to learn by feeling. This may be why poetry and biblical prophecy are linked in the Old Testament—namely, because poetry supplied the prophets with the unique ability to urge the people to a holistic

---

3. This concept was later picked up by the apostle Paul to open the gospel message to those who embraced it in their hearts (cf. Rom. 2:28–29; Col. 2:10–11).

change by painting images that would affect their emotions on behalf of the divine. The *Princeton Encyclopedia of Poetry and Poetics* makes this connection:

> [Hebrew] poetry is intimately linked with prophecy which has no parallel among Eastern or Western people. In spite of the superficial resemblances to ecstatic practices in the ancient East, it is a unique phenomenon. . . . What makes prophets unique poets is a belief and claim that their words are inspired by an all-seeing, all-knowing Power which transcends human wisdom: God. . . . The prophets, who were poets and who couched the simple ideas in images and visions, had an abiding influence on their people and, through them, on the entire world. They may be said to have shaped a nation—perhaps the only example of a people transformed by the magic touch of poetry.[4]

Though not exclusive to poetry, the metaphoric use of the graphic image of circumcision (i.e., cutting away the foreskin) is key to Jeremiah's demand for his people to return to their covenant God. God, through the prophet, calls the people to respond accordingly by "cutting away" anything that is unwarranted or superfluous in their lives—anything that causes them to appear like the nations around them who do not have the unique covenant relationship with the Lord (e.g., idol worship; Jer. 4:1). Jeremiah's circumcision of the heart is characteristic of the prophets' appeal to the affect of the people through the vivid imagery exemplified in poetry.

Calling the people to an internal, sincere response to the Lord, and harking back to God's previously revealed word, seemed to be fashionable among the prophets. Micah uses the poetic devices of parallelism, repetition, and hyperbole to proclaim God's desire for the covenant people to respond in loving obedience to God's former revelation:

> ⁶With what shall I come before the LORD,
>   and bow down before the exalted God?
> Shall I come before him with burnt offerings,
>   with calves a year old?
> ⁷Will the LORD be pleased with thousands of rams,
>   with ten thousands of rivers of olive oil?
> Shall I offer my firstborn for my transgression,
>   the fruit of my body for the sin of my soul?
> ⁸He has shown you, O mortal, what is good.
>   And what does the LORD require of you?
> To act justly and to love mercy
>   and to walk humbly with your God. (Mic. 6:6–8)

4. *Princeton Encyclopedia of Poetry and Poetics*, s.v. "Hebrew Poetry," 338.

This section is replete with poetic aesthetic devices. Repetition is conspicuous in Micah 6:6 by way of parallelism. In the four lines of this verse, the prophet asks two rhetorical questions that both require similar responses. The repetitive questioning is a poetic device used to provide an expected response. In this case, the prophet posits that he can offer nothing that would be worthy of a favorable response by the Lord. The same technique is used again in the next verse, combined with the devices of parallelism and hyperbole. The prophet sets forth the potential offerings of "thousands of rams," "ten thousands of rivers of olive oil," and the overstated suggestion of sacrificing his "firstborn" because of his transgressions. Would the Lord be pleased with these extravagant offerings? No, the prophet implies through the use of aesthetic devices. This, naturally, leads the reader to ask, "What type of offering does the Lord *actually* want?"

The prophet responds that the Lord previously communicated expectations for the covenant community. The Lord requires that people respond to the divine revelation in obedience—to properly carry out justice and lovingkindness and to behave in a humble way. These responses are dispositions of the heart based on embodying God's instruction; they reflect an internalization of the character of the God whom Israel is to serve.

This change in disposition of the heart is also broached in the poetic prophecy of Joel:

> "Even now," declares the LORD,
>   "return to me with all your heart,
>   with fasting and weeping and mourning."
>
> Rend your heart
>   and not your garments.
> Return to the LORD your God,
>   for he is gracious and compassionate,
>   slow to anger and abounding in love,
>   and he relents from sending calamity. (2:12–13)

Again, figurative language is conspicuous relating to the "heart." First, the prophet, speaking on behalf of the Lord, calls the people to return with all of their "heart." Heart is clearly metaphorical in this context, standing in for the essence of the community. The people are being commanded to return to God with all of their being. Second, by calling the people to "rend [their] heart," the prophet is illustratively playing on a familiar phrase in ancient Israel. In other places of the Old Testament, rending the garments was a sign of great anguish (Gen. 37:29; 44:13; Num. 14:6; 2 Sam. 1:11; 3:31;

Job 1:20). Interestingly in the context of Joel, the Lord declares the physical sign of rending one's clothes to be an inadequate response to what is required by the Lord. Returning to God with all of one's heart means rending one's heart—it consists of an internal, transformative experience that is manifested through fasting, weeping, and mourning (Joel 2:13). According to Joel, this type of genuine response might result in the Lord relenting and blessing the people, since "he is gracious and compassionate, slow to anger and abounding in love, and he relents from sending calamity" (2:13; cf. Exod. 34:6).

This call to respond with the heart can be summarized by the parting words of Malachi, who, speaking on behalf of the Lord, commands the people: "Remember the law of my servant Moses, the decrees and laws I gave him at Horeb [Sinai] for all Israel" (Mal. 4:4; see also Deut. 4:9–10; 5:2). Israel was perpetually called to respond to God's Word in obedience, not just to follow arbitrary laws but because their obedience would indicate their reciprocal fellowship with their covenant God. Heart change for Israel meant centralizing God's Word in the very essence of all people.[5]

Moses contextualized the imagery of the heart as the people were about to enter Canaan; Jeremiah, Micah, and Joel used poetic language to appeal to the people and move them to genuinely carry out God's Word in ways that will please the Lord. The varied contextualization of similar language and imagery in poetry lends credence to the suggestion that the principles stemming from these ancient prophetic texts can continue to be contextualized and applied to contemporary situations for modern readers. As the prophets of Israel and Judah called their communities to respond to the Lord in obedience to the revealed Word, so that prophetic voice emerges for contemporary readers who are urged time and again to return to the revealed Word of God with a disposition of obedience. Just as the prophets' readers were called to action by a divine message, delivered in poetic form, that appealed to their affect, so contemporary readers in the faith community are mobilized by the clever poetry of the prophets to serve in ways that align with the revealed character of God. Every generation of readers becomes a new generation of interlocutors for the prophets. The ancient prophets' "you" is now "us" for those in the community of faith who read and embody their prophecies.

---

5. This call back to the Torah is not exclusive to the poetic prophets. Ezra calls the people back to God's written Word and to obedience (Ezra 7:6, 10; Neh. 8:1–8). The major point in this section is that poetry calls the people to their God in a way that uniquely plays on the affect and invokes the reader's imagination.

A Call to the Nations

Several sections of biblical poetic prophecies are seemingly directed at nations outside of Israel (e.g., Nahum, Obadiah, most of Isa. 13–19 and Amos 1–2). Since the messages of these prophecies are targeted to people outside the covenant community, it might be difficult to perceive how they apply to contemporary readers tracking redemptive history through the people of Israel. How do we engage these texts?

A first step to working through this legitimate question is recalling that all of the poetic prophecies under consideration were written in Hebrew. This is a significant fact given that Israel was a relatively small people group in the ancient Near East (i.e., from Egypt to Mesopotamia). Consequently, it is reasonable to suggest that the Hebrew language spoken by the peoples of Israel and Judah simply was not a particularly influential geopolitical language and that it never came close to being the lingua franca of the region.

Many of the people groups of the ancient Near East to whom the biblical prophets directed their messages (e.g., Egypt, Philistia, Assyria, Babylon, Moab, Syria, Edom, Cush) were able to communicate in languages related to Hebrew (e.g., Aramaic, Akkadian, Moabite, etc.). The internal witness of the Old Testament indicates that educated ancient Israelites/Jewish people were well-versed in the languages of the ancient Near East, especially the widely spoken language of Aramaic (Dan. 2:4b–7:28; Ezra 4:8–6:18; 7:12–26; 2 Kings 18:26). Nevertheless, the writers of the prophetic books did not write their compositions in the languages of the nations. Rather, the poetic prophecies about other countries were written in lofty Hebrew jargon, which was a comparatively insignificant language spoken by a small group of people in a vast region.

The prophecy of Nahum provides several straightforward examples of this phenomenon.[6] The book opens with a brief presentation of Nahum as a person (1:1) and immediately transitions into eloquent poetry that recounts the message that Nahum received concerning Nineveh (i.e., Assyria). This transition into poetry is exhibited in Nahum 1:2–8 by the appearance of a partial alphabetic acrostic in Hebrew. Select portions of this acrostic are below with the corresponding Hebrew letters that begin each line in italics:

---

6. Some interpreters do not consider the entirety of Nahum to be about the Assyrians. Additionally, sections of the prophecy, as with other divine messages given to the nations, are overtly directed to the covenant people (e.g., 1:15; cf. Obad. 17–18). The fact that the overall emphasis of Nahum is directed toward a nation other than the covenant people is what is important here.

> (*aleph*) The LORD is a jealous and avenging God.
> (*bet*) His way is in the whirlwind and the storm.
> (*gimel*) He rebukes the sea and dries it up.
> [*dalet* is not clearly represented.]
> (*he*) The mountains quake before him.
> (*vav*) The earth trembles at his presence.
> (*zayin*) Who can withstand his indignation?
> (*khet*) His wrath is poured out like fire.
> (*tet*) The LORD is good.
> (*yod*) He cares for those who trust in him.
> (*kaph*) He will make an end of Nineveh; he will pursue his foes into
> the realm of darkness.

A couple of observations about this poetic section of prophecy highlight how specific this was to readers of Hebrew. The acrostic, though presumably apparent to ancient readers, is somewhat enigmatic in the Hebrew text. The Hebrew letters do not appear at the beginning of every line in the current layout of the Hebrew text, as one might expect; the Hebrew letter *dalet* is not clearly represented; and the acrostic is incomplete, not covering the second half of the Hebrew alphabet. However, whereas it is ideal to have unabridged acrostics (Ps. 119; Prov. 31; Lam. 1), discontinuous acrostic poems are not uncommon in biblical poetry (e.g., Pss. 9–10 are not precisely ordered; Pss. 25 and 34 lack the *vav* line; Ps. 37 lacks the *ayin* line; Ps. 145 lacks the *nun* line). Naturally, accomplished readers of Hebrew poetry still would have recognized this acrostic. It seems as if the author may have been challenging the reader to decipher and internalize the message of the prophecy while decoding the aesthetic device. This is brilliant on behalf of the author and makes for a stimulating reading experience.

There are several other places in Nahum's prophecy in which the prophet uses aesthetic devices that would exclusively have been perceived and understood by those who spoke and/or read Hebrew. For example, as Nahum declares the downfall of the people of Nineveh, he states, "They will be entangled among thorns and drunk from their wine" (1:10). Whereas being said to be "entangled among thorns" and "drunk" might not seem particularly disagreeable to modern sensibilities, Nahum is doing much more than this in Biblical Hebrew. Nahum's creativity can be seen via the transliteration of the Hebrew text (i.e., writing the Hebrew in corresponding English letters): *ki 'ad-ṣirim ṣevukim ukeṣove'am ṣevu'im.*

The transliteration is underlined every time the "s" sound is reiterated. The four main words of this line (excluding prepositions and conjunctions) feature the "s" sound at their beginnings, clearly exemplifying the poetic device of alliteration. Additionally, the final morphemes (i.e., small word units) of three of the words have been bolded. Like many words that end similarly in English, all the words in this line that end in "-im" rhyme in Hebrew when they are pronounced. The word that does not rhyme also ends with an "m" (*sove'am*), exemplifying consonance across the line. Last, as one might imagine, the words *sove'am* and *sevu'im* are related to the same Hebrew-language root, meaning "to imbibe too much alcohol."

This combination of alliteration, rhyme, and consonance would have caught the attention of the original Hebrew-language readers, particularly given the somber tone of the prophecy up to this point. Nahum is not attempting to be endearing by concocting a nursery-rhyme type of jingle and calling his foes childish names. Rather, the prophet uses poetic wizardry to catch the attention of his readers and to inform them of the coinciding repercussions of this immoral state: "They will be consumed like dry stubble" (Nah. 1:10b). The end of Assyria is going to be dreadful, and Israel is seemingly the first to get this breaking news in its language. This should have moved the readers to acknowledge divine justice, mercy, and consolation, given how the tremendous might of the Assyrians was used against Israel after they repeatedly disobeyed the word of the Lord (2 Kings 17:1–18) and how the Assyrians ultimately threatened Judah (18:9–37).

Similar aesthetic devices appear later in another poetic section of Nahum's prophecy that portrays the ruin of Nineveh and her leaders. In Nahum 2:10, the prophet proclaims, "She is pillaged, plundered, stripped!" in reference to the fate of the city (cf. Zeph. 2:13–15). The transliteration of the Hebrew in this line helps us understand the poetic aptitude of the prophet and how this type of statement, though relating to Assyrians, is actually directed to Hebrew speakers: *buqah umevuqah umevullaqah.*

Breaking up the line into individual syllables will help us recognize the poetic value of the statement:

bu-qah	*u-me-vu-qah*	*u-me-vu-lla-qah*

These few words put together in this manner exhibit remarkable poetic genius. First, using rare words or unique conjugations is a conventional poetic device used throughout the Bible, especially in books like Job, Psalms, and Proverbs. As a matter of course, all three of the main words (excluding the conjunctions) in Nahum 2:10a are uncommon, appearing only here in these forms in the Bible. Additionally, the phonetic (i.e., sound) correspondence between these words is striking. Besides the notable assonance and consonance, each word (after the first) contains all the syllables of the previous word.[7] The first two words of verse 10a are likely related to one another in Hebrew and relay the concept of "emptiness." If this is the case, then Nahum's trite "Desolate! Desolation and ruin!" (ESV), in which the exclamation points do most of the work in English, is *really* a clever and elegant articulation of the bareness of Nineveh after it has been ransacked. This proposal seems to be corroborated by the third word in the line (*mevullaqah*), which stems from a root used elsewhere to mean "to lay waste" (Isa. 24:1). The first line of Nahum 2:11 is a prime example of how poetic prophets employ aesthetic devices as their own exclamation points and, in doing so, push readers to be emotionally affected.

In this same context, Nahum uses poetry to jeer at the Assyrian leadership. The taunt begins with an interrogation that hints at the cleverness of the prophet. In one verse, Nahum asks four related questions while using four different words for "lion" (cf. Job 4:10–11):[8]

> Where now is the lions' den,
>   the place where they feed their young [lions],
> where the lion and lioness went,
>   and the cubs, with nothing to fear? (Nah. 2:11)

The repetitiveness of this questioning helps readers perceive that the discussion has progressed from the destruction of the city (Nah. 2:10) to a more specific target represented through the lion imagery. There might be nuances depicted by the use of various words for "lion" in this verse, but one thing can safely be concluded about lions in general: they are ferocious predators. Yet in 2:11, the author depicts the normally savage lion being hunted instead of acting as predator. Nahum 2:12 portrays typical lion activity:

> The lion killed enough for his cubs
>   and strangled the prey for his mate,
> filling his lairs with the kill
>   and his dens with the prey.

Again, transliteration helps us understand what the prophetic poet is doing here.

7. The Hebrew letter *bet* is transliterated with a "b" and a "v" since it can assume two different sounds.
8. Repetition can be used as a powerful poetic device by the prophets. For example, Joel uses four words for "locust" in 1:4.

'aryeh toreph vede gorotayv
umechanneq lelivotayv
vayemalle'-tereph chorayv
ume'onotayv terephah

Poetic aesthetic devices materialize anew when we look at the Hebrew. The bolded sections exemplify consonance that appears in all lines of the verse (*-ayv*). The underlined words in the transliteration depict three related words that are slightly different in form but that all originate from the same Hebrew root that means "to tear." Hebrew readers would have discerned this, sensed the effect of the poetry, and been moved to reflect on the content of the message, as is the result of all impactful poetry.

Based on the context of Nahum's prophecy, it appears that the prophet is depicting the Assyrian leadership as the lions of 2:11–13. Nahum 2:13 is particularly helpful in discerning this metaphorical language

> "I am against you,"
>   declares the LORD Almighty.
> "I will burn up your chariots in smoke,
>   and the sword will devour your young lions.
> I will leave you no prey on the earth.
> The voices of your messengers
>   will no longer be heard."

Those with chariots in this verse are also those who have "young lions" and consume "prey." This is evidently a reference to the Assyrian military conquering other nations. Yet in a dramatic turn of events, Nahum eloquently reverses that imagery and portrays the oppressors being subjugated (2:11). The Lord, the God of Israel, is "hunting" them and will do to the Assyrians what they did to others. This epic reversal carried out in dense poetry was surely intended to make a forceful impact on the ancient reader.

If these messages had been written in Aramaic, more ancient readers would have been able to engage with the original texts closer to the time of the destruction of Nineveh. Yet Nahum communicates these heartrending messages in articulate poetry that was written in Hebrew and not in the languages of the nations. This leaves the reader wondering, Why are the prophecies that are directed toward other nations written in a politically insignificant language of a minority people group of the ancient Near Eastern world? The answer to this question is key to understanding how to read and apply the prophets—especially those who wrote in elevated poetry—in our day and age.

From the Poetic Prophet to the Present Day

Israel may not have been a geopolitical powerhouse in their day, but they were unique in terms of their covenant relationship with the Lord. Israel had a special call on their community to be a living example of the Lord to the nations, being set apart as followers of the detailed verbal revelation that God gave them throughout their history through the Torah, the Prophets, and the Writings. Everything Israel did, from following the legal sections of the Torah that affected daily life to carrying out the details of their religious system, was to represent the Lord as the one true God in their world (Deut. 6:4–9; see also Lev. 11:44). Being the Lord's witness in their world by communicating divine truth through word and deed was inextricably linked to being the Lord's covenant people.

Amid the failures of the covenant community, some of the prophets picked up on this call for God's people to be set apart and to turn back to the Word of the Lord with all of their heart. Others prophesied concerning people groups outside of Israel. As the covenant community discerned what was written about other nations and felt the sentiments provoked by the writer, they were moved to be a prophetic voice to those around them. Through these prophecies, the community further discovered the attributes of the Lord and was called to testify about their God to the nations. The poetic prophets stirred up the covenant people to become a prophetic voice providing hope, encouragement, justice, truth, and when necessary judgment, both within and outside of their community. Simultaneously, the community was to be the paragon of God's love to humanity by exemplifying the unique fellowship they had with the Lord, which was open to all who would respond with their hearts to God's Word.

Just as the ancient covenant people were called to be a prophetic voice to those within and outside of their communities, so contemporary readers of faith can develop a prophetic voice through engaging with and proclaiming the messages of the ancient poetic prophets. As modern readers embrace these prophetic texts, though they were not primarily directed toward us, we become the interlocutors by way of honoring and preserving them as the written Word of God delivered through the prophets. The community of faith is called to positively impact the world around them by sharing the heart of the prophets, calling all to turn and rend their hearts in obedience to God's revealed Word. As we engage and proclaim the messages of the prophets, we become heralds of hope, encouragement, justice, truth, and when necessary judgment, both within and outside of our communities. Simultaneously, the diverse contemporary community of faith is a paragon of God's love to humanity by exemplifying that fellowship with the Lord is available to all who would respond with their hearts to the Word of the Lord.

Though many of the prophets called their communities to a heart response, and though many of them called the nations to heed the voice of the Lord, the covenant community disobeyed their God, and the nations scorned the God of Israel. However, the Lord did not give up on humanity. Rather, the Lord used more prophetic figures and the experiences of the covenant community to provide hope for future restoration. In the next chapter, we will discuss how the poetic servant songs of Isaiah use eloquent poetry to provide future hope for the nations and how God uniquely used the covenant community as this plan of redemption unfolded.

NINETEEN

Who Is Isaiah's Suffering Servant?

Tell them I'm not coming, see? I'd rather be damned than go along with you. I came here to get my rights, see? . . . I'll go home. I didn't come here to be treated like a dog. I'll go home. That's what I'll do. Damn and blast the whole pack of you.

—The Big Man, in C. S. Lewis, *The Great Divorce*

A lack of humility can facilitate the most senseless choices. This is an undeniable conclusion that emerges after observing the decisions made by the diverse group of characters in C. S. Lewis's classic *The Great Divorce*. This story recounts a dream in which a busload of people arrives in heaven and the passengers are faced with the decision of staying there or returning to hell, from where they came. The people, now ghosts in heaven, encounter solid, heavenly spirits who strive to persuade the erstwhile residents of hell to remain in the celestial domain. All that the ghosts ultimately have to do is to humble themselves and concede the obvious—that heaven is a more desirable abode than hell, despite the difficulties associated with giving up all they are familiar with in hell. As a matter of course, almost all the ghosts provide unreasonable excuses to leave the sublime, heavenly realm and go back toward the bus, intent on perpetually residing in the gloomy and undesirable abode of hell.

Though the characters' reasons for returning to hell are absurd, they are, ironically, understandable to readers because they stem from misguided sentiments based on shared human experiences. For example, the Big Man spurns heaven because a murderer known to him is a spirit that endeavors to get him to stay. The haughty disposition of the Big Man emanates not just from the fact that the spirit was a murderer but also from the Big Man's insistence on his perceived "rights," which include being acknowledged as more righteous than a murderer. The Big Man is not adequately self-aware to enter the celestial bliss right before his eyes. He does not recognize that the evidence for a greater good than "rights" is right in front of him in the form of a redeemed murderer inviting him into a place that will bring endless joy. The Big Man is not humble enough to permit the evidence of what he observes to influence his conclusion, and thus he chooses to go "home" and to be damned rather than embrace the better way that is before him. In Lewis's story, he adeptly shows that assertiveness based on arrogance and overconfidence prohibits the ghosts from making logical decisions that would allow them to mature into all that they could be and to experience the pleasures of heaven.

Assertiveness based on arrogance and overconfidence can also hinder Bible reading and deter a person from growing into a more mature reader of biblical texts. This is particularly the case for when we engage with ancient passages that have a generally accepted interpretation within the Christian community. If we have a presumptuous disposition toward the biblical material stemming from preconceived notions of what it *should* mean at the cost of what it *actually* says, then we choose arrogance over humility. Shunning a healthy questioning of our readings of the Old Testament is akin to preferring the comforts of "home," yet this very well may mean choosing to walk back to the familiar bus, imprudently eschewing the possibility to develop as readers of the Bible.

A Sense of the Servant

In the pursuit of Christian self-awareness, reading humbly, and not falling into the trap of scorning the absolute obvious, it is important to make a couple of significant confessions prior to reexamining Isaiah 52:13–53:12. The rhetoric commonly used in popular Bible translations facilitates an understanding of Isaiah's poem as exclusively a *futuristic* prophecy about the person and work of Jesus. Admittedly, one of the reasons that past and present readers have a sense of the identity of this servant is directly related to the fact that the language used in Old Testament translations suggests that the servant song in 52:13–53:12 predicts the vicarious suffering of Jesus.[1]

Some interpreters have had reservations about this overtly Christian interpretation of the passage. Benjamin Sommer weighs in on the interpretation of Isaiah 52:13–53:12 from a Jewish perspective:

> One of the most difficult and contested passages in the Bible, these fifteen vv. have attracted an enormous amount of attention from ancient, medieval, and modern scholars. In particular the identity of the servant is vigorously debated. Although the servant is spoken of as an individual, the reference may well be to the collective nation (or the remnant). Thus, many argue that the servant symbolizes the entire Jewish people. . . . Others maintain that the passage describes a pious minority within the Jewish people; this minority suffers as a result of the sins committed by the nation at large. . . . Other scholars argue that the servant in this passage is a specific individual (cf. 50.4–11 n.). Targum and various midrashim identify the servant as the Messiah. . . . Christians have argued that this passage in fact predicts the coming of Jesus. Medieval rabbinic commentators devoted considerable attention to refuting this interpretation.[2]

Sommer's words help us understand that this passage has not always been interpreted in a way that coheres with Christian intuition. The diverse interpretation of this passage by Jewish people who also hold this text to be sacred should be sufficient to make Christians pause and reflect on whether a *futuristic prophetic* reading of this servant song in its context is warranted. Admitting the inclination to read this passage one way or another is fundamental to challenging one's reading and striving to honestly engage with the text at hand.[3]

It is strikingly obvious that the New Testament writers categorically understood the language of Isaiah's servant song to somehow apply to Jesus; Jesus is portrayed as applying the words of Isaiah 53 to himself (Luke 22:37), and Philip famously preached the gospel message to the Ethiopian eunuch who was reading this passage (Acts 8:26–35). Other New Testament writers also apply this passage to Jesus's life and ministry in some manner (Matt. 8:17; John 12:38; Rom. 10:16; 1 Pet. 2:21–25). Given these facts, there is no doubt

---

1. A futuristic predictive understanding is common in Christian interpretation even though many English-language translations render the prophecy in the past tense.

2. Sommer, "Isaiah," 872.

3. To balance the typical Christian proclivities related to Isa. 52:13–53:12, all biblical quotations of the Old Testament in this chapter are adapted from the Jewish Publication Society's translation (JPS) of the Tanakh.

that Christians *should* believe that Isaiah 52:13–53:12 *somehow* relates to Jesus. There is no sense in trying to act as if we could unsee these passages.

However, honest questions remain concerning the sometimes-curious interpretive methods of the New Testament writers (e.g., the use of Hosea 11:1 in Matt. 2:15). Simply because language from Isaiah's suffering servant song appears in reference to Jesus in the New Testament does not necessarily mean that the Old Testament passage is a *predictive prophecy* in the sense that Isaiah's words were intended to make specific declarations about Jesus's life in advance. The language in Isaiah could have conceivably been appropriated by authors as a rhetorical device either to talk about the Christian Messiah or simply to advance the belief that the fledgling Christian movement burgeoned from ideas like those in Isaiah. Thus for Christians the question is not so much whether Isaiah 52:13–53:12 applies to Jesus in the Christian conscience but, rather, whether this was *predictive prophecy*.

It is impossible to carefully examine all the potential readings of Isaiah's suffering servant song in this chapter. It is possible, however, to examine whether the song lends itself to the type of predictive prophecy that abides in Christian readings of Isaiah 52:13–53:12 in light of the other servant songs and other pertinent sections of Isaiah. In the rest of this chapter, we will attempt to candidly respond to the following question: Does the text of Isaiah 52:13–53:12 invite a reading in its literary context that anticipates a singular, future servant who will eventually play a unique role in the divine plan?

Israel, the "Servant" of the Lord

Isaiah 40 begins with a well-needed word of hope and comfort for the covenant community. Just prior to this encouraging pronouncement, Isaiah relates a narrative in which Hezekiah, the king of Judah, permits Babylonian envoys to view all of his riches. This act greatly displeases the Lord, and, when Isaiah hears about it, he levels a judgment against King Hezekiah and the people of Judah, stating: "Hear the word of the LORD of Hosts: A time is coming when everything in your palace, which your ancestors have stored up to this day, will be carried off to Babylon; nothing will be left behind, said the LORD. And some of your sons, your own issue, whom you will have fathered, will be taken to serve as eunuchs in the palace of the king of Babylon" (Isa. 39:5–7).

An entire reading of the Old Testament clarifies that the Babylonian exile did not come to pass exclusively because of Hezekiah's indiscretion. The community collectively suffered the consequences of turning away from the Lord by being exiled from their land. Jerusalem, the capital of Judah, was eventually captured by the Babylonians during the reign of King Jehoiachin. The king's palace was ransacked, and its valuables were carried off to Babylon. Many political officials, including King Jehoiachin and others, were taken into exile in Babylon (2 Kings 24:10–17). Additionally, the Babylonians destroyed the temple in Jerusalem and carried its valuables and those of the king's palace back to Babylon with them (25:13–17; see also Dan. 1:1–7). Judah was left in ruins, many Jewish people were in exile, and there was eventually no Judean king, no temple, and seemingly no hope for the covenant community.

This is not where the story was meant to end for the community, and thus this is not where the divine word to Isaiah for the people ends either. Into this context, Isaiah speaks a prophetic word of comfort and hope:

> Comfort, oh comfort My people,
> Says your God.
> Speak tenderly to Jerusalem,
> And declare to her
> That her term of service is over,
> That her iniquity is expiated;
> For she has received at the hand of the LORD
> Double for all her sins. (Isa. 40:1–2)

The first verses of Isaiah 40 give the impression of providing consolation for the people as if they already have experienced the negative consequences of their actions. It seems as though the judgment depicted in Isaiah 39 has come to pass and that the community is dismayed, dwelling in exile.[4] The prophet appears to direct his words toward a community that needs to know they have not been forsaken, that God is still for them, and that they are still the covenant people, despite their circumstances. Isaiah communicates that the covenant people will continue to serve a special role in God's plan by uniquely functioning as the Lord's servant. Isaiah takes up servant speech

---

4. This drastic change in tone is one of several reasons some scholars posit that Isa. 40 begins a section of the book that was written by an author other than the one responsible for chapters 1–39. Additionally, scholars propose that there is another, distinct section toward the end of the book consisting of chapters 56–66. Thus it is common to hear of a tripart division of the book of Isaiah consisting of the initial section written by Isaiah of Jerusalem (1–39), Deutero-Isaiah (40–55), and Trito-Isaiah (56–66). For further discussion from a broadly evangelical perspective, see Block and Shultz, *Bind Up the Testimony*. In my opinion, the prophetic voice that anticipates future events like the Babylonian invasion of Judah could very well be the same voice that creatively speaks to a future audience that will experience the comfort of the Lord, since their position as the covenant community of God had not changed despite their troublesome circumstances.

to say that there is still a bright future for the people, even though they have suffered the repercussions of their transgressions:

> 8But you, Israel, My servant,
> Jacob, whom I have chosen,
> Seed of Abraham My friend—
> 9You whom I drew from the ends of the earth
> And called from its far corners,
> To whom I said: You are My servant;
> I chose you, I have not rejected you. (41:8–9)

"Israel," "Jacob," and the "Seed of Abraham" (through Isaac [Gen. 17:19–21]) are all in parallel to one another in the three lines of Isaiah 41:8. The descendants of Israel remain the covenant community simply because God chose them (Isa. 44:1). Irrespective of their waywardness and the divine judgment leveled against them, the Lord has not cast them off, since they are God's treasured possession (Deut. 7:6–11; 10:15; 14:2; Ps. 135:4). Accordingly, Isaiah claims that the Lord will fortify and continue to use Israel in a unique way (Isa. 41:10). But the question remains as to what role the Lord's servant will play from here on, given the difficult political circumstances that considerably weaken their community. What does it mean that Israel remains the Lord's servant, and how will this ultimately manifest, given the hardship that is to face them without a temple, a king, or a land, and, thereby, no political power in the exile?

Reading successively provides more information regarding how the Lord will continue to use the covenant community in the divine plan despite their vulnerable position as an exiled people group. The seed of Abraham, Isaac, and Jacob is called back to its age-old and unique charge of being a testimony to the one true God of Israel. Being witnesses of the Lord was one of the ways in which the covenant people were to function as God's servant:

> My witnesses are you
> —declares the LORD—
> My servant, whom I have chosen.
> To the end that you may take thought,
> And believe in Me,
> And understand that I am He:
> Before Me no god was formed,
> And after Me none shall exist. (Isa. 43:10; see also v. 12)

The community was a witness of the Lord insofar as the people correctly represented God's singularity. The ministry of the covenant people is to be the Lord's witnesses in the nations in which they will eventually dwell, testifying to their God's uniqueness. The prophet Isaiah repeatedly emphasizes this central principle:

> Do not be frightened, do not be shaken!
> Have I not from of old predicted to you?
> I foretold, and you are My witnesses.
> Is there any god, then, but Me?
> "There is no other rock; I know none!" (Isa. 44:8)

Monotheism was a fundamental theological principle that was reiterated throughout the history of Israel while they were in their land. Yet idolatry was one of the main struggles of the covenant community and was part and parcel to Israel's and Judah's exiles (2 Kings 17:7–23; Jer. 44:1–6). Isaiah calls the people back to be the unique witnesses of the Lord, the God of Israel— the only God—wherever they are located in that moment. Representing the Lord to the nations while in locations other than the land of Israel will be a way Israel can play the role of being the Lord's servant, even in exile.

Briefly surveying these select passages in which the Lord's servant is mentioned in Isaiah shows that the title in question can indeed refer to the covenant community. Interpreters who suggest that "the servant of the Lord" refers to Israel in the notable Isaiah 52:13–53:12 passage have repeated and indisputable precedents justifying this reading. The question that remains is whether readers should understand Israel to always be the referent of the servant of the Lord. To this topic we now briefly turn our attention.

"Servant(s)" of the Lord?

Earlier in the book, Isaiah communicates a word from the Lord in which the prophet himself is called the divine servant: "And now the LORD said, 'It is a sign and a portent for Egypt and Nubia. Just as my servant Isaiah has gone naked and barefoot for three years, so shall the king of Assyria drive off the captives of and the exiles of Nubia, young and old, naked and barefoot and with bared buttocks—to the shame of Egypt!'" (Isa. 20:3–4).

In the case of Isaiah 20:3, the servant language explicitly refers to Isaiah the prophet, showing that this designation does not *necessarily* signify the covenant community and *can* represent a singular servant (22:20; 37:35). In this passage, Isaiah the divine servant is called by the Lord to perform an unconventional exploit that is to serve as a portent for a sociopolitical event that God is going to bring to pass. Isaiah's divinely appointed mission in

20:3–4 is to testify to another, more broad-ranging event that will transpire in the future in accordance with the divine plan. This observation concerning the various significances of the Lord's servant is key to interpreting other servant passages in Isaiah. In distinct passages in the book, readers encounter ambiguity concerning the identity of the Lord's servant. For example, the Lord's servant makes an enigmatic appearance at the beginning of Isaiah 42:

> ¹This is My servant, whom I uphold,
> My chosen one, in whom I delight.
> I have put My spirit upon him,
> He shall teach the true way to the nations.
> ²He shall not cry out or shout aloud,
> Or make his voice heard in the streets.
> ³He shall not break even a bruised reed,
> Or snuff out even a dim wick.
> He shall bring forth the true way.
> ⁴He shall not grow dim or be bruised
> Till he has established the true way on earth;
> And the coastlands shall await his teaching. (Isa. 42:1–4)

Isaiah 42:1 seems to depict the covenant community, the Lord's servant, being called to represent the Lord to the nations. However, the precise identity of the servant of the Lord grows ambiguous as one reads through this passage in the context of the entire book of Isaiah. For example, the servant language in the second half of Isaiah 42:1 is reminiscent of Isaiah 11:1–11, which tells of an occasion in which the Lord promises the divine spirit. This passage depicts the emergence of a significant figure upon whom the Lord's spirit will also rest (11:2). It is prophesied that the "Stump/Root of Jesse" in Isaiah 11 will bring about righteous judgment, particularly by paying close attention to society's most vulnerable (11:4–5). Similarly, the servant of the Lord in 42:3 seems to be particularly concerned about bringing forth justice on behalf of the weak, which is evident through the parallelism of the first two lines of the verse. The servant will not "break" or "snuff out" those in vulnerable positions. The servant will uphold the integrity of all people irrespective of their strength and prominence. Executing justice and establishing righteous judgment—especially for the oppressed—is understood elsewhere in Isaiah to be a ministry of the Lord, the God of Israel (Isa. 2:1–4; 57:15; see also Pss. 9:8; 146:7). The portrayal of the servant in Isaiah 42:1 corresponds with that of another important figure in Isaiah and shares characteristics with the biblical portrayal of

God, so as to arouse the curiosity of those who engage with 42:1–4 while reading entirely.[5]

Another question concerning the identity of the figure in Isaiah 42 stems from the scope of the servant's ministry. In Isaiah 42:4, the Lord's servant is depicted as bringing forth justice to the coastlands—to the nations outside of the covenant community.[6] In Isaiah 11, peace that also far transcends the covenant community is to be brought about by the Root of Jesse (11:11–16). In both passages, the ministry of this servant upon whom the Spirit of the Lord rests will have a far-reaching impact on nations outside of Israel. Isaiah 11 suggests that a singular figure from the people of Israel through the lineage of Jesse will accomplish this feat. The servant of the Lord and the stump/root of Jesse share similar functions, raising the possibility that the singular figure of 11:1–11 might somehow be related to the servant in 42:1–4.

As readers continue to engage with the rest of Isaiah 42, more information is revealed concerning the Lord's servant through a metaphor relating to light:

> [6]I the Lord, in My grace, have summoned you,
> And I have grasped you by the hand.
> I created you, and appointed you
> A covenant people, a light of nations—
> [7]Opening eyes deprived of light,
> Rescuing prisoners from confinement,
> From the dungeon those who sit in darkness. (42:6–7)

At first glance, Isaiah 42:6 seems to clarify the ambiguity of the servant from the preceding verses. Here, there appears to be a distinct reference to the covenant people[7] and their unique task of being a representative of the Lord, the God of Israel, to the nations through imagery related to light. Light can be used as an agent to make things visible that would normally not be easily seen. This seems to be how the concept of light is used in 42:6, since Israel being a "light of nations" is followed by a reference to opening the eyes of those "deprived of light" (i.e., the blind) in the next line. Perhaps the

---

5. Elsewhere in the prophets, servant language can refer to a futuristic Davidic figure (cf. Ezek. 34:24; Zech. 3:8).

6. The term "coastlands" likely represents people outside of Israel, since it is paralleled with "nations afar" in 49:1 and "sons from afar" in 60:9 (cf. Gen. 10:5).

7. This phrase can be literally translated "for a covenant of people." The meaning of this exact phrase is uncertain. This translation in Isa. 42:6 reflects an understanding that the descendants of Israel were the Lord's covenant community, whom God uniquely used in the divine plan. See more on how this phrase could be translated below.

covenant community being a light causes people to "see the light"—that is, to understand that the Lord is the one true God.

The imagery changes in the last two lines of Isaiah 42:7 from the servant providing light to the servant freeing prisoners. This imagery is a bit more difficult to discern if it exclusively relates to the covenant community in exile, given that they were subjects to other nations. How could the people of Israel provide any type of freedom for anyone when they did not have freedom themselves?

Reading Isaiah 49 provides some clarification to this question. In this chapter, Isaiah connects the servant of the Lord to the salvation of the Lord. Isaiah 49:5–6 states,

> [5]And now the LORD has resolved—
> He who formed me in the womb to be His servant—
> To bring back Jacob to Himself,
> That Israel may be restored to Him.
> And I have been honored in the sight of the LORD,
> My God has been my strength.
> [6]For He has said:
> "It is too little that you should be My servant
> In that I raise up the tribes of Jacob
> And restore the survivors of Israel:
> I will also make you a light of nations,
> That My salvation may reach the ends of the earth."

A plain reading of Isaiah 49:5 seems to indicate that the Lord speaks to an individual servant, distinct from the covenant community, whose mission is to bring the people back into fellowship with their God.[8] However, reading this verse in the context of the chapter complicates this straightforward interpretation. For example, the prophet depicts Israel as the Lord's servant in 49:3: "And He said to me, 'You are My servant, Israel in whom I glory.'" Given the clarity of this statement that appears so nearby, identifying the servant as Israel in this chapter seems to be the most reasonable conclusion. However, going back a couple more verses calls even this conclusion into question. In 49:1, the prophet invokes imagery of the mother's womb as he does when explicitly referencing the servant in verse 5. Verses 1–2 read

---

8. There is a textual issue in line four of verse 5 ("That Israel may be restored to Him") in the Hebrew manuscript. The literal reading of this line based on the Hebrew text could be "But Israel will not be gathered," perhaps implying that the servant will only return "Jacob" to the Lord. The JPS version quoted above accepts a slight change to the traditional Masoretic Text to make sense of the apparent disparity and to coincide thematically with Isa. 49:6.

together seem to depict a singular person being separated for the Lord's purposes. By the time readers get to 49:5, it seems clear that the prophet uses servant language in various ways. In just the first four verses of the chapter, the prophet could have potentially been speaking of himself, the whole covenant community, a portion of the community, or even some other, unnamed servant.

At any rate, the servant in Isaiah 49:5 is appointed by the Lord to return Jacob and restore Israel. Therefore, it appears as if the Lord's servant in this passage is not a stand-in for Israel but, rather, another individual or entity who will usher in a new season in which the people will be drawn back to God. With this understanding, the final half of verse 6 becomes particularly ambiguous. Who will restore the covenant community so that it might be a "light of nations"? In being a light of nations, how will the community bring the Lord's salvation to the ends of the earth? Ironically, the ambiguity is not clarified by the prophet's reiteration of the concepts of salvation, freedom, light, and darkness just a few verses later while referencing the servant of the Lord yet again:

> [8]Thus said the LORD:
> In an hour of favor I answer you,
> And on a day of salvation I help you—
> I created you and appointed you a covenant people—
> Restoring the land,
> Allotting anew the desolate holdings,
> [9]Saying to the prisoners, "Go free,"
> To those who are in darkness, "Show yourselves." (49:8–9a)

Since the "covenant people" *seem* to be the servant in this passage, the imagery *appears* to reflect the idea that the Lord will use the collective group to participate in remarkable future events. The Lord promises divine assistance to the servant so that the servant might restore what was destroyed, liberate prisoners, and call them into the light. Yet the phrase translated "covenant people" in Isaiah 49:8 can be literally rendered "for a covenant of people" as in 42:6.[9] The use of the phrase in this context leaves readers wondering whether the reference is to the people group as the covenant people or to another entity appointed "for a covenant of people." The interpretation of this translation is admittedly hard to discern.

Adding to the uncertainty relating to the servant's identity is the fact that the imagery in Isaiah 49:8–9a is strikingly similar to the imagery used for the

---

9. See note 7 above.

"anointed" figure on whom the Spirit of the Lord dwells in 61:1–4. Particularly noteworthy is that this figure is appointed

> as a herald of joy to the humble,
> To bind up the wounded of heart,
> To proclaim release to the captives,
> Liberation to the imprisoned. (61:1)

The phrase "liberation to the imprisoned" contains a Hebrew word normally used for opening the eyes (*pakach*; Isa. 35:5; 37:17; 42:7). In this verse, the prophet presents a liberator who facilitates restoration and provides comfort to the vulnerable, while using a word that alludes to the motif of providing vision for those who previously could not see. The servant of the Lord shares these same characteristics. The speaker of Isaiah 61:1–4 appears to be an individual person on whom the Spirit of the Lord dwells. Perhaps, then, the servant of the Lord might also refer to a singular individual who will bring about the Lord's salvation by showing people light, setting people free, and all the while, caring for the vulnerable.

The ambiguity embedded in multiple servant passages close to one another, combined with the identification of the servant with other personages in Isaiah, leads readers to suspect that the imprecision is an intentional ploy by the author. The inspired poet's crafty, polyvalent (i.e., having more than one meaning) servant language provokes us to perpetually wonder to whom or what the "servant" might refer. This vagueness stimulates us to deliberately read the entire text. It is with this disposition that we engage with the renowned servant song in Isaiah 52:13–53:12.

The Suffering Servant in Context

There already exist multiple interpretive options for us when we encounter the Lord's servant again in Isaiah 52:13. These include but are not limited to

- the covenant community of Israel (or, perhaps, a faithful portion thereof);
- Isaiah the prophet; and
- another individual figure who shares characteristics with (an)other personage(s) in Isaiah's prophecy but whose full identity remains ambiguous.

The major issue with settling on a consistent interpretation of the referent to the Lord's servant is that, quite frankly, Isaiah does not invariably endow the phrase with one meaning. Isaiah's language relating to the Lord's servant indicates various referents in proximity to one another, to the point that we may have difficulty distinguishing when the prophet switches from one referent to another. It is up to us as readers to be sensitive to the poetic prophet's stylistic expressions while carefully discerning the topic at hand. Perhaps the poetic prophet has us exactly where he wants us—inquisitive enough to continue thoughtfully engaging with the text, but not so completely bewildered as to revert to despair.

The suffering servant song begins by highlighting the protagonist's menial beginnings. The servant is introduced as particularly unremarkable to behold, to the point where his appearance and the public derision of him makes it seem as if no one should expect any tangible good from him (Isa. 52:14; 53:2–3). Yet the servant is exalted by the Lord and unpredictably has an outsized impact on the nations outside of Israel (52:13, 15). In Isaiah 53 the language of the song transitions to reflect images of the Lord's servant that we have not observed up to this point in Isaiah. Particularly striking is the motif that the servant will suffer on behalf of the transgressions of others. Isaiah 53:4–6 states,

> [4]Yet it was our sickness that he was bearing,
> Our suffering that he endured.
> We accounted him plagued,
> Smitten and afflicted by God;
> [5]But he was wounded because of our sins,
> Crushed because of our iniquities.
> He bore the chastisement that made us whole,
> And by his bruises we were healed.
> [6]We all went astray like sheep,
> Each going his own way;
> And the LORD visited upon him
> The guilt of all of us.

In this passage, the servant becomes the victim of divinely imposed distress for the sake of others to bring about peace for them (Isa. 53:4–5). This is particularly evident in the two sets of parallel lines in verse 5. In the first two parallel lines of the verse, the servant is "wounded" and "crushed" for the "sins" and "iniquities" of others. The result of the servant's suffering is revealed in the last two lines of the verse. The servant's "chastisement" and "bruises" bring about wholeness and healing to those for whom he vicariously suffered.

It is important to note that the prophet speaks in the first-person plural in this section of the composition ("our," "us," "we"). By doing so, he distinguishes himself from the servant while including himself in the community that receives the benefits of the servant's actions. Though the referent of the Lord's servant could conceivably change, the use of the first person in these verses, and again in verse 8, suggests that the prophet does not speak of himself as the servant of the Lord in this song. Additionally, the first-person pronouns include the prophet in a broader community that will benefit from the servant's hardship. Thus it is unlikely that the prophet is indicating that the community, or even a portion of the people, will suffer on behalf of itself. Isaiah appears to be speaking of a servant—not to be confused or conflated with the prophet or the covenant community. This individual servant of the Lord depicted in Isaiah 52:13–53:12 vicariously suffers divinely appointed affliction because of the waywardness of others (53:6). Poetic language relating to vicarious suffering continues as the servant is likened to a sacrificial lamb:

> He was maltreated, yet he was submissive,
> He did not open his mouth;
> Like a sheep being led to the slaughter,
> Like a ewe, dumb before those who shear her,
> He did not open his mouth. (53:7)

The personification of the lamb, and the parallel ewe, is particularly important to interpreting this passage. The significance of this imagery can be elucidated by a reference to a passage in Jeremiah in which the prophet likens himself to a lamb being led to the slaughter. Concerning his own condition of peril, Jeremiah states,

> For I was like a docile lamb
> Led to the slaughter;
> I did not realize
> That it was against me
> They fashioned their plots:
> "Let us destroy the tree with its fruit,
> Let us cut him off from the land of the living.
> That his name be remembered no more!" (11:19)

Realizing that his enemies have plotted against him (Jer. 18:18), Jeremiah portrays himself as a placid lamb being led to the slaughter, just like the Lord's servant in Isaiah. According to Jeremiah, the personified lamb represents an individual person who is "slaughtered" because of the treachery of others. Jeremiah's enemies plot to treat him as if he were a wicked person, cutting him off from the land of the living and blotting out his name and memory

(Pss. 83:4; 109:15; Prov. 10:7). This is the type of treatment that the servant is set to receive in Isaiah's song.

> By oppressive judgment he was taken away,
> Who could describe his abode?
> For he was cut off from the land of the living
> Through the sin of my people, who deserved the punishment. (Isa.
>   53:8)

The Lord's servant in Isaiah is treated as if he were the one who transgressed, and he is cut off from the land of the living. Yet the suffering of Isaiah's lamb is not ineffectual like in the scenario presented by Jeremiah; it is vicarious and substitutionary in nature, and it is ultimately efficacious for the covenant community, among others. The lamb in Isaiah bears the iniquities of others and in this way provides intercession for those who transgressed:

> Out of his anguish he shall see it;[10]
> He shall enjoy it to the full through his devotion.
>
> "My righteous servant makes the many righteous,
> It is their punishment that he bears;
>
> Assuredly, I will give him the many as his portion,
> He shall receive the multitude as his spoil.
> For he exposed himself to death
> And was numbered among the sinners,
> Whereas he bore the guilt of the many
> And made intercession for sinners." (53:11–12)

The Lord is somehow pleased that the servant bears the sin and punishment of others, suffering at the divine will to make other people righteous (Isa. 53:4, 10). Thus toward the end of the composition the Lord provides recompense to this personified lamb who vicariously endures anguish to provide intercession for sinners, making them honorable instead of transgressors. The Lord's servant, a personified lamb, receives "the many as his portion."

Once Isaiah mentions the image of the lamb and the fact that people benefit from its suffering, it becomes possible to track a thread concerning the servant

---

10. The JPS renders this line generally according to the Masoretic Text. The Great Isaiah Scroll from the Dead Sea Scrolls and the Old Greek versions all provide the phrase "he will see light." This reading could be theologically significant for Christians who believe that Jesus is the Lord's suffering servant. Given that light can be a metaphor for life, some might see a reference to Jesus's resurrection in the reading preserved by these manuscripts.

of the Lord in the latter part of Isaiah. In Isaiah 39, the prophet declares that judgment is coming by way of the Babylonians. Yet the community is immediately comforted by the communication to ancient Israelites and to all subsequent readers that God has not cast away his covenant community. Israel is still appointed to play a unique role in the divine plan as the Lord's servant, a "light of nations." In 52:13–53:12, the servant is portrayed as a lamb whose suffering will be beneficial to the covenant community, the prophet himself, and the nations. It seems then that Isaiah might be depicting Israel as ultimately being the Lord's servant and a light to the nations through the individual servant of the Lord presaged in several servant passages and highlighted in 52:13–53:12. Maybe one of the points of this culminating servant song is to convey that Israel will perpetually serve as a light to the nations through an individual servant who will extend the legacy of the covenant community by suffering to make people from Israel and the nations righteous.

History of Reception

The imagery of a lamb that suffers instead of the community is not new to those who read the Bible entirely. The same motif appears in the story of the Passover (Exod. 11–12; see chap. 8 above). In this narrative, the people of Israel are commanded to slaughter an unblemished lamb at twilight on the day of the Passover and to smear its blood on the doorpost and lintel of the houses in which they eat it. The blood of this slaughtered, unblemished lamb is to deliver the people from the destruction that would have come upon them if the lamb had not died (12:3–13). The lamb will die so that the people do not have to, and thereby, the slaughter of the lamb will play an intercessory role on behalf of the community. The Passover lamb will bring about freedom from the penalty of perpetually disobeying God that will be endured that horrid night in Egypt. Only those who have the blood of the Passover lamb on their dwellings will be spared. The slaughtered blameless lamb will intervene on behalf of the people, saving the firstborn from imminent death. After the death of the Passover lamb, the people will be liberated from slavery and brought into a covenant with the Lord their God at Sinai (Exod. 13–14; 20).

Thus when Isaiah uses the lamb imagery, he seems to play on a trope that is fundamental to the history of the people of Israel. Isaiah uses the model for freedom depicted in the Passover based on a sacrificial lamb to denote a spiritual liberation—a freedom from carrying the burden of one's own transgressions. The Lord's servant, the blameless lamb, delivers others from the consequences of their sin, intercedes for them, and pleases the Lord by making many righteous.

It is difficult to know how ancient readers of Isaiah close to the time of the prophetic composition would have understood the imagery of a personified lamb representing an individual vicariously carrying the sin of others to make them righteous. However, what *is* possible to see is how these passages were understood by the writers of the New Testament, who believed that they were perpetuating the tradition of ancient Israel. When the New Testament writers interpreted the lamb imagery and applied it to Jesus, they joined Isaiah in using and furthering a pattern that was deeply embedded in the collective history of the people of Israel.

For example, when John the Baptist observes his cousin Jesus walking toward him, he exclaims, "Look, the Lamb of God, who takes away the sin of the world!" (John 1:29; see also v. 36). In John's exclamation, there are remnants of the imagery of the Passover that were received in Isaiah 53:7 and applied to Jesus as the Lord's servant and the personified lamb. By this, New Testament readers can observe that John the Baptist was participating in a tradition of interpretation that preceded him (see also Rev. 5:6). John adapts imagery that was not simply predictive but also socially and theologically impactful, since it would have been part of the consciousness of his community at that time.

Peter's take on the lamb imagery is quite significant given that it asserts that the blood of Jesus was efficacious like that of the Passover lamb. Peter tells the recipients of this letter, "For you know that it was not with perishable things such as silver or gold that you were redeemed from the empty way of life handed down to you from your ancestors, but with the precious blood of Christ, a lamb without blemish or defect" (1 Pet. 1:18–19). The blood of the unblemished lamb, Jesus, liberated the people from their former, wrongheaded trajectory. Peter further expounds on this allusion to the lamb, making extensive reference to Isaiah's suffering servant song:

> "He committed no sin
> and no deceit was found in his mouth."

> When they hurled their insults at him, he did not retaliate; when he suffered, he made no threats. Instead, he entrusted himself to him who judges justly. "He himself bore our sins" in his body on the cross, so that we might die to sins and live for righteousness; "by his wounds you have been healed." For "you were like sheep going astray," but now you have returned to the Shepherd and Overseer of your souls. (2:22–25)

Peter connects many of the dots related to the lamb imagery for his readers in these verses. Jesus, like Isaiah's lamb, obediently suffered with the purpose of making others righteous, to make others whole (cf. Matt. 8:17). People are like sheep who have gone astray, according to Peter, but they can be brought back into the fold by the vicarious suffering of the good shepherd (see John 10:11–18).

The New Testament writers were keen readers of the Old Testament texts, and they picked up on themes and motifs that were applicable in their times. After observing and experiencing what Jesus did on behalf of the people, they justifiably applied the imagery associated with the Passover and the suffering servant to Jesus in a way that would encourage their readership to respond to their claims that Jesus was the ultimate embodiment of the personified lamb (who is likened to a suffering servant of the Lord in Isa. 52:13–53:12). Isaiah provided ancient readers hope in the expectation that someone great would come from the covenant community to bear their and others' burdens for the sake of making them righteous. The New Testament writers appropriately adopt this theme and apply it to Jesus as the ultimate fulfillment of the suffering servant figure. In this sense, New Testament readers can confidently state that Isaiah 52:13–53:12 is predictive prophecy.

Conclusion

Contemporary Christian readers are compelled to approach the texts of ancient Israel with the utmost humility, recognizing the legitimate distances between them and us. We must consciously strive to refrain from importing what we want the text to say *just to fit our Christian convictions*, regardless of what the text might actually say. We must endeavor to be self-aware enough to permit the evidence of what we observe in the text to influence our conclusions, irrespective of the consequences on our prefabricated systems of theology. We do this so as not to simply return to the bus when our interpretations are challenged and thereby doom ourselves to return to our theological comforts rather than choosing the better way that is before us.

The endless discussions about the Lord's servant passages in Isaiah, and especially the poem in Isaiah 52:13–53:12, are indicative of the fact that a legitimate ambiguity exists. We cannot shun good questions about these passages, and we certainly should not be overconfident in our interpretation of ambiguous passages. It is precisely through this ambiguity that Isaiah eventually presents the imagery of the lamb, tying the Passover to the suffering servant and providing the people future hope of restoration. New Testament writers used this model to depict the person and the work of Jesus, thereby providing hope for restoration with God through the blood of this servant.

Postscript

I promise nothing complete; because any human thing supposed to be
complete, must for that very reason infallibly be faulty. . . . My object
here is simply to project the draught of systematisation of cetology. I am
the architect, not the builder.

—Ishmael, in Herman Melville, *Moby-Dick*

Cetology is the scientific study of whales, a branch of zoology that far transcends my training as a Biblicist. Nevertheless, it is safe to say that in the
mid-nineteenth century, when Herman Melville wrote the famous novel
Moby-Dick, less was known about the vastness of the seas and the different
species of whales therein. Contemporary science and technology have surely
contributed to the study of whales, and correspondingly, it is presumably
feasible to develop a more comprehensive and detailed list than the one that
the protagonist Ishmael provides for readers in *Moby-Dick*. Ishmael's words
are thus prophetic in a sense. He suggests that striving for comprehensive-
ness is ill-advised since, ultimately, information will be disclosed that reveals
shortcomings in the list of whales that he is compiling. No human thing is
complete, and even the proposal of such an idea is erroneous, according to
Ishmael.

Developments in science and technology do not simply provide more information. They also expand the boundaries of the subject matter. In the case of
cetology, scientific and technological developments have certainly improved
our understanding of the whales that Ishmael lists in *Moby-Dick*, but they
have also revealed the likely unanticipated vastness of the seas and, with this,

the potential of discovery that transcends what once could have been imagined. The comprehensive assessment of whales that was an impractical feat for Ishmael to accomplish when *Moby-Dick* was written likely still eludes oceanographers in light of our better grasp of the immensity and depths of the seas. In this manner, Ishmael's assessment concerning cetology applies broadly to many disciplines: it is best to build an understanding on known information at any given time while remaining aware that further details will eventually emerge that provide more information and broaden our awareness of what still needs to be learned.

Any attempt at a comprehensive guide to engaging with the Old Testament "must for that very reason infallibly be faulty," as Ishmael would say. The sea of Old Testament studies is too deep, too broad, too rich, and too fertile for its interpretation to be restrained to the borders of one staging of its contents. Rather, similar to Ishmael's list of whales, the object of this book was to project a "draught of systematization" of engaging the Old Testament well to encourage Bible students to persevere in their reading. While not comprehensive in any of the areas broached, this book, like an architect, sketches a blueprint of how to erect a compelling framework for reading every word of the Old Testament as important to us as contemporary Christian readers.

Thank goodness that omniscience is not a prerequisite for engaging the Old Testament well. On the contrary, having an awareness of our own proclivities as readers and a willingness to admit gaps in our knowledge engenders an inquisitiveness that provokes us to closer readings. Acknowledging our human finiteness and approaching the text with a disposition of humility are prerequisites to maximizing the efficacy of our engagement with the Old Testament. Intellectual modesty facilitates a curiosity that lends itself to reading texts deliberately, asking good questions while interpreting, and learning from all of the divine words of the Old Testament text. As we engage with the Old Testament humbly, successively, entirely, and deliberately, not only do we become better readers, but those texts that may have previously seemed ridiculous become applicable to our lives, and we become further empowered to proudly identify with the entirety of the Bible as our book.

Readers who believe the Old Testament to be God's Word do not just receive information from texts but also participate in an exchange that provokes corresponding life change. When responding to the principles advanced in the texts of the Old Testament by conforming more to the character of God, we "practice what we preach"—that the entirety of the Old Testament is the inspired Word and is useful for instruction in the church today (2 Tim. 3:16–17). By engaging all of the texts of the Old Testament and responding with an increased devotion to God, we practically employ them as inspired Scripture.

My illustrative readings were intended to demonstrate how engaging the Old Testament well might yield results that are relevant to modern readers.

There is a glaring irony in a book that encourages reading humbly and then provides confident readings of the Old Testament texts. I hope that my readings are assertive and sensible but not rigid. They are certainly not settled. You may disagree with my interpretations; in fact, I expect that some readers will. For the record, disagreeing with me, or any other author's readings of Scripture, is perfectly legitimate. However, where there is dissent, it becomes the responsibility of the reader to propose a more reasonable interpretation of the passage at hand. In developing and arguing for Old Testament readings superior to mine, readers will be compelled to deeply engage with the Old Testament, and thereupon, the goal of the book will still be accomplished.

A book that emphasizes engaging with the Scriptures well might be as revealing to contemporary readers as modern technology might have been to nineteenth-century sailors. Disclosing the vastness of the topic being studied calls those interested into deeper exploratory waters. Once our eyes are opened to how we *can* improve as readers, we realize how much more we *actually need* to improve at engaging the text, and how much more work there is to be done. This is a significant realization for readers of the Bible because it draws us closer to the revealed Word, permitting us to better discern the character and plan of God.

It is impossible to know of everything that inhabits the depths of the vast seas. Knowing this, *Moby-Dick*'s Ishmael provides enough information for nonexperts to follow along as he and his comrades take to their deep-sea journey in search of a whale. Perhaps there is just enough information in a resource like this one to provoke readers to participate on the journey of engaging the entire Old Testament well. In full disclosure, the seas are scary and intimidating, exploring slows you down, you will have to go deeper and probe longer than you might imagine, and there is always the possibility of finding something unanticipated. Indeed, it is safer and easier to stay on dry land and neglect exploration for the sake of self-assurance and certainty. Yet personal growth and formation are spurred by deliberately stepping out onto the waters and participating in the act of discovery. Once there, we realize how vast the waters are, how much we have been missing, and how much more there is to engage.

Bibliography

Bartor, Assnat. *Reading Law as Narrative*. Atlanta: Society of Biblical Literature, 2010.

Berlin, Adele. *Dynamics of Biblical Parallelism*. Rev. and expanded ed. Grand Rapids: Eerdmans, 2008.

―――. *Poetics and Interpretation of Biblical Narrative*. Winona Lake, IN: Eisenbrauns, 1994.

―――. "Reading Biblical Poetry." In *Jewish Study Bible*, ed. Berlin and Brettler, 2184–91.

Berlin, Adele, and Marc Zvi Brettler, eds. *The Jewish Study Bible*. 2nd ed. New York: Oxford University Press, 2014.

Block, Daniel I., and Richard L. Shultz, eds. *Bind Up the Testimony: Explorations in the Genesis of the Book of Isaiah*. Peabody, MA: Hendrickson, 2015.

Collins, Billy. "On Turning Ten." In *Sailing Alone around the Room*, 63–64. New York: Random House, 2002.

Day, John. "Baal (Deity)." In *The Anchor Bible Dictionary*, edited by David Noel Freedman, 547. New York: Doubleday, 1992.

Foster, Benjamin R. *Before the Muses: An Anthology of Akkadian Literature*. 3rd ed. Bethesda, MD: CDL, 2005.

Frame, John. *The Doctrine of the Word of God*. Phillipsburg, NJ: P&R, 2010.

Fuhr, Richard Alan, and Gary E. Yates. *The Message of the Twelve: Hearing the Voice of the Minor Prophets*. Nashville: B&H Academic, 2016.

Gentry, Peter J. *How to Read and Understand the Biblical Prophets*. Wheaton: Crossway, 2017.

―――. "The Text of the Old Testament." *Journal of the Evangelical Theological Society* 52 (2009): 19–45.

Golding, William. *The Lord of the Flies*. New York: Penguin Books, 2016.

Good, Edwin M. *Irony in the Old Testament*. 2nd ed. Sheffield: Almond Press, 1981.

Greenstein, Edward L. "Biblical Law." In Holtz, *Back to the Sources*, 83–104.

———. *Essays on Biblical Method and Translation.* 2nd ed. Atlanta: Scholars Press, 2020.

———. "How Does Parallelism Mean?" In *A Sense of Text: The Art of Language in the Study of Biblical Literature*, 41–70. Jewish Quarterly Review Supplement: 1982. Winona Lake: Eisenbrauns, 1983.

———. "The Riddle of Samson." *Prooftexts* 1 (1981): 237–60.

Hamilton, Mark W. *A Theological Introduction to the Old Testament.* New York: Oxford University Press, 2018.

Hernández, Dominick S. *Illustrated Job in Hebrew.* Wilmore, KY: GlossaHouse, 2020.

———. "Metaphor and the Study of Job." *Hebrew Studies* 61 (2020): 391–415.

———. *The Prosperity of the Wicked: A Theological Challenge in the Book of Job and in Ancient Near Eastern Literature.* Piscataway, NJ: Gorgias, 2022.

———. *Proverbs: Pathways to Wisdom.* Nashville: Abingdon, 2020.

Holtz, Barry W., ed. *Back to the Sources: Reading the Classic Jewish Texts.* New York: Summit Books, 1984.

Kaiser, Walter C., Jr. *Old Testament Documents: Are They Reliable and Relevant?* Downers Grove, IL: InterVarsity, 2001.

Lakoff, George, and Mark Johnson. *Metaphors We Live By.* Chicago: University of Chicago Press, 1980.

Lakoff, George, and Mark Turner. *More Than Cool Reason: A Field Guide to Poetic Metaphor.* Chicago: University of Chicago Press, 1989.

Lee, Harper. *To Kill a Mockingbird.* New York: Perennial, 2002.

Lewis, C. S. *The Complete C. S. Lewis Signature Classics.* New York: HarperCollins, 2002.

———. *Mere Christianity.* In *The Complete C. S. Lewis Signature Classics*, 1–118. New York: HarperCollins, 2002.

———. *Reflections on the Psalms.* In *The Inspirational Writings of C. S. Lewis*, 131–209. New York: Inspirational Press, 1994.

Lichtenstein, Murray H. "Biblical Poetry." In *Back to the Sources: Reading the Classic Jewish Texts*, edited by Barry W. Holtz, 105–27. New York: Summit Books, 1984.

Postell, Seth, Eitan Bar, and Erez Soref. *Reading Moses, Seeing Jesus: How the Torah Fulfills Its Purpose in Yeshua.* 3rd ed. Bellingham, WA: Lexham, 2017.

Preminger, Alex, ed. *Princeton Encyclopedia of Poetry and Poetics.* Princeton: Princeton University Press, 1986.

Roth, Martha T. *Law Collections from Mesopotamia and Asia Minor.* 2nd ed. Atlanta: Scholars Press, 1997.

Sommer, Benjamin D. "Isaiah." In *Jewish Study Bible*, ed. Berlin and Brettler, 763–899.

Sternberg, Meir. *The Poetics of Biblical Narrative*. Bloomington: Indiana University Press, 1985.

Tolkien, J. R. R. *The Hobbit*. New York: Houghton Mifflin, 1997.

Würthwein, Ernst. *The Text of the Old Testament: An Introduction to the Biblia Hebraica*. Translated by Erroll F. Rhodes. Revised and expanded by Alexander Achilles Fischer. 3rd ed. Grand Rapids: Eerdmans, 2014.

Scripture Index

Subject Index

tabernacle, the, 23–25, 131, 134, 136, 148
Tale to Two Cities, A (Dickens), 180–81,
    192–93
temple, Jerusalem, 166, 179
    ark of the covenant, 23–24, 26, 166, 167
    destruction, 167–68, 179, 261
    Second Temple period, 37n9, 44, 69n1
    Solomon and, 167–68, 170–71, 175
Tanakh, 37–38
Ten Commandments, 20–23, 74–75
textual issues, 34–35
time, 12
    and distance, 38–39, 40–41
    narrative, 63–65
To Kill a Mocking Bird (Lee), 97–98, 110
Tolkien, J. R. R., 164–65
Torah, the, 19, 25, 26, 37, 59–61, 68, 138
    adultery, 156–58
    Canaan conquest, 113–14
    Joshua, book of, 100–101, 103
    legal portions, 69–75, 76–83, 86–87
    narrative, 79–83
    Oral Torah, 69n2
    prophets, 228–29

redemption, 140–41
    truth telling, 106–7
trust, 34, 52, 110, 142–43
truth telling, 106–7
Turner, Mark, 192, 195

underreading, 48–50
underworld, 216–19
Uriah the Hittite, 61, 155, 156–59, 160–61

war, 106, 195–96
whales/cetology, 277–78
wisdom embodied, 202–3
wisdom, 166–67
    traditional, 132, 215, 219–22
Word of God, 25n7, 28–29, 255–56, 278–79
    as animate, 24–25
    authority, 48–49
    Book of the Law, 23–24, 26–27
    fellowship with God, 19–20, 24–25, 27–29, 42
    organic inspiration, 45–48
    physical and spiritual life, 24–25, 27

Zophar, 212, 215, 220, 222